A WORLD OF DIFFERENCE

Other books by Kenneth Richard Samples

Without a Doubt: Answering the 20 Toughest Faith Questions

Prophets of the Apocalypse: David Koresh and Other American Messiahs (with others)

The Cult of the Virgin: Catholic Mariology and the Apparitions of Mary (with Elliot Miller)

Lights in the Sky and Little Green Men: A Rational Christian Look at UFOs and Extraterrestrials (with Hugh Ross and Mark Clark)

A WORLD OF DIFFERENCE

PUTTING CHRISTIAN TRUTH-CLAIMS
TO THE WORLDVIEW TEST

KENNETH RICHARD SAMPLES

BakerBooks
Grand Rapids, Michigan

Published by Baker Books
a division of Baker Publishing Group
P.O. Box 6287, Grand Rapids, MI 49516-6287
www.bakerbooks.com

Printed in the United States of America

Library of Congress Cataloging-in-Publication Data
Samples, Kenneth R.
    A world of difference : putting Christian truth-claims to the worldview test / Kenneth Richard Samples.
        p.   cm.
    Includes bibliographical references (p.   ) and indexes.
    ISBN 10: 0-8010-6822-3 (pbk.)
    ISBN 978-0-8010-6822-5 (pbk.)
    1. Christianity 2. Christianity and culture. 3. Church and the world. I. Title.
BR121.3.S26 2007
239—dc22   2007021817

To the memory of Jesse Alexander Samples Jr.
(1918–1985)

7th Army, 44th Infantry Division, 71st Infantry Regiment, Company C,
European Theatre of Operation, United States Army, World War II

My father was a member of that great generation of American patriots
who helped save the world from fascist tyranny and oppression.
Their decisive victory in Europe and in the Pacific guaranteed
the freedom that billions of people enjoy today.
May their courage, devotion to duty, and selfless sacrifice
be remembered with respect and gratitude.

CONTENTS

FIGURES AND TABLES

Figures

Tables

ACKNOWLEDGMENTS

Many people either encouraged me in the writing of this book or directly contributed to improving the book's overall quality. Honoring this debt of gratitude begins with acknowledging my family. My wife, Joan, is an extraordinary person. She supported me throughout the writing process and patiently endured the hundreds of hours I spent hibernating in the "dungeon" (our walk-in bedroom closet) both writing and editing the manuscript. Joan also courageously and selflessly nursed me back to health when I experienced the catastrophic health crisis described in this book.

My children were also a big help along the way. Oldest daughter Sarah competently and generously helped with many of the word processing tasks, while middle child Jacqueline graciously prepared meals when her mother was working the late shift at the hospital. And my youngest, Michael, kept me well supplied with ice-cold drinks and helped me check the many quotations included in the book. My love for my family remains the *sine qua non* (essence) of my life.

Valuable editorial support came from a number of exceedingly qualified people. My friend and colleague Robert M. Bowman Jr. provided editorial suggestions that strengthened the scholarly quality of the manuscript.

The Reasons To Believe (RTB) editorial team worked skillfully to improve the manuscript's readability and accuracy. I'm especially grateful to Patti Townley-Covert for her excellent editorial work and encouragement. RTB editors Kathy Ross, Joe Aguirre, and Adam Martinez also offered valuable suggestions on improving the manuscript. The careful work of Sandra Dimas in preparing the indexes, Marj Harman's diligent efforts in checking the notes and bibliography, Diana Carrée's help on some of the tables, and Phillip Chien's computer assistance is also greatly appreciated.

RTB's scholar team including Hugh Ross, Fuz Rana, Dave Rogstad, Jeff Zweerink, and Bob Stuart reviewed parts of the manuscript and provided invaluable advice and support.

For the professionalism and gracious assistance of the people at Baker Books, I remain thankful. In particular, special thanks to Baker's acquisitions editor Robert Hosack for his support and to Paul J. Brinkerhoff for his astute editorial queries and counsel.

It's also important to acknowledge the Consistory of Christ Reformed Church in Anaheim, California—especially pastor Kim Riddlebarger, who allowed me to present much of the material in this book to my weekly Sunday school class. I have also benefited from the support of church friends such as Larry Keith, Cliff Steele, Gary DeBoer, Peggy Burke, Duane Ratzlaff, Judy Sniegowski, Winona Taylor, Donna Earnheart, Glenn Bulthuis, Vince Martinez, Les and Lorri Connard, and Wes and Lynn Hoffmaster.

My friends and teaching colleagues—including Douglas Wessell, Joseph van de Mortel, Robert Dargatz, Martin Schramm, and Dave Andrews—have inspired and challenged me over the years concerning the subject of worldview thinking. For their input, I give thanks.

My father, Jesse Alexander Samples Jr., to whom the book is dedicated, and his World War II band of brothers left a precious legacy of liberty.

Finally, glory and honor to the Triune God: Father, Son, and Holy Spirit.

Faith seeking understanding,
Kenneth Richard Samples
2007

INTRODUCTION

CULTURE CLASH

Why is it that two people can look at the very same issue or event but come to fundamentally different conclusions? Human beings—born, raised, and educated in the same culture (perhaps even the same home)—can nevertheless have opposing visions about the nature of reality, truth, and goodness. Even two people who embrace religion can have monumental disagreements in their basic outlook.

Stark contrasts in perspective are especially pronounced since the events of 9/11. An actual clash of civilizations appears to be taking place. How can people understand this antithesis of viewpoints? Some specific examples illustrate the problem.

A Terrorist Trigger

American President George W. Bush and Muslim extremist Osama bin Laden represent diametrically opposed positions. Bush considers the total destruction of the Twin Towers, damage to the Pentagon, and all the deaths that have resulted from terrorist actions as a moral outrage. He believes the mass murderers who perpetrate this ongoing mayhem must be brought to justice.

Thus, President Bush leads the way in a strategic war against Islamic terrorists. A devout evangelical Christian, he asks for God's help in bringing swift and decisive recompense to these "evildoers." Bush assesses terrorist acts largely in moral terms rather than strictly political, economic, or social terms. This basic moral evaluation has shaped his course of action not only in the war on terror, but in numerous other leadership decisions as well.

Osama bin Laden represents a completely different view. He considers the United States to be the "great Satan," a country that for decades has manipulated the political events in the Middle East for its own selfish interests. This extremist leader and his followers believe terrorist actions to be expressions of devotion to Allah and ask his help to win the jihad (holy war) against their vision of evil.

These differences are not merely political, economic, or cultural, though such factors carry real importance. Nor do opposing perspectives arise strictly from two distinct religious traditions, Christianity and Islam, which actually share some common beliefs and values. The differences run far deeper than mere religious doctrine.

Philosopher Ronald H. Nash points out the touchstone that accounts for these differences: "Many disagreements among individuals, societies, and nations are clashes of competing worldviews."[1] The diversity makes a world of difference—one with global consequences.

A Country Divided

The clash of cultures is evident not just among nations but also within them. In the presidential elections of 2000 and 2004, strong political, social, and moral differences separated Americans into *red* and *blue* states. People in the United States have become increasingly polarized (perhaps more so than at any time since the Civil War), not just politically but also in the underlying beliefs that shape their worldviews.

Real and substantive differences separate Americans on the great questions of life and death—abortion, physician-assisted suicide, euthanasia, capital punishment, and war, among others. Bioethical issues such as stem-cell research and cloning ignite and fuel hot debate. Even the traditional definition of marriage and family relationships has come under scrutiny.

Some astute observers of political, social, and cultural trends claim that the United States is undergoing a cultural civil war, one in which differences run far deeper than just the traditional sparring between political parties.

When the media mistakenly attribute these skirmishes to political perspectives alone, they ignore more fundamental issues. People hold conflicting views on such ultimate concerns as truth, reality, ethics, and values. These profound divisions make a world of difference—they can either unite a country or tear it apart.

A Family Tragedy

The case of Terri Schiavo (the brain-damaged Florida woman who died in 2005 after her feeding tube was removed) shows how opposing positions can even devastate families. Many variables (familial, medical, and legal) generated a tremendous conflict between Terri's husband and her parents, but the crucial clash arose from philosophical differences.

Michael Schiavo looked at the poor quality of his wife's life and concluded that the most merciful act would be to remove her feeding tube so she could die. Keeping her alive served no purpose. Autonomy gave Terri the "right to die." As an individual, she (or her representative) could make the ultimate decisions about life and death. To a significant degree, this belief in self-determination is rooted in the secular approach to life born out of a naturalistic worldview.

On the other hand, Robert and Mary Schindler saw their daughter as a disabled person whose physical vulnerabilities required care. Terri's life deserved to be preserved because she was, in spite of severe health problems, a living human being. Her "life" in and of itself was sacred (valuable, unrepeatable, and endowed with dignity). Terri's parents argued for a "right to life," given by God.

Life-and-death decisions reveal underlying worldviews. And those belief systems can make a world of difference—one that either unites families during a difficult time or tears them apart.

My Own Life-or-Death Drama

A few years ago, around Thanksgiving, a serious illness threatened my life. Upon hearing the news that I might soon die, my own belief system helped me make sense of the world. It provided a grand perspective and interpretation for what is real, true, rational, good, valuable, and beautiful—even in the face of death.

That experience solidified my commitment to help others understand the concept of worldviews and how they impact individuals, societies, and nations. Because beliefs precede behavior, understanding what a worldview is, being familiar with its component elements, and learning to evaluate differing worldviews can equip people to deal more wholesomely with harsh reality and with each other. Such knowledge can make a world of difference to every individual.

The Importance of This Book

Today's intensified cultural clash of thought underscores the need for a clear and relevant introduction to the topic of worldview thinking. Contrasting belief systems and the need to understand those variant points of view have never been more apparent or more important.

Evangelicals can greatly benefit from thinking "worldview-ishly." Unfortunately, most do not. It appears as if the concept is largely either unknown or untried among most individual Christians.

The lack of appreciation for worldview-thinking negatively impacts doctrinal literacy, apologetic understanding, evangelistic fervor, and the living of a God-honoring life. Pollster George Barna's survey in 2003 revealed discouraging news: "Only nine percent of born-again Christians hold a biblical worldview." Barna further stated that "most Americans have little idea how to integrate core biblical principles to form a unified and meaningful response to the challenges and opportunity of life."[2]

This study also underscored that how a person *thinks* significantly influences his *actions*. A Christian who understands his worldview and can practically apply it exhibits an overall lifestyle that corresponds to a much greater degree with traditional Christian ethics and values. A believer who appreciates and values the historic Christian worldview is more likely to honor his marriage vows and avoid sexual promiscuity, divorce, and addiction to drugs and alcohol. That individual is also more likely to educate his children in the doctrines of the faith. In other words, a person's worldview powerfully and dynamically impacts his moral choices in life.

About This Book

A number of good books already examine various aspects of worldviews. They greatly enhanced my study (evidenced by the many quotations and references contained in this work). Still, I wanted to define and explain this critical area of thought (see part 1, chapters 1–2) in what proved for me to be a life-changing manner. Logical thought patterns establish and enhance sound reasoning and expose fallacies that lead to flawed worldview thinking (see chapters 3–4).

Spelling out a worldview in considerable detail and clarity can put a belief system to the test in several significant ways. Because I'm an evangelical Christian and consider this historic worldview to be the most cogent and viable, I've chosen to use it to demonstrate how this evaluation works (see part 2, chapters 5–11). Any other position can be examined by applying the same rigorous standards.

In addition, integrating theological systems with their accompanying philosophical aspects is an ongoing process that warrants continued effort. In that process everyone stands to gain a much deeper understanding of how differing systems of thought apply to all of life. An awareness of the bona fide competitors in the marketplace of ideas—naturalism, postmodernism, pantheism, and Islam—equips individuals to better defend their beliefs when engaged in discussions or debate with others (see part 3, chapters 12–15). Everyone can benefit from learning to understand the viewpoint(s) they oppose.

This book is intended to represent a historic Christian worldview perspective. Undoubtedly, much of the content of this book could be embraced by all major branches of conservative Christendom (especially chapter 6 on the Apostles' Creed). However, other parts of the book clearly convey a distinctive Protestant evangelical perspective (for example, chapter 7 on Scripture). And still other parts of the book reflect the particular Augustinian-Reformed theological consensus (such as the discussion of God's sovereignty and providence in chapter 9).

It is my hope that this work will help Christians think deeper and more comprehensively about their worldview and as a result that their thoughts and lives will be enriched. By learning to evaluate alternative philosophical and religious views from a distinctly Christian worldview perspective, evangelicals can greatly enhance their approach to such issues as education, evangelism, apologetics, prayer, worship, and other elements of living.

I also hope that skeptics and seekers explore the content of this book. Understanding what the historic Christian worldview is all about and how it fares with its philosophical and religious competitors can change lives. Testing and evaluating truth-claims is the best way to discover where the truth lies, and knowing that makes a world of difference.

Soli Deo Gloria,
Kenneth Richard Samples
Easter 2007

PART 1

DEVELOPING A WORLDVIEW PERSPECTIVE

1

SHADES OF REALITY

A worldview, then, is a set of beliefs and practices that shape a person's approach to the most important issues in life.

Michael D. Palmer, *Elements of a Christian Worldview*

*S*everal *years ago, I lived in a small city in the desert where summers seemed to last about eight months of the year. Due to the glaring sunshine, I decided to buy a pair of sunglasses I'd seen advertised on television. These highly touted spectacles claimed to block the dangerous blue light released from the sun. They were designed to protect their wearer from the sun's rays and at the same time maximize visual clarity.*

When I received these "shades," I soon discovered they had both optical strengths and weaknesses. Indeed, the glasses did a good job of blocking the sun's powerful glare. When I wore them on a bright day, I could look directly up into the sky and not be overwhelmed by the sun's brilliance. Things seemed so clear upon looking through the lenses that at first I wondered whether there was actually any glass in the frames. Reality, so to speak, seemed to come into sharper focus.

Over time, however, I noticed that these same glasses contained some disturbing defects. For example, they distorted certain colors. Orange appeared yellow, while yellow appeared white.

One day when I visited a snack shop, this problem kept me from finding my favorite flavor of Wrigley's chewing gum. Without reading the label, I couldn't differentiate Juicy Fruit from Spearmint. The lenses made the distinctive yellow wrapping of Juicy Fruit indistinguishable from the white wrapping of Spearmint.

This color distortion soon became more than merely annoying. It was downright dangerous. While driving, the lenses in the sunglasses affected the appearance of traffic signals. When approaching an intersection I couldn't determine which color was lit. Green always appeared dim so I couldn't tell whether to stop or go. For safety's sake (and to avoid getting a ticket) I had to either glance above the lenses or remove them altogether.

Ironically, the same pair of sunglasses that at times enhanced visual perception, at other times distorted it. Reality passed through the lenses before my eyes, and as it did so, those lenses affected my interpretation. My interpretive vision depended upon the spectacles that sat upon my nose.

What in the World Is a Worldview?

In the simplest terms, a worldview may be defined as how one sees life and the world at large. In this manner it can be compared to a pair of glasses.[1] How a person makes sense of the world depends upon that person's vision, so to speak. But can ultimate reality be shaped by the philosophical or worldview "glasses" an individual wears? How can the strengths and weaknesses of worldview perspectives be tested by the proper application of experience and reason?

A worldview functions in much the same way as a pair of glasses through which a person sees the world. The interpretive lens helps people make sense of life and comprehend the world around them. Worldviews also shape people's understanding of their unique place on Earth. Sometimes worldviews bring clarity, and other times they can distort reality.

Derived from the German term *Weltanschauung*,[2] the word *worldview* refers to the cluster of beliefs a person holds about the most significant issues of life—such as God, the cosmos, knowledge, values, humanity, and history. These beliefs (which may in reality be right or wrong or a combination thereof—not unlike the visual clarity or distortion given by glasses) form a big picture, a general outlook, or a grand perspective on life and the world.

In more technical terms, a worldview forms a mental structure that organizes one's basic or ultimate beliefs. This framework supplies a comprehensive view of what a person considers real, true, rational, good, valuable, and beautiful. In this vein, philosopher Ronald H. Nash defines a worldview as "a conceptual scheme by which we consciously or unconsciously place or fit everything we believe and by which we interpret and judge reality."[3]

Similarly, philosophers Norman L. Geisler and William D. Watkins describe a worldview as "an interpretive framework through which or by which one makes sense out of the data of life and the world."[4] Worldview perspectives involve much more than merely a set of intellectual beliefs. However, thinking of a worldview in terms of a basic conceptual system is critical. Rather than a disconnected or disparate group of unrelated beliefs, a carefully examined and reflective worldview consists of a network of interconnected ideas that form a unified whole.

This system of beliefs then responds to the big questions of life, focusing particularly upon issues central to human concern. These issues especially include thoughts about the human predicament (why man is the way he is and why he faces the challenges he does). And, these concerns involve how human beings derive meaning, purpose, and significance.

Philosopher Michael D. Palmer explains some of the ways a worldview functions: "Through our worldview, we determine priorities, explain our relationship to God and fellow human beings, assess the meaning of events, and justify our actions."[5] A person's worldview supplies a general context for life, providing a vision of what one considers authentically real.[6]

Life's Road Map

More than just an interpretive lens, a worldview perspective shapes, influences, and generally directs a person's entire life. Because people behave as they believe, their worldviews guide their thoughts, attitudes, values, interpretations, perspectives, decisions, and actions.

Living a well-balanced life based on realistic values requires thinking about basic and critical questions. When a worldview attempts to answer them, it functions like a chart or plan used to navigate through the journey of life (though the distortions of the sunglasses must be kept in mind).

An accurate road map supplies valid directions that profoundly guide a person's life decisions. Therefore, a well-thought-out course, or worldview, needs to answer twelve ultimate concerns that philosophers identify as "the big questions of life":[7]

1. **Ultimate Reality**: What kind of God, if any, actually exists?
2. **External Reality**: Is there anything beyond the cosmos?
3. **Knowledge**: What can be known and how can anyone know it?
4. **Origin**: Where did I come from?
5. **Identity**: Who am I?
6. **Location**: Where am I?
7. **Morals**: How should I live?
8. **Values**: What should I consider of great worth?

 9. **Predicament**: What is humanity's fundamental problem?
 10. **Resolution**: How can humanity's problem be solved?
 11. **Past/Present**: What is the meaning and direction of history?
 12. **Destiny**: Will I survive the death of my body and, if so, in what state?

When a worldview elucidates reasonable answers to these ultimate questions, life (and death) issues become much more comprehensible and easier to get through.

Does Everyone Have a Worldview?

Every person thinks about the big questions of life to some degree. People who grasp the worldview concept and seriously reflect on the subjects involved undoubtedly develop more functional and coherent belief systems than those who do not.

Unfortunately, many people consider philosophical reflection in general—and worldview consideration in particular—a waste of time. Ironically, however, even this position of apathy reveals a philosophical viewpoint (in that the sentiment "philosophy is a waste of time" is itself a philosophical position). Philosophy is difficult, if not impossible, to avoid. A generally unexamined or scarcely examined approach to life may explain why so many people hold underdeveloped, disjointed, and poorly understood worldviews. Though such incomplete positions may be difficult to articulate, they do exist.

The randomly developed interpretive lens by which many people view life lacks an appropriate systemization and integration of beliefs based on such logical considerations as coherence, correspondence, and explanatory power (see chapter 2). As a result, individuals with fragmented or uninformed worldviews tend to take a smorgasbord approach in their perspectives, usually motivated by preference and convenience. However, this approach typically suffers from the fatal flaw of incoherence (internal inconsistency). The optical defects in this type of interpretive lens distort a comprehensive vision of reality.

Where Do Worldviews Come From?

A person's worldview orientation begins very early in life and is formed by multiple factors. These influences coalesce and have a cumulative effect in developing an individual's broad outlook on life. Philosopher Patrick J. Hurley explains where the development of one's worldview starts:

> Beginning in infancy, our worldview emerges quietly and unconsciously from enveloping influences—culture, language, gender, religion, politics, and social

economic status. As we grow older, it continues to develop through the shaping forces of education and experience.[8]

Some of these elements are more important than others. For example, religious training (or the lack thereof) has a much greater impact on shaping a basic worldview than language, gender, or economic status. In fact, throughout much of history in both the East and West, a person's religious framework has established the very core of his broader worldview.

Many people, as they mature, retain the same worldview they inherited, but do so only after examining it to decide if they want to continue living according to its principles and values. Upon approaching adulthood, most young people begin to examine what they've been taught and then decide whether the beliefs of their upbringing are really their own or just a system on loan from their parents.

While worldview orientation is usually inherited or adopted from one's family and culture, it can also be deliberately chosen through reflection and analysis. Thus, people may challenge their childhood influences and make a change. This alteration can obviously be significant and is referred to in philosophy as a paradigm shift. To modify the classic reflective statement by the Greek philosopher Socrates, there comes a time for some when *the unexamined worldview is not worth believing and living out*.

Worldviews are often adopted first, then questioned and examined through testing, and ultimately accepted or rejected. (The process of testing a worldview is explored in chapter 2.) People, therefore, need not feel trapped by the worldviews they inherit but rather can test those life perspectives to see if they stand up to appropriate scrutiny.

What Are the Major Components of a Worldview?

While a comprehensive world-and-life view touches on virtually every area of a person's life, six central areas of belief—theology, metaphysics, epistemology, axiology, humanity, and history—make up the conceptual heart of a worldview. These components should not be viewed in isolation but rather as unfolding integral parts that overlap and influence each other. The types of questions involved with each area of study are clarified in the sections that follow.

1. Theology (Concept of God)

No worldview is neutral with regard to the question of God. *Every* viewpoint makes basic assertions about God or ultimate reality, either affirming (theology) or denying (atheology) the existence of a divine being.[9] Theology is so important that typically what a philosophical perspective says about God is that viewpoint's defining feature (for example, *atheism* literally means "no-god-ism," *pantheism* literally means "all-is-god-ism," and *polytheism* literally means "many-gods-ism").

Theology attempts to answer essential questions about the existence, nature, and attributes of God. These fundamental interrogatives include: Does God actually exist? Is there one God or many gods? Is God a personal or impersonal being? Is God infinite or finite? What is God's relationship to the space-time-matter world? Has God revealed himself to humanity? Does God perform miracles? Can human beings have a relationship with God? If so, how?

These considerations about God powerfully impact the way people interpret truth, reality, right and wrong, and good and bad. For example, an individual's view of such ethical issues as the "right to life" (in relating to abortion) and the "right to die" (in relating to euthanasia) is usually shaped by a commitment either to secularism (often atheism) or religion (for example, a Judeo-Christian form of theism).

Ideas have consequences, and ideas about God typically have profound consequences. The reason why is because the question of God touches upon the issue of *ultimate* reality, which then influences all questions of truth and values.

To be neutral and dispassionate when it comes to the God question is difficult for many, if not most, people. Atheists often seem to get angry when they discuss God. Christians and Muslims, among others, are passionate enough about God to proselytize. For many reasons, theology matters.

2. Metaphysics (View of External Reality, Especially the Cosmos)

Metaphysics[10] is concerned with the ultimate nature, structure, and characteristics of reality.[11] This broad category covers both questions about the study of being (ontology) and the study of the universe (cosmology). Answers are sought to questions such as: Is ultimate reality mind, matter, or spirit? Can reality be apprehended by the five senses? Is the space-time-matter world the sole reality? Is the origin of the universe natural or supernatural? Why is the universe orderly rather than disorderly and chaotic? How can such things as time, change, and cause-effect relationships be explained?

These questions might seem theoretical or speculative, but how a worldview answers them significantly impacts the way a person sees her place and self in the grand scheme of things. What is considered *real* and *true* strongly influences the so-called practical areas of life and affects what one perceives to be *good* and *valuable*.

For example, if an individual believes the cosmos is all there is and that he is a mere physical entity, he will look at life and death in one distinct way. However, a person who believes that a realm exists beyond the material world and that people possess an immortal soul will see life-and-death issues very differently. Appreciating these metaphysical differences of perspective may help when trying to understand why people hold contrasting positions on controversial ethical issues.

3. Epistemology (Theory of Knowledge)

Epistemology[12]—the fundamental study of knowing—is the investigation of the origin, nature, limits, and validity of knowledge.[13] Some of its most important inquiries are: What is knowledge? How is knowledge acquired? What roles do the five senses, reason, and revelation play in the process of knowing? Can one be certain of anything and, if so, under what conditions? Is belief in the existence of God rational? What is the proper relationship between faith and reason? What is truth? Is truth absolute or relative? What is the relationship between knowledge and belief?

Like metaphysical questions, epistemological inquiries have important practical ramifications. For example, what people "know" and what they can "prove" profoundly influence views on jurisprudence, science, education, and even on difficult ethical matters, such as abortion. What can be known and proven about when life begins and what constitutes actual human life powerfully impacts the abortion debate. This dispute continues to rage and tends to be one of the major issues that divides Americans.

4. Axiology (Study of Values)

The discipline of axiology doesn't have anything to do with axes or hatchets. Rather, it involves asking questions concerning the origin, nature, meaning, and criteria of values.[14] There are three basic types of criteria—moral values, value theory (the worth or importance of things in general), and aesthetics.

Moral values[15] focus on identifying what is "right." That determination involves the systematic study of appropriate human conduct. Probing questions include: What is the ultimate good? Is morality relative or absolute? Are ethics invented or discovered? How does one ground or justify one's ethics? What is God's (or ultimate reality's) relationship to moral principles?

The Terri Schiavo case that received intense media coverage in the spring of 2005 divided a country over the "right to die" issue. People's positions were strongly influenced by their understanding of and commitment to certain values. The culture clash taking place in America today often focuses on issues relating to moral values because a person's worldview frames his moral/ethical understanding.

Value theory is concerned with the worth of things in general (other than morals). Value theory asks: What do people value (God, material things, money, pleasure, freedom, education) and why? How does (or should) a person assign worth or value? What is of ultimate value? How do values affect other areas of thought?

Aesthetics encourages analysis of the idea of beauty and how people respond to it (taste). This discipline examines attitudes, values, and standards as they pertain to people's judgments about what is beautiful—in film, painting, literature, music, photography, and architecture among other things. Typical questions are: Is beauty merely subjective—"in the eye of the beholder"—or is there some objective standard? Does society imitate art or does art imitate society? Why do human beings have an aesthetic and creative sense? How is aesthetic value related to moral values and to other focal points of one's worldview, such as God, ultimate reality, and knowledge?

A generation ago, the operative question in attempting to understand the spirit of the age (German *Zeitgeist*) might have been to inquire about the most popular books of the time. Today, the operative question might be to inquire about the most popular films. Movies have a profound influence on the way people, especially the young, view the world around them.

Actor and producer Mel Gibson's blockbuster movie *The Passion of the Christ*, released in 2004, raised aesthetic questions with far-reaching worldview implications. Often, the most acclaimed and impactful movies draw their story lines from books (as this one did from the Bible).

5. Humanity (View of Human Nature)

The course of studying humanity, often called anthropology, concerns the origin, nature, problems, and destiny of human beings. It raises such questions as: Are people merely the product of undirected, natural processes (naturalistic evolution) or are they special creations of God? What are human beings in relation to animals? Do people possess an immaterial soul? Are human beings good, bad, or neutral? Are people innately rational or irrational? How does a person derive meaning, purpose, and significance? How does God relate to mankind's basic predicament? What is the final destiny of humankind: extinction, immortality, or reincarnation? What kind of afterlife exists, if any?

In the twenty-first century, bioethical questions keep appearing in the news. Such issues as embryonic stem cell research and cloning raise important questions about what it means to actually be human and the value and dignity of each individual human life. These questions address ultimate human concerns that bring a worldview into focus and are second in importance only to the question of God.

An additional consideration directly related to a person's view of humanity, as well as his view of God, is the issue of theodicy—the study of the origin, nature, and resolution of the problem of evil.[16] Questions connected with this concern include: Why isn't the world the way many people think it should be? What is the origin and cause of evil? Why does God allow evil to exist? Does the existence of evil prove or disprove an ultimate standard of goodness? What role do humans play in the problem of evil? What about natural disasters and calamities?

Examples of "moral and natural evil," as philosophers refer to them, are easy to identify. The Holocaust perpetrated by the Nazis against the Jews during World War II constitutes maybe the most glaring example of sheer moral evil the world has ever beheld, though the murderous purges perpetrated by the communists in the former Soviet Union and in Mao Tse-tung's China may rival the Nazi atrocities. The terrible tsunami that killed a quarter of a million people living in countries in the vicinity of the Indian Ocean just after Christmas 2004 supplies an example of a natural calamity or natural evil. So does Hurricane Katrina, which ravaged the United States Gulf Coast in the summer of 2005.

6. History (Study of Unfolding Historical Events)

History as a component of a worldview raises questions not only about the past but also about the future.[17] Questions about the nature, direction, and purpose of historical events include: What is the meaning and significance of history? Where is history going? Is history cyclical or linear? Is history the product of purely natural factors or of divine providence? Has God intervened in history? What can be known from history? What will unfold in the future for humankind and the physical universe?

The Christian worldview in particular is deeply connected to history (see chapter 6, about the Apostles' Creed). According to the New Testament, the birth of Jesus Christ took place under the reign of Caesar Augustus (Luke 2:1), and Jesus's crucifixion, death, and bodily resurrection from the grave happened when Pontius Pilate was the Roman governor of Judea (Matt. 27:11–14). The Christian church emerged in a particular historical context (the Roman Empire) and in a given time period (first century A.D.). The religion also developed through a historical time period (the first and second millennium A.D.), which is why the faith is often referred to as "historic Christianity." Most other religions have a more tenuous and sketchy relationship to historical fact.

But Christianity also makes predictions about the future, specifically about the return of Jesus Christ to the earth as Lord and King and about such monumental events as God's raising the dead and judging humanity for their deeds while living upon Earth. Christianity is rooted deeply not only in the factual events of the past (history) but also in promises for the future (in the *eschaton*, the last or final things of human history[18]).

Which Worldview Is Best?

The way a person sees life and the world as a comprehensive whole is his world-and-life view. This perspective is analogous to a pair of glasses. The collection of beliefs an individual holds about the most important questions of life—such as God, the world, knowledge, values, humanity, and history—colors his interpretation of each day's experiences and observations. That view then shapes and influences his entire existence including his ideas and actions.

This general context for life, this vision of what is authentically real, functions as a road map to guide and direct a person's living. Virtually everyone has a worldview, though people's belief systems often tend to be underdeveloped and poorly articulated.

Because various worldviews come to fundamentally different conclusions about the big questions of life, logic and reason mandate that not all perspectives can be true. The rational choice of one particular position ought to be made—and can be made—via testing and evaluation. The next chapter gives guidance for that challenging but worthwhile process.

Discussion Questions

1. What does it mean that a worldview provides a general context for life? How do worldviews function like a road map for living?
2. Why do many people avoid reflecting upon the big questions of life? What role do distraction and diversion play when avoiding thought about ultimate issues?
3. Many philosophers consider metaphysical and epistemological questions to be the foundational questions of philosophy. Why might that be the case?
4. What factors tend to influence which worldview one will embrace? What factors seem most important?
5. Why does a particular (worldview) perspective on God and humanity tend to be supremely important?

For Further Study

Geisler, Norman L., and William D. Watkins. *Worlds Apart: A Handbook on World Views*. 2nd ed. Eugene, OR: Wipf and Stock, 2003.

Nash, Ronald H. *Worldviews in Conflict: Choosing Christianity in a World of Ideas*. Grand Rapids: Zondervan, 1992.

Palmer, Michael D., comp. and ed. *Elements of a Christian Worldview*. Springfield, MO: Logion, 1998.

Plantinga, Cornelius Jr. *Engaging God's World: A Christian Vision of Faith, Learning, and Living*. Grand Rapids: Eerdmans, 2002.

Sire, James W. *The Universe Next Door: A Basic Worldview Catalog*. 3rd ed. Downers Grove, IL: InterVarsity, 1997.

2

Testable Truth

Like it or not we are stuck with the tough decision as to which one of the world views is true. Therefore, we must find a good way to test their claims to truth.

Norman L. Geisler and William D. Watkins, *Worlds Apart*

Looking grim, the emergency room doctor came over and stood beside the gurney on which I lay, a CAT scan image gripped in his hand. He held it up to the light, looking as though he hoped something in the picture had changed. Then, he spoke quietly: "I need to have a few words with you in private, before talking to your wife. She's waiting outside."

Before coming to the hospital, I'd barely been able to get out of bed. My head still pounded in pain. But surely I was only suffering from a bad case of the flu.

Unfortunately the doctor saw my condition differently: "I'm afraid your brain scan shows multiple brain lesions. I'm transferring you to another hospital where some specialists can evaluate your condition." Then he left the room.

Numb, I began to wonder—Is this my time to die?

My wife came in a few minutes later with tears in her eyes. Gently, she took hold of my hand and leaned in close. Joan whispered, "I wish it were me rather than you."

A team of doctors examined me at the other hospital. After a few days they told me they weren't certain as to the cause of my suffering. The worst-case scenario would be brain cancer. If that were the diagnosis—and they had little doubt—it would be quite serious.

Desperately I tried to get my mind around what was happening. A life-threatening illness was about to test me to the very core of my being.

Discerning Truth

A person's worldview shapes his vision of what is real, true, right, and valuable. It is the prism through which one makes sense of life and death. Controversial ethical issues such as abortion, euthanasia, capital punishment, and war are powerfully impacted by worldview considerations. Therefore it is critical to have a view that is genuinely clear and distinct.

The problem, however, is that the major worldview options available conflict and collide with one another. They do not agree about what constitutes ultimate reality. Naturalism claims nature is the sole reality. Pantheism asserts that all is God and God is all. Theism insists that the world is the product of an infinite, personal, Creator God.

Diverse worldviews come to fundamentally different conclusions about the big questions of life. Therefore, logically, they cannot all be true. But how can individuals possibly know which belief system most closely aligns with reality—which one they should choose?

20/20 Vision

Careful worldview thinking demands a logical evaluation of the various interpretations of reality offered in the marketplace of ideas. By applying methods of critical thinking to the various aspects of each particular worldview, the accuracy of that belief system can be analyzed to determine how well it actually fits reality. To pass logical muster an adequate worldview will score high on a comprehensive set of tests.

These tests examine worldviews for coherence, balance, explanatory power and scope, correspondence, verification, practicality, livability, diversity of support, and competitive competence.[1] Each evaluation contributes increasing insight into a worldview's adequacy. Rather than being completely distinct, these tests overlap and impact each other. They work in a complementary fashion to guide a person into a viable outlook—one that shapes attitudes and decision making from the most important basis: truth. A well-thought-out worldview, grounded in reality, can even be a lifeline in the face of death.

1. Coherence Test: Is a particular worldview logically consistent?

A foundational test for the truth of a worldview evaluates its coherence or logical consistency. Truth will always be wholly consistent within itself, displaying internal logical harmony. The coherence test stresses the crucial unity and relatedness of all truth. Therefore any logical inconsistency in the basic elements of a worldview is a mark of essential error.

The fundamental law of logic (the law of noncontradiction) states that two contradictory statements cannot both be true at the same time and in the same respect (see chapter 3). Genuine contradiction in the central claims of a worldview signifies a false belief system. Scholar and author A. J. Hoover has said, "If I find an egregious contradiction in a system, this makes me want to look at another system."[2]

A satisfactory worldview will also avoid self-stultification. This problem occurs when a statement asserts a particular principle that, if applied back to that statement, contradicts it (in other words, the claim fails to meet its own standard). For example, the statement "There is no truth" is self-stultifying because it purports to assert the "truth" that there is no truth (this important concept is further developed in chapter 3).

Further, to avoid being self-defeating, a worldview must provide a sufficient and meaningful basis for rationality itself. A worldview that cannot account for the rational process itself cannot possibly be true but would instead be incoherent.

There must be legitimate grounds for reason and argumentation in a sound worldview. People must, in fact, be capable of authentic intellectual deliberation. (Chapters 12 and 14 show how related problems impact naturalism and pantheism.)

Coherence is a necessary condition for truth but not a sufficient one. In other words, truth must contain coherence, but coherence isn't all that is needed in order to possess truth. Philosopher L. Russ Bush explains what truth requires: "It is conceivable, however, for a system of thought to demonstrate a measure of rational consistency (given its assumptions) and yet still be false. Failing to achieve consistency is a mark of error, but it takes more than abstract consistency to demonstrate truthfulness."[3]

Incoherence shows that a worldview *must* be false; coherence shows that a worldview *may* be true. As important as coherence is, more is needed for a worldview to pass the ultimate truth test.

2. Balance Test: Is the worldview properly balanced between simplicity and complexity?

A valid worldview will be "neither too simple nor too complex."[4] All things being equal, the simplest worldview that does justice to all aspects of reality deserves preference. In other words, when confronted with two seemingly equal explanatory hypotheses, the simplest or most economical explanation should be granted logical deference.

This famous principle has been called "Ockham's Razor"[5] after a Christian medieval philosopher. The term "razor" is a metaphor for cutting away unnecessary elements in an explanation. Yet some distort this principle of simplicity by failing to recognize that it also includes the principle of necessity. The simplest or most economical explanation may indeed deserve initial preference over the complex explanation. However, the simplest theory may actually end up being simplistically inadequate, while a more complex view may do a better job of accounting for all of the facts. Ockham's Razor addresses both the need for simplicity and the need for explanatory adequacy.

Testing for balance between *simplicity* and *complexity* is a useful barometer of the ultimate accuracy and reasonableness of a worldview. A credible interpretation of reality will be neither overly simple nor unnecessarily complex. In short, the simplest, fully orbed worldview possesses superior explanatory power. The test for balance guards against both *superfluous* and *simplistically inadequate* explanations of reality.

3. Explanatory Power and Scope Test: How well does a worldview explain the facts of reality ("power"), and how wide is the range of its explanation ("scope")?

A viable worldview explains the phenomena of the material realm and life in sufficient detail. This description should account for what can be observed external to humanity (the physical universe) as well as internal to the same (hopes, desires, aspirations, and so on). An adequate belief system explains a broad range of data.

The more profound the explanatory power, the greater the assurance that one is encountering a truthful vision of reality. Thus the best explanation has both specificity of detail (power) and acceptable breadth (scope). Professor Robert A. Harris provides a helpful explanation of this worldview test:

> When detectives examine a crime scene, their goal is to develop a narrative of events—a story—that explains as many of the details of evidence as possible in as plausible a way as possible. In other words, they develop a hypothesis that covers the facts. Similarly, a worldview might be seen as a hypothesis that aims to take into account as many of the observed phenomena of the world, life, and experience as possible in a coherent, unified way. The more phenomena that can be reasonably and plausibly explained by a given hypothesis, the greater is that hypothesis' explanatory power.[6]

4. Correspondence Test: Does a particular worldview correspond with well-established, empirical facts, and does it correspond to a person's experiences in the world?

The correspondence test includes two identifiable parts: *facts* of the world and *experiences* in the world—yet the two overlap. The claims of an adequate worldview must match with the observed world, the way it really is. The widely accepted correspondence theory of truth says that "truth equals what corresponds to reality."[7] A person's ideas must coincide with the actual state of affairs in the world. Thus, a reasonable worldview is not lacking in factual support.

An individual's personal experience of the world also really matters. No worldview can be truly acceptable if it is genuinely at odds with a person's established experiences. Philosopher Ronald H. Nash states that "no worldview deserves respect if it ignores or is inconsistent with human experience."[8]

5. Verification Test: Can the central truth-claims of the worldview be verified or falsified?

A viable worldview makes claims that can be tested and proven true or false. The scientific enterprise operates on the basis of the verification/falsification principle. Hypotheses and theories are subjected to appropriate and continued testing. Over time they are either verified (confirmed) or falsified. While absolute confirmation of a specific scientific perspective is not possible given the basic inductive nature of science, a theory that withstands extensive testing is considered a well-established truth or fact.

On the other hand, a nonfalsifiable claim that cannot be investigated, evaluated, and critiqued carries little rational weight. If there is no way (at least in principle) to falsify a view, then by the same standard there is no way to verify it. Testability increases a worldview's intellectual credibility. The concept of "testable truth" contains persuasive power.

6. Pragmatic Test: Does the worldview promote relevant, practical, and workable results?

An acceptable worldview must be sensible and workable and, therefore, "externally livable." This pragmatic approach applies to both society and individuals. A worldview should meet people's needs, both theoretically and practically. A realistic vision must work in everyday life. It should provide direction to people and help them solve problems.

However, the pragmatic test cannot be the principal test for truth because expediency and usefulness presuppose some relation between human activity and ultimate reality (or possibly revelation). That is, something can only be considered "useful" if it can be known that such a use is a good thing in the real world. Something can "work" only in light of the purpose or goal toward which it is being "worked." And purpose presupposes that there is something real, true, and good.

Workability thus assumes a metaphysical (view of reality) and epistemological (theory of knowledge) foundation by which the practical component can be defined. Philosopher Douglas Groothuis identifies this notion of workability for one particular worldview: "Christian faith teaches that it works (or bears spiritual fruit) only because it is true."[9] On the other hand, the Eastern philosophies strike many as practically unworkable. For example, for the nation of India to advance technologically it, in large measure, had to divorce itself from the metaphysical claims of Hinduism.

7. Existential Test: Does the worldview address the internal needs of humanity?

Worldviews must account for real human needs, desires, and aspirations. They should address man's need for meaning, purpose, and significance—and explain why man is the way he is. According to philosopher Søren Kierkegaard (1813–1855), a worldview as a broad philosophy of life should propose a viable reason for people to live and to die. A satisfactory worldview illumines man's existential predicament.

The actual living out of a worldview should fill a person's life with meaning and purpose. An internally livable worldview supplies genuine existential satisfaction.

The diverse worldview tests examined thus far are important individually. But is there a way to draw these tests together so that they illuminate the whole picture?

8. Cumulative Test: Is the worldview supported by multiple lines of converging evidence that together add increasing support for its truth-claims and extend the breadth of its explanatory power?

The best worldview does not depend upon only one particular argument or piece of evidence to make its case.[10] Nor does it depend upon passing one specific worldview test at the expense of the others. Rather, a genuinely acceptable worldview has multiple strands of supporting evidence. These diverse lines of evidence build a cumulative case in support of a worldview and ultimately demonstrate its genuine and broad explanatory power.

Cambridge professor C. S. Lewis seems to have had this concept in mind when he described his reason for believing in the truth of Christianity. He said, "I believe in Christianity as I believe that the Sun has risen, not only because I see it, but because by it I see everything else."[11] For Lewis, the Christian worldview illumined the world and all of life, particularly the enigmatic human condition. The multiple strands of evidence in support of the Christian worldview had resulted in a cumulative case argument for the faith.

9. Competitive Competence Test: Can the worldview successfully compete in the marketplace of ideas?

A suitable position should also be able to accept and adjust to new data, respond to reasonable challenges, and offer an insightful critique of competing systems. Worldviews need to be sufficiently firm yet somewhat pliable and responsive to objections and changes. The ability to adjust makes for a successful contender and workable belief system in the marketplace of competing ideas.

In contrast, a worldview that cannot compete in this way is usually sent into philosophical retirement. Its viability is firmly questioned and its adherents gradually dwindle. To some extent the worldview of deism, especially popular in the eighteenth century, has suffered this fate.[12] An effective worldview must successfully compete in the "intellectual Coliseum." As scholar Ravi Zacharias notes: "A world view is not complete in itself until it is able to refute, implicitly or explicitly, contrary world views."[13]

The worldview that scores well on all nine tests deserves consideration as a feasible option in the quest for a truthful perspective on reality.

Truth Once Tested

A. J. Hoover cautions that even the best worldviews come with limitations: "A good worldview does not have to be perfect to be held by reasonable men. . . . Every worldview has a few loose ends, a few bits of data left unexplained, just as every big court case has a few uncoordinated facts scattered here and there."[14]

No worldview is perfect in explaining reality. Instead, a worldview functions much like a scientific model in its attempt to provide a broad and general explanatory theory about reality. Lack of perfection should not prevent anyone from evaluating various positions and embracing the one that scores highest on the nine critical tests.

The study of logic helps develop the critical thinking skills necessary to explore and evaluate competing worldviews. Principles of reason must be appropriately applied in this process. No one in search of truth can afford to miss the next chapter's logic lesson.

Discussion Questions

1. Which worldview test do you consider to be the most important? Why?

2. In what order would you apply the tests? Why?
3. Can a worldview be imperfect yet still be a viable option for a rational person? If yes, how so? If not, why not?
4. What does it mean that logical coherence is a necessary but not a sufficient condition for determining truth?
5. What does it mean for a worldview to be externally and internally livable?

For Further Study

Bush, L. Russ. *A Handbook for Christian Philosophy*. Grand Rapids: Zondervan, 1991.

Corduan, Winfried. *No Doubt about It: The Case for Christianity*. Nashville: Broadman & Holman, 1997.

Harris, Robert A. *The Integration of Faith and Learning: A Worldview Approach*. Eugene, OR: Cascade, 2004.

Hoover, A. J. *The Case for Christian Theism: An Introduction to Apologetics*. Grand Rapids: Baker, 1976.

Wainwright, William J. *Philosophy of Religion*. Belmont, CA: Wadsworth, 1988.

3

LOGIC 101 AND
CHRISTIAN TRUTH-CLAIMS

Even though most people who reject Christianity treat it as a refuge for enemies of reason, the truth is that there may be no worldview in the history of the human race that has a higher regard for the laws of logic.

Ronald H. Nash, *Worldviews in Conflict*

Test everything. Hold on to the good.

1 Thessalonians 5:21

*T*he value of a coherent and logical worldview wasn't just important to me while I was lying in a hospital bed due to a life-threatening health crisis. It began making a distinct impression on me as a young college student when I attended an academic debate between a Christian and an atheist. It was fascinating to hear those two debaters going back and forth arguing their respective cases for and against belief in God's existence. As they spoke, I outlined their points to better evaluate each position.

During the question/answer periods, I very much wanted to ask the atheist about his bold and staunch claim that God does not exist. Specifically, I wanted to find out how he could know that. But, being a bit self-conscious and realizing hundreds of people would hear this critical question—which, frankly, I wasn't *sure was all that well-thought-out—anxiety got the better of me, and I decided against going to the microphone.*

Fortunately, however, the debaters stayed afterward. One-on-one they fielded questions for the few who remained. I approached the atheist and shook his hand, thanking him for his efforts. Then I asked if it were correct to define atheism as the claim that "no god or gods are real" or that "no god or gods actually exist."

After some quibbling about the exact meaning of certain terms, the atheist essentially agreed that these two statements accurately reflected his position. I then asked, "If atheism asserts that 'no god is real' or that 'no god actually exists,' then isn't it making a universal claim about 'all reality' and 'all existence'?"

In other words, as a point of logic,[1] doesn't the atheist, for his claim to be valid, have to know all about reality and existence to rightly exclude any and every god? For example, to claim with any validity that there are no entities of a particular type (gods) in a given circle or set (reality), doesn't a person need a complete or comprehensive knowledge of that circle or set (reality)?

I concluded my remarks by asserting that the atheist position could be valid only if atheists could justify their implicit claim to have a comprehensive knowledge of all reality and/or all existence. This position of seeming omniscience is, of course, beyond the capacity of any human being.

The atheist responded by saying that an incoherent god could not exist regardless of humanity's limited knowledge.

"That may well be true," I replied, "but then in order to maintain one's atheism, a person must bear the burden of showing that every conceivable concept of God is actually incoherent. This feat seems beyond the atheist's capacity."

At that point other people in line interrupted impatiently with their questions and comments. While that exchange marked the end of my first discussion with an adamant atheist, it nevertheless furthered my belief in the value of logic when considering worldviews. No perspective of reality can offer legitimate help unless it withstands logical scrutiny.

Choosing a Logical Worldview

The ability to think rationally and critically is indispensable for a person to choose a reality-based world-and-life view and to successfully evaluate other positions. Moreover, in order to analyze the subject of worldviews, from the historic Christian perspective or otherwise, the bare elements of logic are necessary.

Both Christians and non-Christians can appreciate that the Bible itself promotes intellectual virtues and that believers are called to value and pursue the "life of the mind" as a gift from God. The general consensus throughout church history has been that faith and reason are compatible (see chapter 5).

The Life of the Mind

The Christian worldview highly values logic and rationality, which find their source and ground in God.[2] As the only creatures made in the image of God,[3] human beings possess profound intellectual faculties. Humans alone read and think—pursue, discover, and reflect upon the truths of logic, mathematics, science, philosophy, and the arts. Only human beings develop a comprehensive world-and-life view and philosophize about whether their belief systems best match reality.

Curiously enough, even the very concept of a *worldview* presupposes that humans are capable of the type of serious philosophical, religious, and moral reflection that the Bible uniquely attributes to divine image bearers.[4] Both the Old and New Testaments call for people to love God with their entire beings,[5] and this holistic approach certainly includes developing and using the extraordinary minds God has given. According to Scripture, true "wisdom, knowledge, and understanding" are rooted in reverence for God and his revealed Word.[6]

Intellectual virtues such as discernment, reflection, testing, analysis, and renewal of the mind are biblical imperatives.[7] Therefore pursuing the "life of the mind" to the glory of God is an important component in the Christian's overall devotion. Using divinely given faculties to think clearly and carefully about the most important issues of life pleases God.[8] By contrast, mental sloth, gullibility, prejudice, and especially intellectual dishonesty bring dishonor to Christ. A mindless or anti-intellectual approach to the Christian faith does not correspond to a genuine understanding of many Old and New Testament passages.

History corroborates this view. Judaism and Christianity have (in many parts of the world) led the spread of literacy and education. This thriving connection to literacy is simple to understand: if a Jew or Christian can't read, then he or she can't easily study the Word of God.

A Brief Survey of Logic

Studying logic helps order a person's thinking like no other academic discipline. Understanding the laws of logic and the basic rules of argumentation greatly enhances a person's thinking skills and thus promotes a more rational view of the world and life. And, if a classroom is any indicator, a refresher course could be extremely beneficial for many people (see sidebar titled "Classroom Quotes: Logic Laughter").

In the following introduction to the fundamental principles of reasoning, biblical truth-claims are used to illustrate the rationality of the historic Christian worldview.

Classroom Quotes:
Logic Laughter

"But Professor Samples, if I can't attack my opponent's character, I have nothing left."

"Because of women's intuition, women don't need logic. Men do."

"I thought I was a good student, until I took your class!"

"Professor Samples, I'm sorry I failed the first two exams, but it's not my fault. It's actually yours."

"What should I be thinking about when I'm listening to your lecture?"

Comments like these not only make interacting with students a great deal of fun, they also confirm the tremendous need for introductory logic instruction.

Three Foundational Laws of Logical Thought

The study of logic considers three laws of thought as bedrock principles: the law of non-contradiction, the law of excluded middle, and the law of identity.[9] Their importance to human thought and discourse cannot be overstated. These logical anchors, so to speak, can be stated to reflect a metaphysical perspective (what is or is not—being) or an epistemological perspective (what can be true or not true—truth).[10]

The Law of Noncontradiction: "A" cannot equal "A" and equal "non-A"

Nothing can both *be* and *not be* at the same time and in the same respect.

A statement cannot be both true and false at the same time and in the same respect.

The **law of noncontradiction**, the foundational principle for all logical thinking, reveals the nature of contradictory relationships. A contradiction in logic reflects a very specific relationship. Two statements are contradictory if they negate or deny each other. Contradictory statements cannot both be true, and they cannot both be false. Rather, contradictory statements have opposite truth value: exactly one statement is true; the other is false.

The qualifying phrase "at the same time and in the same respect" is a critical component. Statements can be both true and false at different times and in different ways, but they cannot be both true and false at the exact same time and in the exact same way. In light of this, the logical relationship between the following statements should be considered:

"Jesus Christ is God Incarnate."   "Jesus Christ is not God Incarnate."
(historic Christianity)   (Judaism, Islam)

These two statements (which form the cores of distinctly different religious perspectives) stand in a contradictory relationship to each other. They negate or deny each other—the statements cannot both be true (nor can they both be false) at the exact same time and in the exact same way. If one statement is assumed true, then the other must be false. The statement on the left asserts that Jesus Christ (the subject term) is included in the category of God Incarnate (the predicate term), whereas the statement on the right excludes Jesus Christ from the category of God Incarnate.

The two statements thus have opposite truth value. Both cannot be simultaneously true; rather, exactly one statement can be true and the other false. Thus, if the declaration "Jesus Christ is God Incarnate" is true, then any theology or religion that affirms the contradictory statement "Jesus Christ is not God Incarnate" must be false. On the other hand, if the statement "Jesus Christ is not God Incarnate" is true, then the claim of historic Christianity that "Jesus Christ is God Incarnate" must be false. A person cannot logically affirm that two contradictory religious beliefs (or worldviews) are both true.

The Law of Excluded Middle: "A" is either "A" or "non-A"

Something either is or it is not.

A statement is either true or false.

Applying the **law of excluded middle** to the contradictory statements above (whether Jesus is or is not God Incarnate) shows that truth can be found in only one statement or the other. The law of noncontradiction can be thought of as indicating that "not both" are true, whereas the law of excluded middle subtly reveals that "either one or the other" must be true (no middle ground is possible). For example, the law of excluded middle says either Jesus Christ is God Incarnate, or he is not God Incarnate; one of those two statements must be true (and the other one false). The claim cannot be made that there is "some truth" in both statements. If the terms are used consistently and clearly, a choice must be made—either Jesus Christ is, or he is not, God Incarnate.

The Law of Identity: "A" is "A"

A thing (person, event, judgment) is what it is.

A true statement is true.

The **law of identity** conveys that something is identical to itself and different from all other things. With the subject term of the statements above being none other than Jesus Christ, if that statement is true, then he cannot be someone else ("A" is "A").

Without exception the laws of noncontradiction, excluded middle, and identity apply to all matters of thought and hold true for any and all worldviews. Therefore, the truth-claims of other religions can also be subjected to these principles.

Logicians have traditionally considered these three principles to be both necessary and inescapable because all thought, correspondence, and action presuppose their truth and application. The laws are therefore said to be *"ontologically real"* (defining the ultimate characteristics of reality), *"cognitively necessary"* (no coherent thinking is possible without their application), and *irrefutable* (their attempted refutation presupposes their use in refuting them).[11]

Four Logical Relationships

Recognizing the principle of noncontradiction as foundational to logic (and necessary for a well-thought-out worldview), four logical relationships—contradictory, contrary, subcontrary, and subalternation—must be compared and contrasted. These relationships are obtained when statements fitting two or more of the following categorical propositions are compared with one another:

Universal affirmative proposition	**A**: All "S" are "P."
Universal negative proposition	**E**: No "S" are "P."
Particular affirmative proposition	**I**: Some "S" are "P."
Particular negative proposition	**O**: Some "S" are not "P."

Note: A, E, I, and O represent the standard categorical propositions;
S = subject term and P = predicate term.

The four logical relationships can help in understanding how differing religious and worldview claims relate one to another. These assertions can stand in different logical relationships in terms of truth.

A **contradictory relationship** expresses opposite truth value (exactly one statement true, and exactly one statement false). Propositions **A** and **O** have a contradictory relationship, as do **E** and **I**. A specific example of a contradiction relating to the nature of Christ could read:

A: "All of the divine nature was in Christ."	O: "Some of the divine nature was not in Christ."
(orthodox Christian view)	(unorthodox view)

Only one of these Christological statements can be true.

A **contrary relationship** means not both statements are true (though both statements may be false). The **A** and **E** propositions stand in a contrary logical relationship. A set of religious truth-claims could be stated:

A: "All world religions are true."   E: "No world religions are true."
(pluralism)   (atheism)
I: "Some (at least one) world religions are true."
(historic Christianity)

A contrary relationship differs from contradictory: the two universal statements (**A** and **E**) can both be false if the particular statement (**I**) is true. The two universal statements are said to be *contrary*, not contradictory, because although they cannot both be true, it is possible for both of them to be false. On the other hand, statements **E** and **I** are *contradictory*: either no religion is true, or at least one religion is true.

In a **subcontrary relationship**, not both statements are false (though both statements may be true). Propositions **I** and **O** stand in a subcontrary logical relationship.

(I): "Some of Jesus's attributes are divine."   (O): "Some of Jesus's attributes are not divine" (but human).

Logically speaking, both of these statements cannot be false, but they could both be true. And, according to historic Christian Christology (the study of the person and nature of Christ), both are true. This example illustrates that Jesus Christ can have both divine and human attributes without necessarily defying reason.

Subalternation relationships show how truth in the universal statements guarantees truth in the corresponding particular statements (but not vice versa) and how falsity in the particular statements guarantees falsity in the corresponding universal statements (but not vice versa). For example, suppose it is true that:

(A) All the canonical Gospels reflect eyewitness testimony about the life of Jesus of Nazareth.

Then it must also be true that:

(I) Some (at least one: the Gospel of John, for example) of the canonical Gospels reflect eyewitness testimony about the life of Jesus of Nazareth.

In this example, since the universal affirmative proposition (**A**) is true, then it follows logically that the corresponding particular affirmative proposition (**I**) is also true. Truth then flows from the universal proposition to its corresponding particular proposition (both **A** and **I** are affirmative or inclusive statements).

Falsity flows only from the particular to its corresponding universal proposition. For example, suppose it is false that:

(O) Some canonical Gospels are not divinely inspired.

Then it is also false that:

(E) No canonical Gospels are divinely inspired.

In this example, a false particular negative proposition (**O**) makes its corresponding universal negative proposition (**E**) false as well (both **O** and **E** are negative or exclusive statements).

> If this material is new, then take a few minutes and review the difference between *contradictory*, *contrary*, *subcontrary*, and *subalternation* logical relationships. Experts on the brain and the mind say that a person's thinking skills improve the more they're used. Neurological experts even say that sustained and rigorous intellectual stimulation is one component in helping to ward off dreaded diseases of the brain such as Alzheimer's.

Self-Referentially Absurd Statements

Self-referentially absurd statements both affirm and deny the same basic meaning. This problem occurs when an asserted principle contradicts itself. People often make such philosophical statements without realizing what's really being said.

"I hate to say it, but the truth is that there is no truth." (***The claim of "no truth" is itself expressed as truth.***)

"All truths are half-truths." (***Then this truth must be a half-truth—or maybe a quarter truth!***)

"You can never know anything for certain." (***People who say this are often quite certain when they say it.***)

"My belief is that I only believe in what I see." (***But aren't beliefs, such as the one expressed in this sentence, conceptual and thus invisible?***)

"I accept the principle that one should only believe in things that have evidence to support them." (***And where is the evidence for this principle?***)

These last two examples are especially intriguing:

"My daddy *told* me, 'Only believe half of what you see and none of what you *hear*.'" (***Was Daddy believed when he said this?***)

"Professor Samples, I would like to give you a few reasons why logic is invalid." (*Isn't logic being used to dismiss logic?*)

> Each of the above statements is self-referentially absurd. What makes them so? Remember, a self-referentially absurd statement is a statement that asserts a particular principle that, if applied back to that statement, would contradict it (in other words, it fails to meet its own standard).

Reasoning: Ordered Thought

The Greek philosopher Aristotle (384–322 B.C.) referred to logic as a "tool" or "instrument" that helps order thinking so a person can arrive at truthful, rational conclusions. Though Aristotle certainly did not invent the principles of logic, he was the first to systematize them.[12] By using these standards of correct reasoning a person can appropriately evaluate the worldview claims made by various belief systems.

Logic is all about proving things through the proper use of arguments. Such arguments aren't verbal fights, bitter controversies, or heated disagreements. Rather, as logician Patrick J. Hurley explains, a logical argument is "a group of statements, one or more of which (the premises) claim to provide support for, or reasons to believe, one of the others (the conclusion)."[13] An argument, then, consists of two essential parts: (1) a claim (or conclusion) and (2) support (or premises) for the claim in the form of reasons, evidence, or facts.

Logician T. Edward Damer asserts that "an argument is a supported opinion."[14] If, however, a claim is made without any support to substantiate or justify that claim, then an opinion has been expressed—but no argument. Opinions simply convey the thoughts and/or feelings of a speaker or writer at a given time. Because they don't attempt to prove anything (lacking support), opinions are not arguments.

Sometimes a series of facts, evidence, and reasons (potential premises) is presented without an actual claim being made. Without a specific assertion, the observer is left with a bunch of interesting data but no argument. (For example, in informal conversation, the conclusion is frequently left unstated but is implied or understood in context.) However, to have an argument, a claim (conclusion) must be made and supported (with premises).

A good argument requires that the premises genuinely support the conclusion or entail it. This necessary connection between the premises and the conclusion is called an inferential relationship. With this proper connection established an argument is considered valid or strong. A breach in this relationship results in a breakdown or failure of the argument to prove its conclusion. The argument would then be classified as invalid or weak. Various fallacies (errors in reasoning) describe breakdowns in the all-important premise(s)/ conclusion relationship. Some of these problematic thinking processes are addressed in the next chapter.

For the conclusion of an argument to be adequately supported, all premises must be true, and the argument must employ correct reasoning in using them. In a sound or cogent argument, the premises must support the conclusion in five different ways. Using these standards guides a person's reasoning on the logical **TRACK**:[15]

True support: All premises must be factually true or intellectually accept- able. Even one false premise in an argument defeats the argument. At the same time, it's worth remembering that sometimes premises represent acceptable views more than demonstrable truths.

Relevant support: The premises must be connected, readily applicable, or pertinent to the conclusion. As Damer explains: "A premise is relevant if its acceptance provides some reason to believe, counts in favor of, or makes a difference to the truth (or falsity) of the conclusion."[16]

Adequate support: The premises must provide enough support—"sufficient in number, kind, and weight"[17]—to justify the conclusion. This point applies to arguments dealing with empirical facts, such as scientific or historical matters. Genuine support supplies all the crucial reasons necessary to back up the conclusion with appropriate depth.

Clear support: The premises must possess essential clarity of thought and expression, thus avoiding vagueness (being blurred or fuzzy), ambiguity (multiple meanings), and grammatical error. Thinking, speaking, and writing should reflect logical unity.

Knowledgeable support: The premises must qualify as knowledge (warranted, true belief), avoiding unwarranted presumption. Good premises are not based upon easily challenged assumptions but instead on those beliefs that supply legitimate proof or evidence for accepting the conclusion. Good argu- ments also anticipate and rebut alternative viewpoints and/or challenges.

Logic is an indispensable tool for investigating various worldview perspec- tives. And knowing what constitutes a good argument greatly assists a person in discovering a rational vision of life. Understanding that the premises of an argument must be true, relevant, adequate, clear, and knowledgeable helps keep a person's thinking on the right track.

Three Types of Logical Arguments

Awareness of the distinctions between different forms of arguments can help substantiate or refute individual belief systems. The pursuit of a worldview that can withstand logical scrutiny requires an ability to think through the arguments to determine how a particular position holds up. Three basic forms of reasoning—deductive, inductive, and abductive—can be used in this important process.[18]

Deductive

These arguments are constructed in such a way as to produce conclusions that follow with certainty or logical necessity from the premises. In a valid deductive argument, the inferential link (reasoning process) between the premises and conclusion is so well-connected that it guarantees or ensures the conclusion. If the premises are true, then the conclusion must also be true. If the logical structure of a deductive argument fails to preserve the truth of the conclusion, then the argument is invalid.

Deductive arguments, if constructed properly (that is, if valid), produce certain conclusions. And if the argument is valid with true premises, the argument is considered sound. The conclusion, therefore, must certainly be true. The shortcoming of deductive reasoning is that deductive arguments apply to a very limited number of areas (principally formal logic).

The following is a classic example of a deductive argument:

All men are mortal.
Socrates is a man.
Therefore, Socrates is mortal.

Three other popular deductive forms—*modus ponens, modus tollens,* and disjunctive syllogism—should also be understood.[19]

MODUS PONENS (AFFIRMING THE ANTECEDENT)

If P, then Q.	(The first term [P] is called the antecedent and the
P.	second term [Q] is called the consequent.)
Therefore Q.	

For example:

If you trust in Jesus Christ as the divine Messiah, then you are redeemed.
You do trust in Jesus Christ as the divine Messiah.
Therefore, you are redeemed.

MODUS TOLLENS (DENYING THE CONSEQUENT)

If P, then Q.	(The first term [P] is called the antecedent and the
Not Q.	second term [Q] is called the consequent.)
Therefore not P.	

For example:

If it's Easter, then it's Sunday.
It's not Sunday.
Therefore it's not Easter.

DISJUNCTIVE SYLLOGISM (DENYING THE DISJUNCT)

Either P or Q.	(A disjunct refers to an "either . . . or" statement.)
Not Q.	
Therefore P.	

A syllogism refers to the form of an argument that has exactly two premises followed by the conclusion.

Chris is either a man or a woman.
But Chris is not a woman.
Therefore, Chris is a man.

Remember, for these deductive arguments to be valid their forms must be exact.

Inductive

Inductive arguments are constructed in such a way as to produce conclusions that follow only *probably* from the premises. Unlike deductive arguments, inductive arguments cannot guarantee the truth of a conclusion. A strong inductive argument offers enough evidence to make the conclusion *likely* (or highly likely). If the premises prove insufficient to support the conclusion, then the argument is considered weak (inadequately supported).

The strength of an inductive argument (unlike the validity of a deductive argument) can fluctuate from strong to stronger. While inductive arguments by definition lack certainty, in most real-life situations, *probability* is the best a person can hope for. Therefore most arguments end up being inductive in nature. Though these arguments have limitations, they nevertheless remain a common and indispensable form of reasoning.

This inductive argument supplies an example:

Adolf Hitler was a dictator and an evil man.
Hideki Tojo was a dictator and an evil man.
Benito Mussolini was a dictator and an evil man.

Joseph Stalin was a dictator and an evil man.

Mao Tse-tung was a dictator and an evil man.

Kim Il Sung was a dictator and an evil man.

Idi Amin was a dictator and an evil man.

Pol Pot was a dictator and an evil man.

Saddam Hussein was a dictator and an evil man.

Therefore, it is highly likely that the next dictator to appear on the world scene will be an evil man.

The conclusion of this argument is probable, at best, though an objective analysis of history makes it all the more probable. (With respect to world-views, a viable conceptual system should be able to account for the evil [see chapter 16] committed by these aforementioned dictators.)

Contrasting Deduction and Induction

The following flow charts illustrate and explain the process for evaluating deductive and inductive arguments:[20]

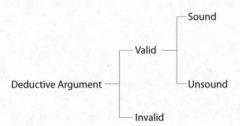

Validity: The conclusion of a valid deductive argument does, in fact (upon inspection), follow with certainty from the premises (a solid inferential connection exists between the premises and conclusion).

Soundness: All the premises of a sound argument must be true or acceptable (ensuring a certainly true conclusion).

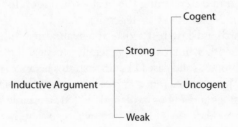

Strength: The conclusion of a strong inductive argument does, in fact (upon inspection), follow probably from the premises (the premises provide substantial evidence to support the conclusion).

Cogency: All the premises of a cogent argument must be true or acceptable (producing a probably true conclusion).

Table 3.1 contrasts deductive and inductive arguments.[21]

Table 3.1
Deductive versus Inductive Arguments

Deductive Arguments	Inductive Arguments
Certainty of conclusions (primary distinction)	Probability of conclusions (primary distinction)
No new information in the conclusion	Possible new information in the conclusion
From general to particular (usually)	From particular to general (usually)
From cause to effect (usually)	From effect to cause (usually)
A priori reasoning (prior to experience)	*A posteriori* reasoning (from experience)
Philosophical reasoning (typically)	Scientific reasoning (typically)
Argument forms are valid or invalid	Argument forms are strong or weak
Arguments are sound or unsound	Arguments are cogent or uncogent

Abductive

Arguments that attempt to arrive at the best explanation for an event or a given series of facts are called abductive. Unlike deduction, abduction provides no certainty in its conclusions but, like induction, yields more or less probable truth.

In contrast to induction, however, abductive reasoning doesn't try to predict specific probable outcomes. Rather, this method tries to provide the best broad explanatory hypothesis. Abductive reasoning can be helpful for determining which explanation of a given event is most likely true. For example, a person may use an abductive approach in seeking the best explanation for the origin of man (naturalistic evolution versus biblical creation). An abductive approach may also be used in determining the best explanation for the life of Jesus of Nazareth (divine Messiah versus legendary figure).[22]

No single hard-and-fast test exists for evaluating the superiority of one hypothesis over another, but logicians generally accept six criteria for determining the best explanation. A solid case (1) demonstrates balance between complexity and simplicity, (2) shows coherence, (3) corresponds to the facts, (4) avoids unwarranted presumptions and ad hoc explanations, (5) is testable, and (6) successfully adjusts to accommodate possible counterevidence. The hypothesis that scores highest on these criteria has genuine explanatory power and scope. However, a poor explanatory hypothesis can result in an erroneous belief system.

The abductive form of reasoning isn't as common as deduction and induction. However, when it comes to evaluating competing explanatory hypotheses, abductive arguments can be both preferable and invaluable. Being able to draw an inference to the best explanation is often crucial in evaluating competing worldview claims.

A Mindful Approach

Logic is all about constructing and evaluating arguments. The three standard ways these arguments take shape are through deductive, inductive, and abductive reasoning. Becoming skillful in their use can lead a person to rational and truthful conclusions, and this is especially true about worldviews.

To think logically brings order to one's thinking. Appreciating the crucial laws and relationships in logic, understanding the problems inherent in self-referentially absurd statements, and discovering three ways to correctly construct arguments reveals that rational order.

Sound reasoning is also indispensable when formulating and evaluating worldview claims. The next chapter explores common flaws that hinder the reasoning process and ten ways to avoid them.

Discussion Questions

1. What intellectual virtues are mentioned in Scripture as models for believers?
2. In a clear, concise, and correct way, explain the three foundational laws of logic.
3. Why do many logicians consider all significant thought, speech, and action to be dependent upon these foundational laws of logic?
4. Clearly and concisely explain the four logical relationships as applied to Christian truth-claims.
5. Explain the differences between deductive, inductive, and abductive arguments.

For Further Study

The Life of the Mind

Adler, Mortimer J., and Charles Van Doren. *How to Read a Book*. Rev. ed. New York: Simon & Schuster, 1972.

Moreland, J. P. *Love Your God with All Your Mind: The Role of Reason in the Life of the Soul*. Colorado Springs: NavPress, 1997.

Noll, Mark. *The Scandal of the Evangelical Mind*. Grand Rapids: Eerdmans, 1994.

Williams, Clifford. *The Life of the Mind: A Christian Perspective*. Grand Rapids: Baker, 2002.

The Study of Logic

Damer, T. Edward. *Attacking Faulty Reasoning: A Practical Guide to Fallacy-Free Arguments*. 4th ed. Belmont, CA: Wadsworth, 2001.

Geisler, Norman L., and Ronald M. Brooks. *Come, Let Us Reason: An Introduction to Logical Thinking*. Grand Rapids: Baker, 1990.

Hurley, Patrick J. *A Concise Introduction to Logic*. 8th ed. Belmont, CA: Wadsworth, 2003.

Kreeft, Peter. *Socratic Logic: A Logic Text Using Socratic Method, Platonic Questions, and Aristotelian Principles*. 2nd ed. South Bend, IN: St. Augustine's Press, 2005.

4

STRAIGHT THINKING

Do not conform any longer to the pattern of this world, but be transformed by
the renewing of your mind.

Romans 12:2

*Though I was not afraid of dying per se, I did feel great sorrow about the idea
of leaving my wife and three young children. In my hospital bed, though
multiple brain lesions made thinking difficult, I reflected as never before on a
statement made by my favorite Christian philosopher, Augustine (A.D. 354–430).
The words seemed written especially for me: "I was born into this life which leads
to death—or should I say, this death which leads to life?"[1]*

*My faith and worldview were being put to the test in the crucible of pain and
suffering. It was the greatest challenge of my life. But I was fortunate to have already
spent many years thinking carefully about what I believed and why I believed
it. To try to sort out my beliefs while undergoing a great trial would have been
overwhelming. Embracing sound reasoning and avoiding fallacious reasoning were
fundamental to my discovery of a rational and livable world-and-life view.*

Genuine learning often involves knowing both what to do and what not
to do. With crucial logic lessons, this awareness of how or how not to think
is all the more true. Thinking straight means first coming to understand the
standard patterns of correct reasoning (like those discussed in chapter 3).

Second, it involves avoiding faulty patterns of thought that can shipwreck the rational process.

A direct and necessary connection exists between logic and worldview orientation. Coherent worldviews may be true, whereas incoherent worldviews must be false. Inadequate and unacceptable worldviews inevitably flow from convoluted reasoning.

Learning how to avoid common missteps in the reasoning process helps protect thinking and equips a person to recognize and appreciate what a solid worldview foundation looks like.

Ten Ways to Avoid Fallacious Reasoning

A fallacy occurs when an argument contains a specific defect.[2] This mistake in the reasoning process causes an argument to break down (or fail to adequately support the conclusion). And left unrecognized, that failure (depending upon its magnitude) can seriously distort the lens through which one sees reality. Understanding and correcting fallacies can clarify a person's perception and thereby dramatically impact worldview thinking. (Warning: Some of these fallacies have Latin names, but plain English makes their explanations easy, even fun, to explore and understand.) The following ten strategies help thinkers avoid the pitfalls of fallacious reasoning:

1. Focus critical attention on backing an argument with solid support (evidence, facts, reasons), and avoid irrelevant emotional appeals.

When irrelevant emotional appeals replace solid premises (authentic support for the conclusion), a deceptive type of fallacy occurs. Though these fallacious claims clearly lack logical relevance, they sometimes go undetected because they contain psychological appeal.[3] This emotional effect tends to linger long after the appeal is made. Three types of emotionally based fallacies are common:

Argumentum ad baculum: "An appeal to force." This fallacy replaces real support for a given conclusion with a *threat*. The constituted intimidation may be either physical or psychological, and it may be expressed explicitly or implicitly. Sometimes referred to as the "appeal to the stick," this approach simply conveys the point that a person must "accept a particular conclusion *or else.*" The following examples illustrate this fallacy:

Bin Laden to the Saudi royal family—

"You must break off all cooperation with the United States and denounce America as an imperialistic enemy of Islam. This is your moral obligation.

And if you do not, Allah will surely use his agents to topple your puppet government."

Doctoral advisor to graduate student—

"Your arguments critiquing Darwinian theory are certainly provocative and clever, but pay heed that no student will ever successfully defend a doctoral dissertation at this institution while challenging the biochemical basis for evolutionary thought. You may want to consider revising your position in light of this ongoing precedent."

The first example involves more of a physical threat, while the second entails one more psychological in nature. It should be noted, however, that the threat in both cases is irrelevant to the issue at hand.

Argumentum ad misericordiam: "An appeal to pity." While instructors tend to be good at the appeal to force, students tend to be masters of the appeal to pity. This fallacy replaces legitimate support for a conclusion with an attempt to evoke sympathy. An emotional appeal of this type, though logically irrelevant, is nevertheless often successful because it plays upon another person's sense of compassion. The following examples demonstrate this fallacy:

Student to instructor—

"I know I failed the exam last week, but the events surrounding Hurricane Katrina have really bothered me. My family and I used to live in New Orleans, so I deserve to retake the test."

Pro-choice advocate speaking at a pro-abortion rally—

"If abortion on demand is outlawed, then desperate women will seek illegal back-alley abortions with rusty coat hangers, leading to untold harm and thousands of needless deaths."

Not only is this last example an unproven assumption about what would result in society if abortion on demand were outlawed, but the appeal intentionally attempts to evoke sympathy on the part of the listener. This appeal to pity is not based on reason but on emotion.

Argumentum ad populum: "An appeal to the people." Human beings have certain psychological needs. They want to be accepted, respected, and included. The appeal-to-the-people fallacy plays on these human needs in order to get a conclusion accepted. This appeal to popular sentiment can have a powerful result, especially when exploiting the enthusiasm of a crowd. An historical example of this bandwagon approach illustrates the problem:

Hitler Youth leader to student (ca. 1938)—

"Our Führer Adolf Hitler's policies must be good for Germany—just look how the large crowds salute him. You too should join our victorious patriotic movement."

A more contemporary example demonstrates how a congressman used this approach in opposition to Operation Iraqi Freedom:

"World opinion is clearly against U.S. military action in Iraq. If most of the people around the world condemn it, this war must be morally wrong!"

The question should be asked: Does the number of people who believe in something make it morally right or wrong? Should a person appeal to popularity or to reason?

Appeals to force, pity, and people may attract attention but in reality represent nothing more than irrelevant emotional manipulation. Solid premises must be logically relevant to the conclusion.

Genetic fallacy. This reductionistic argument selectively ignores logical relevance. It evaluates a thing, event, or idea solely in terms of its origin, and then carries that appraisal into the present while disregarding relevant changes. The trouble with this approach, however, is that things often change over time.

Psychology instructor to class—

"Belief in God arises from fear—primarily fear of the unknown and especially fear of death. Reason and logic have nothing to do with belief in the divine."

This Freudian example confuses a supposed origin of belief in God with its epistemological warrant (justifying reasons). First, the view that belief in God initially arose from fear of death is a doubtful assumption that presumes a naturalistic bias (man invented God as a psychological projection). And, second, even if the belief had come about through human fear, plenty of arguments still offer logical justification for a rational belief in God.

2. Openly acknowledge and seek to fairly justify any worldview presuppositions, thus avoiding inappropriate presumption.

Presumption is fatal to logical arguments because logic is about proving things. Wishful thinking, begging the question, and the complex question are common fallacies of presumption.

Wishful thinking. The logical error of wishful thinking consists in assuming that because someone *wants* a particular thing to be true, it *must* be true (or assuming that because a person doesn't want something to be true, it isn't). The problem with this approach is that the "wishing" is treated as a premise in support of a desired conclusion. However, mere wishing doesn't make something true or false.

> "I don't want the world to have an objective meaning, so for me it doesn't. Therefore I am free to do as I please with my life and create my own subjective reality."

> "If we commit mass suicide together, then our souls will join the mother ship that is following the Hale-Bopp Comet. Don't worry that the spacecraft can't be observed."

> "I am positively confessing that God will give me unlimited health, wealth, and prosperity! Sickness, poverty, and death cannot even touch me!"

All three of these examples illustrate wishful thinking instead of reasoned reflection.

The wishful thinking fallacy assumes the "truth" it should attempt to prove through an argument. The mere wishing for or desiring of something does not affect the objective truth or falsity of that which is longed for.

Petitio principii: **"Begging the question."** The begging-the-question fallacy also assumes that which should be proved. This fallacy occurs when an argument (1) conceals an essential premise, (2) bases a premise on the truth of the (as yet unproved) conclusion, or (3) technically goes in a circle.[4]

> "All the greatest scientists in the world believe that Darwinian evolution is a fact. If they didn't believe this they wouldn't be great scientists."

> "Of course David Koresh was the messiah. All of his followers at Waco believed it. And he personally taught his intimate followers about his messianic claims."

These two arguments are circular in nature and thus beg the question rather than prove the conclusion.

Complex question. This fallacy raises questions that carry built-in, unproven conclusions. Two examples are:

> "Hey, Henry, have you stopped plagiarizing other people's works yet?"

> "By the way, Bob, do you still use insulting racial epithets?"

These questions presume fact, in this case a person's guilt, and then ask a further question based upon that assumption. They cannot be answered satisfactorily with a mere yes or no. An appropriate answer from Henry may be: "I have never plagiarized the works of others." And, from Bob, "I have never used epithets."

3. *Exercise caution in analyzing causal relationships and conceptual comparisons.*

Careful thinking and especially worldview reasoning require an understanding of causal relationships. However, cause-and-effect connections can be difficult to track and logical mistakes can easily creep in. Three types of the "false cause" fallacy—*post hoc ergo propter hoc, non causa pro causa,* and the oversimplified cause have premise-conclusion relationships that reflect either an "imaginary causal connection" or merely a "minor causal connection."[5] The "slippery slope" and "faulty analogy" are two special types of the false cause fallacy.

Post hoc ergo propter hoc: **"After this, therefore because of this."** This type of reasoning insists that because A precedes B, then A must have caused B. But temporal succession alone does not mean that A actually caused B. The connection in time may be merely coincidental. The following example illustrates:

> "Baseball legend Ted Williams batted over .400 in the 1941 major league baseball season. Just a couple of months after this accomplishment the Empire of Japan attacked Pearl Harbor. Wow. A batting slump on Williams's part might have kept America out of World War II."

This example reasons accordingly: "after Williams hit .400, therefore because Williams hit .400." The amazing batting feat of the one they called "The Splendid Splinter" obviously had no causal connection to the Japanese surprise military attack upon Pearl Harbor on December 7, 1941. Mere temporal succession is not enough to make a causal connection. (To be exact, Williams hit .406 that season. No major leaguer has reached a season batting average of .400 or higher since.)

This type of conclusion (A preceded B, therefore A caused B) is sometimes drawn by religious leaders who attribute national tragedies and natural disasters to God's judgment against human sin (calamity happens after human sin; therefore calamity happens because of human sin). For example, some evangelical Christian leaders suggested that the events of 9/11 resulted from God's judgment upon America for the sins of abortion and homosexuality. Similarly, after the December 2004 tsunami that killed almost a quarter of a million people in countries surrounding the Indian Ocean, some Muslim leaders suggested that Allah had destroyed these people because of their lack of strict devotion to Islam.

From a biblical perspective, while God holds both the power and authority to mete out divine judgment in response to human sin, even against the particular sins of particular nations, this type of cause-and-effect reasoning is tricky to say the least. If a case is going to be made for interpreting calamity as a divine judgment, then the argument needs to be characterized by careful biblical, theological, historical, and moral reasoning. Otherwise, this type of reasoning may simply be an embarrassing example of the *post hoc ergo propter hoc* form of the false cause fallacy.

Non causa pro causa: "Not the cause for the cause." This fallacious form of reasoning simply misidentifies the actual cause of an effect.

> "Big cities typically have a high crime rate. They also have a lot of churches. To slow down the crime rate, the cities may want to shut down some of those churches."

Many reasons can be cited for large cities' high crime rates, but the abundance of churches within them would not likely be one of them.

Oversimplified cause. This fallacy occurs when an effect has multiple causes, but only one cause is identified.

> "President Ronald Reagan won the Cold War."

This statement constitutes an oversimplified cause. While President Reagan may be considered an extraordinary world leader and a critical player in bringing down the Soviet Union (especially in its later stages), other important people and issues made significant contributions. American presidents Truman, Eisenhower, Kennedy, Nixon, and Ford played central roles during critical stages. And Pope John Paul II, with his spiritual and moral influence in Eastern Europe, may actually have had more to do with the toppling of the Soviet Union than President Reagan. In addition, political and economic deficiencies in the Communist system played a significant role in its ultimate demise, as did reform policies (glasnost and perestroika) instituted by Soviet premier Mikhail Gorbachev. While Reagan's leadership was crucial, many world leaders share in the great victory of freedom and democracy over Soviet totalitarianism.

Slippery slope: "Domino fallacy." The slippery slope fallacy is a special type of false cause committed when someone asserts that a particular action or event will set off a chain reaction of events leading ultimately to devastating consequences. The problem lies in the lack of sufficient reason and/or evidence to ensure that the domino effect will indeed occur.

Thought Box: Analogical Reasoning

Some pro-life advocates compare the phenomenon of abortion on demand in America to the Jewish holocaust in Nazi Germany. This analogy often generates a sharp reaction and for good reason:

"If pro-life advocates really believed that abortion constitutes an actual holocaust on par with what transpired in Nazi Germany in the 1940s, then they would readily justify shooting abortion doctors. But they do not."

A different line of reasoning makes use of the analogy but avoids the fallacy:

Abortion on demand in America may be today's greatest moral issue. As a moral controversy it seems both like and unlike what went on in Nazi Germany in the 1930s and 1940s. Defeating the German war machine in World War II was certainly the only way to stop the systematic extermination of the Jews and other ethnic minorities. Killing individual SS soldiers was a moral necessity, for they were the actual perpetrators of this cataclysmic crime.

Shooting abortion doctors in America would *not* be the moral equivalent of killing SS soldiers in World War II. Mothers of aborted children are willing participants. If abortion on demand is to be stopped, then the hearts of these women must be transformed to place value on the lives they would otherwise terminate.

Killing abortion doctors would be morally misguided and repugnant, dangerous to the innocent, and deeply flawed as a strategy to combat abortion. One can rightly view abortion on demand as a type of holocaust yet adamantly repudiate the killing of abortion doctors.

Sound reasoning can correct faulty analogies.

Sometimes Christian groups issue dire warnings of imminent societal collapse as a result of prostitution and pornography and other moral ills. In doing so they often come close to committing the slippery slope fallacy. Although the devastating social effects of these sexually oriented sins can be catalogued, to argue directly against these activities as being harmful to individuals and society may be more appropriate and reasonable than to argue along the lines of a moral chain reaction, which is usually difficult to prove.

Faulty analogy. According to Hurley, "Analogical reasoning may be the most fundamental and most common of all rational processes."[6] Careful thinkers therefore must give prudent consideration to the common arguments derived from analogy.

An analogy attempts to argue that because two things share some similarities, then they likely have other traits in common. For example, if X and Y share attributes a, b, c, and d, and X has attribute e, then it is likely that Y has that distinctive as well. Analogies break down, however, when the things compared are trivial or superficial to the issue at hand (the conclusion).

Good analogies compare things that have solid connections, directly relate to the conclusion, and pay careful attention to dissimilarities. Arguments from analogy are inductive in nature and therefore suggestive at best. As a result they are not conclusive. (The thought box on the previous page supplies a provocative example of analogical reasoning.)

4. Present substantive evidence in support of an argument.

At least three distinct fallacies need to be avoided to support sound reasoning. These types of errors in thinking are especially common when it comes to promoting a particular worldview. Appeals to untrustworthy authorities, appeals to ignorance, and hasty generalizations betray weaknesses when offered in support of a belief system.

Argumentum ad verecundiam: "An appeal to an untrustworthy authority." Nothing is wrong with appealing to a genuine authority to buttress an argument. However, some so-called authorities may be unqualified or untrustworthy.[7] Alleged authorities may lack expertise or necessary abilities, or they may be inclined to bias or prejudice.

This fallacy is frequently committed when an authority speaks outside of his specialized field. For example, advertising often uses a famous person to pitch a product in an area very different from his own. The opinion of a physicist on philosophical questions or of a biologist on ethical questions may or may not be well-informed, but either way those personalities speak outside their areas of expertise. The same can be true of philosophers (though some of them don't consider anything to be outside their area of expertise). Supposed authorities who remain unnamed or unidentified have no bearing on the matter at all.

Argumentum ad ignorantiam: "An appeal to ignorance." This fallacy occurs when the premises fail to prove anything definite, and yet a specific conclusion is still drawn. Such an error typically takes the form of arguing for an assertion on the basis that it has not been proved false, or that it is false solely because it has not been proved true.

Ignorance on a particular point proves only a lack of knowledge on that point; that is why the premise of this fallacy fails to prove its conclusion. The reasonable thing to do if something is not proved is to reserve judgment. Conclusions drawn from premises that fail to prove anything—an appeal to ignorance—prove nothing.

Atheists who claim that no evidence exists for God are susceptible to this fallacy. Thinking God's existence unproven, atheists often go further concluding that God does not exist. Assuming, for the sake of argument, that God's existence can't be *proved* does not mean his existence has been *disproved*. Yet, some atheists argue that atheism should be presumed until convincing evidence for God is established. This strikes some theists as being little more than an "arbitrary intellectual imperialism."[8]

Hasty generalization. This faulty form of inductive reasoning draws a general conclusion before enough evidence has been gathered to support it. The particular collection of samples may be far too small or not randomly selected and therefore inadequate to support the generalized conclusion. Solid generalizations should be based on fair, carefully examined, and abundant data. Generalizations use an inductive form of reasoning that, at best, only shows probability.

One such example states:

> "I've worked with three born again Christians. All three were obnoxious and had a holier-than-thou attitude. Born-again people and their churches are a bunch of hypocrites."

Christians as sinful people whom God has forgiven are certainly capable of exhibiting bad behavior and poor attitudes, but to judge a whole group of people based upon the actions of a few individuals represents a hasty (or sweeping) generalization.

5. Ensure that the arguments reflect clarity of thought and expression.

Two fallacies, equivocation and amphiboly, demonstrate the problems that occur when words are ambiguous or sentences violate grammatical rules.

Equivocation. This error occurs when the conclusion of an argument depends upon the multiple uses (ambiguity) of a term. Usually the lack of clarity involved leads to a faulty conclusion as the following examples illustrate.

> "I'm a nobody. Nobody is perfect. Therefore I am perfect."

> "Some dogs have fleas. My dog has fleas. Therefore, my dog is some dog."

In the first example the word "nobody" carries the confusion, whereas in the second example, the word "some" changes meaning.

Amphiboly. In an amphiboly, the conclusion depends upon an ambiguous statement (improper grammar or syntax) that causes the reader or listener to draw an erroneous conclusion. For example:

> "Professor Samples's son Michael likes World War II more than his father. But how can a boy like a war more than he likes his own dad?"

Does Michael Samples enjoy studying World War II more than Professor Samples likes studying World War II? Or does Michael actually like the war more than he likes his dad? Surely, the former clarifies the correct meaning.

6. Identify the right kind of evidence necessary to make a good argument.

Category mistake. This error in reasoning mixes ideas or categories that do not belong together. Apples are compared with oranges.

"That musical arrangement (without lyrics) is morally evil!"

"What does the color red smell like?"

"Why can't God (an invisible transcendent Spirit being) be seen?"

While these examples seem obvious in isolation, identifying such category mistakes can alleviate potential distortions when considering worldviews. For example, some worldviews reject the existence of God because the divine being is not perceived by the five senses of humans. However, this type of reasoning needs to confront what historic Christianity teaches about the doctrine of the Incarnation (see chapter 8).

The ability to handle arguments (especially those of opponents) with fairness and integrity is a critical intellectual virtue and a core principle of sound reasoning. This "intellectual golden rule" or "principle of charity" calls for treating others' arguments with the same degree of care and detailed attention a person expects toward his own. Observance of rules seven through ten helps ensure a respectful approach. Critiquing the worldviews of other people needs to be done respectfully.

7. Respond directly to an opponent's argument and avoid character-related issues unless they are the logical issue.

Argumentum ad hominem. The standing order of General George S. Patton Jr. during the Second World War was to "attack, attack, attack, and, if in doubt, attack again!" That approach may have worked well for the U.S. Army in Europe during World War II, but when it comes to a logical engagement, an attack must focus on the argument and not on the person.

The *ad hominem* fallacy (argument against the person) occurs when someone presents his point and a competitor ignores that point and attacks the opponent's character instead. This tactic is not only rude and offensive but also logically unacceptable because it violates two core principles of reasoning. First, a person has an intellectual responsibility to respond to the content of an argument. Second, a person's character is irrelevant to whether his argument is valid. Even morally flawed people can present sound arguments.

This fallacy comes in three identifiable varieties:

Abusive: directly denouncing character (old-fashioned name-calling). The American political scene supplies two easy examples:

"Democrats are just a bunch of unpatriotic, Communist morons!"

"Republicans are a gang of heartless, greedy Nazis!"

Circumstantial: raising special circumstances in an attempt to discredit a person's motives (also known as "poisoning the well"):

"Christian-oriented scientists who argue for the big bang and for an old earth are clearly compromisers, for they care more about what their secular scientific colleagues think than they do what the Word of God clearly teaches."

It is possible that scientists who are Christians actually believe in big bang cosmology and an old Earth because they are intellectually convinced these views are consistent with both solid scientific evidence and sound biblical exegesis.[9] The focus should be on an opponent's arguments, not on a person's alleged motives.

Tu quoque: accusing the other person of hypocrisy as an attempt to avoid personal criticism (*tu quoque* is Latin for "you too"). A husband and wife illustrate this variety of the *ad hominem* fallacy:

"Yes, Honey, I maxed out the MasterCard by buying too many books on Amazon.com. But you spent even more on that couch. Frankly, when it comes to household items your spending is simply out of control!"

To criticize a person's character may be appropriate—*if* the person's character is the logical issue at hand. For example, jurors in a courtroom need to know if a witness has been found guilty of perjury in the past. In this case believability is closely connected to the issue of discerning truth. However, unless character is relevant, personal attacks are not.

When victimized by an *ad hominem* attack, it's tempting to respond in a similar manner, but a more effective and appropriate response is to highlight the attack's logical irrelevance. Then attention can be refocused on the relevant argument. Once the focus is on the issue and not on a person, listeners (even opponents) are more likely to consider and be persuaded by the arguments offered.

8. Take the time and effort to gain a correct understanding of an opponent's position.

Straw man. When one person distorts the argument of another and then proceeds to critique that misrepresentation (whether in writing or speaking), he commits the informal logical fallacy known as attacking a straw man. A straw man may be an extreme or exaggerated version of another's position or an oversimplification of it.[10] Any criticism of a distorted view lacks relevance.

This fallacy was so named because of the ease with which a straw image can be knocked down as opposed to a real man made of bone and muscle. So too, it is easier to dispose of an exaggerated or simplistic argument than a well-balanced and substantive argument. For example, critics of the Trinity doctrine often allege that this doctrine is unbiblical because it teaches three Gods. However, this objection is a straw man because in fact the doctrine of the Trinity affirms the existence of only one God who subsists as three persons.

The straw man fallacy is often committed in a face-to-face argument (especially a heated one) because a person may be thinking about her response instead of listening carefully. A good way to avoid misrepresentation and irrelevance is to restate an opponent's argument back to him. ("Let me make sure I understand your argument. Are you saying . . . ?"). This practice can produce positive results, including better listening, clearer understanding, and more successful communication.

People appreciate being heard and, when they are, often become more open to other perspectives and possible critique. Attitude and demeanor, not just arguments, affect persuasion. Understanding the worldviews of others can be difficult. Yet a spirit of fairness is indispensable.

9. Stay on topic when offering a rebuttal.

Red herring. Closely associated with the straw man error is the red herring fallacy. When someone diverts attention from the real issue by focusing on an extraneous or secondary matter he leads his opponent down an unproductive side trail. (The herring fish was reportedly used in English fox hunts to try to draw hunting dogs off track.) A change in subject (even if subtle) results in a loss of logical relevance.

Diversionary tactics (such as the red herring) violate the "appropriate response" principle—a critic's responsibility to focus any critique or rebuttals on the real question at hand.[11] One can avoid being the victim of this fallacy by maintaining a consistent focus, identifying where an argument got off track, and reminding an opponent of the authentic core of the debate.

The following illustration shows how a shift in the topic, even if somewhat related, takes the focus off the relevant issue:

> "You have argued against the so-called plague of abortion on demand based upon your pro-life convictions. But war, famine, and disease cause millions of deaths every year throughout the world. Shouldn't we be addressing those issues?"

The main point—the intentional killing of unborn humans because they are unwanted—has been shifted to unrelated deaths.

10. Render a fair assessment of all evidence for an opponent's position.

Suppressed evidence. Compounding other errors in argumentation is the commonly committed fallacy of *suppressed evidence*. It occurs when an arguer emphasizes only the evidence that supports his or her position while suppressing counterevidence that may point toward—or even require—a different conclusion.

The rules of logic and good reasoning compel truth seekers to deal honestly and transparently with facts, evidence, and all relevant data. A candid admission of tentativeness about one's own position (or worldview) reflects a refreshing and attractive intellectual integrity. When evidence points away from one's own position, it is better—even obligatory—to acknowledge a compelling argument than to shade the truth or engage in intellectual dishonesty.

Unfortunately, a strong temptation to engage in deck-stacking makes the fallacy of suppressed evidence easy to commit. Given this reality, if an advocate for one position appears to have ignored or diminished appropriate evidence against that position, then by all means an opponent should make the broader picture known.

Ardent advocates of Darwinian evolution commit the fallacy of suppressed evidence when they emphasize only the data that seems to support their position but ignore or suppress relevant challenges (e.g., narrow time constraints, a lack of a clear and viable biochemical pathway, the sudden emergence of complex life-forms and ecosystems, the problem of repeated evolution, etc.). However, to be fair, sometimes Christians also fail to admit the challenges to their worldview. While historic Christianity has some good answers in response to the problem of evil, pain, and suffering, theodicy (justifying God's goodness in a world that contains evil) nevertheless remains a challenge to those who embrace this world-and-life view.

Intellectual Integrity

The passionate pursuit of truth demands nothing less than a commitment to sound reasoning and honorable intellectual exchange. Arguments shaped by logical and moral/ethical principles establish well-reasoned and persuasive positions able to withstand scrutiny and everyday reality, as well as life-and-death situations. Incorporating the essential virtues of honesty, fair play, and charity increases a person's ability to defend any particular position.

Part 2 presents and explains the Christian theistic worldview in greater depth. This section begins with the Christian vision of truth, knowledge, and history.

Discussion Questions

1. What is a fallacy?
2. Why do fallacies often go undetected? How can one guard against fallacious thinking?
3. State the ten principles that help order one's thinking.
4. What fallacies are especially relevant with regard to worldviews?
5. Why is intellectual integrity critical in the life of the Christian?

For Further Study

Damer, T. Edward. *Attacking Faulty Reasoning: A Practical Guide to Fallacy-Free Arguments*. 4th ed. Belmont, CA: Wadsworth, 2001.

Hurley, Patrick J. *A Concise Introduction to Logic*. 8th ed. Belmont, CA: Wadsworth, 2003.

Kreeft, Peter. *Socratic Logic: A Logic Text Using Socratic Method, Platonic Questions, and Aristotelian Principles*. 2nd ed. South Bend, IN: St. Augustine's Press, 2005.

EXPLORING
THE CHRISTIAN
WORLDVIEW

5

A CHRISTIAN VISION OF TRUTH, KNOWLEDGE, AND HISTORY

The Bible does not present truth as a cultural creation of the ancient Jews or the early Christians. They received truth from the God who speaks truth to his creatures, and they were expected by this God to conform themselves to this truth.

Douglas Groothuis, *Truth Decay*

More than ten years of teaching philosophy and religion courses at a public college convinced me of how entrenched relativistic thinking is in the minds of many students today. This mindset impacts thinking about such critical realities as truth, knowledge, and even history. Students often expressed the basic thought that "there are no absolutes." They believed truth to be subjective in nature and dependent upon an individual's own perceptions, opinions, and experiences.

Unfortunately, many professors present a relativistic view of truth and morality but do not expose the monumental problems involved with this approach. But, then again, many of those professors may also be unaware of the insurmountable difficulties inherent in a relativistic perspective.

When it comes to truth, knowledge, and history, relativism is ubiquitous in Western culture. Christians who desire to communicate effectively the unique truth-claims of their faith in today's culture must be prepared to confront this wave of relativistic sentiment.[1]

While historic Christianity represents the faith of millions of believers through the centuries, the term "Christian theism" refers to the comprehensive worldview position. Therefore, Christian theism, as a broad and vibrant world-and-life view, involves far more than a mere personal relationship with God. It's a system of thought with truth, knowledge, and history as central components. The necessary and objective foundation for these crucial realities comes from the God of the Bible.

This infinite and personal God, the one who made the physical realm, is also responsible for the world's intelligibility and the unfolding of historical events. As a result, the classical Christian position on truth, knowledge, and history differs significantly from the relativistic spirit so common in today's world. The Christian worldview is rooted in absolute truth.

A Christian Theistic View of Truth

The Bible does not contain a technical philosophical discussion on the theory of truth. Nevertheless, this concept is a critical topic because Scripture claims to reveal absolute truth about God, about human beings and their condition, and about what God has done for humanity through Jesus Christ. General principles, therefore, concerning the nature of truth can be inferred from the scriptural revelation. The key biblical words for truth (Hebrew: 'ĕmet; Greek: alētheia) convey the ideas of stability, faithfulness, reliability, and honesty.[2] They also convey the idea of conformity to reality (or fact) and accuracy as opposed to error.[3]

Both the Old and New Testaments express the concept of truth by drawing critical contrasts between truth and falsity, truth and error, and complete truth as opposed to partial truth.[4] A "correspondence theory of truth" is generally presupposed. Christian philosophers J. P. Moreland and William Lane Craig define this approach as "the idea that truth is a matter of a proposition (belief, thought, statement, representation) corresponding to reality; truth obtains [is apprehended] when reality is the way a proposition represents it to be."[5]

Truth equals, represents, or matches reality. If an individual's thinking on a particular issue corresponds with the actual state of affairs (the way things really are—reality), then she knows the truth.

This basic understanding reflects the scriptural view. New Testament scholars D. A. Carson and Douglas J. Moo state: "Though 'truth' in Scripture can refer to more than propositional truth, propositional truth certainly lies within its embrace."[6] Seven crucial points set this historic Christian position apart from other worldviews (such as skepticism in general and postmodernism in particular, see chapter 13) that question or reject the idea of ultimate truth.[7]

1. God is ultimate truth.

In the Bible, God describes himself as being real, true, and alive[8] rather than being unreal, false, and dead like the gods conjured through counterfeit human idolatry.[9] According to historic Christianity, God is the ultimate and unchanging truth and the necessary real being that stands behind the created order. He also is the source and ground of all truth.

The ultimate veracity of God's moral character demonstrates reliability and faithfulness.[10] As a result of these attributes, his written Word reflects those same traits. It also carries his authority.[11] The Triune God of the Bible claims to be the greatest truth that all human beings should seek to discover and come to know personally.

> Now this is eternal life: that they may know you, the only true God, and Jesus Christ, whom you have sent.
>
> John 17:3

2. Jesus Christ is the truth of God Incarnate.[12]

According to the New Testament, the infinite, eternal, and transcendent God (in this case the second person of the divine Godhead—the Son or Living Word) has taken on a human nature and become man in the person of Jesus Christ.[13] Jesus of Nazareth is the truth of God in human flesh. While God's truth permeates the world through both creation and providence, the truth of God also came to humankind in a person.

As the God-man, Jesus proclaimed: "I am the way and the truth and the life. No one comes to the Father except through me" (John 14:6). Jesus is the only way of salvation because he perfectly possesses and reflects the divine *truth* and *life* that are exclusive qualities of God Almighty.[14] This special revelation of the life, death, and resurrection of God Incarnate has now been embodied in the New Testament Scriptures (the written Word, see chapter 7).

> The Word became flesh and made his dwelling among us. We have seen his glory, the glory of the One and Only, who came from the Father, full of grace and truth.
>
> John 1:14

3. All truth is God's truth, and he has revealed it to humankind.

God is the metaphysical foundation of all that is true.[15] Truth is logically coherent and corresponds to reality; the same is true of God's thoughts and knowledge. He knows all correct propositions and possesses a perfect knowledge of all things.

When human thoughts cohere and correspond with reality, people apprehend truth as well. As they discover the content of general revelation (studied in logic, philosophy, history, literature, science, values, law, and other disciplines), human beings know the truth of God. When understood and interpreted properly, the knowledge revealed by God in general revelation (via the created order) corresponds to the truth revealed by God in special revelation (via Scripture).

Christian thinker Robert A. Harris notes: "There is no conflict between Scriptural truth and any other truth. Apparent conflicts involve conflicts of interpretation (either of Scripture or of external facts). All truth is God's truth, and God does not contradict himself."[16] Truth that extends from God's nature and character is unified.

Sanctify them by the truth; your word is truth.

John 17:17

4. Truth is objective, knowable, and applicable.

The truth God revealed through both general and special revelation (creation and Scripture) is objective in nature.[17] It is the way things really are—independent of human subjective experience and man-made conventions. (This reality does not rule out the need for the subjective application of truth in one's life.) Truth, then, from the human standpoint is *discovered* not *invented*. Human beings can know the facts because God made people with the necessary capacities to apprehend what is true (see *imago Dei*, chapter 10).

This assertion doesn't mean, however, that human beings know all truth perfectly or that they don't have to work very hard at comprehending it. But some truth can be understood and applied to the human condition, especially as aided by the goodness of God to all people. Even though fallen in sin, the human race—by God's common grace—retains this basic capacity.[18]

Propositional language also conveys authenticity.[19] Because the Creator made human beings in his image, they are "networked" to think and speak the same language. God accommodates himself to the finite limitations of human beings whenever he reveals truth in a way they can understand. Because of truth's objectivity, availability, and knowability—the failure to seek it dooms an individual to live an inauthentic life that has monumental consequences now and forevermore.

Then you will know the truth, and the truth will set you free.

John 8:32

5. Truth is universal, absolute, and unchanging.

Central to historic Christian belief is the reality of Christ's unique lordship.[20] He is God, King, and Ruler over all.[21] The truth about this lordship is universal in nature—meaning it is true for all people, at all times, everywhere. It is not conditioned by culture but is without exemption, exception, or qualification.

Christian philosopher and apologist Douglas Groothuis explains: "The truth of the gospel is not subject to any human veto or democratic procedures. Jesus was not elected Lord by humans but was chosen by God; nor can he be dethroned by any human effort or opinion or insurrection."[22]

The lordship of Jesus Christ is therefore absolute, not dependent upon human will or conventional agreement. Christ's lordship is unchanging and permanent. Christian truth-claims concerning Christ (his identity, mission, and message) stand in direct opposition to the relativistic spirit currently so in vogue.

> Jesus Christ is the same yesterday and today and forever.
>
> Hebrews 13:8

6. Truth excludes whatever is contrary as falsehood.

An appeal to two unique Christian truth-claims helps with exploration of this critical point. First, *Jesus Christ is God Incarnate*. If true, then this assertion's denial (Jesus Christ is *not* God Incarnate) must by necessity be false, because two contradictory statements cannot both be true at the same time and in the same way (see chapter 3). The truth of Jesus being God Incarnate negates or denies its opposite (see, for example, 1 John 4:1–6). Further, this bold declaration that Jesus is God in the flesh is either true or not true, for clearly no middle position is available.

Second, *Christ's unique lordship* excludes all others who make the same claim. That means he alone is Lord. Indeed, the claims of his competitors (Caesar, Krishna, Allah, Hitler, and so on) must be false, and they must be imposters.[23] Christian truth-claims about Jesus may seem intolerant in light of present-day, politically correct cultural standards, but *if* Christ is in fact who he said he was, then these claims are the necessary and correct conclusions of sound logical reasoning.

To proclaim "Jesus is Lord" is, by necessity, an exclusive and logically intolerant claim. Unfortunately, popular appeals to tolerance often come at the expense of truth. Under the right conditions, tolerance[24] can be a valued Christian virtue, but never when it compromises genuine truth.

> Salvation is found in no one else, for there is no other name under heaven given to men by which we must be saved.
>
> Acts 4:12

7. To deny the reality of truth is self-defeating.

The skeptical attempt to deny the existence of truth ends up being self-defeating. This nullification results because all attempts to dismiss truth constitute claims about truth itself. Christian philosopher Gordon Clark succinctly explains the logical problem that results from denying truth:

> The skeptic asserts that nothing can be known. In his haste he said that truth was impossible. And is it true that truth is impossible? For, if no proposition is true, then at least one proposition is true—the proposition, namely, that no proposition is true.[25]

The chapters on logic showed that a self-referentially incoherent statement lays down a principle which, when applied back to itself, results in a contradiction (see chapter 3). The denial of truth is one such contradictory statement because it inevitably results in an assertion about truth itself.

God has made a world and human beings in that world in such a way that truth cannot legitimately be dodged. Sinful creatures inevitably try to avoid facing the truth in innumerable ways with devastating consequences[26]—but the God of all truth ensures that truth inevitably prevails in all things.

> For this reason I was born, and for this I came into the world, to testify to the truth. Everyone on the side of truth listens to me.
>
> John 18:37b

"The Truth, the Whole Truth, and Nothing But the Truth"

In all fields, truth must be pursued to arrive at a correct understanding of life. Objective reality should never be feared, and nothing less should be settled for. When an individual pursues and grasps the truth, he tracks with its Author.

The Christian worldview considers God as ultimate truth. The person of Jesus Christ reveals that truth to humankind in an objective, knowable, and applicable way. All truth is God's truth. It is universal, absolute, and unchanging and excludes whatever is contrary as falsehood. To deny truth's reality is self-defeating. These seven points show why the historic Christian view of truth is absolute. And they refute any possibility of inappropriate relativistic thinking. They also impact the Christian vision of knowledge.

A Christian View of Knowledge

What is knowledge? How does it arise? What can human beings actually know and how can they know it? And what limitations do people face in the process of knowing?

The Bible does not contain a technical epistemological theory within its pages. Epistemology (from the Greek *epistēmē*: "knowledge") refers to the study of the origin, nature, limits, and validity of knowledge. However, as in the case of truth, general principles related to the concept of knowing can be derived from Scripture. The key biblical words for knowledge (Hebrew: *yādaʿ, nākar;* Greek: *oida, ginōskō*) convey the idea to "know," "recognize," or "understand"; and this knowing applies in various ways to God, the world, and general comprehension. In Scripture, knowledge can be of a personal and experiential nature.[27] It can also be of a propositional nature.[28]

Though no one strict approach to the question of knowledge finds complete agreement within Christianity, several universally accepted points represent a consensus among Christians.[29]

1. Extreme skepticism is self-defeating.

Like the universal denial of truth, extreme skepticism with regard to knowledge is self-defeating and therefore false. The skeptic's reasoning ("one cannot know") backfires for surely he at least claims to know that he doesn't know—an assertion which is self-referentially incoherent or absurd. Logical reflection reveals that at least some knowledge is both possible and, in fact, actual.

2. Knowledge is possible with God as its source and foundation.

The Bible indicates that human beings can attain genuine knowledge of God, the self, and the world.[30] God created both the world and humankind and his objective existence is the fixed reference point that makes authentic knowledge possible.

The Creator sustains the universe and the mind and sensory organs of man in such a way that they correspond with each other and with him. Because man is created in God's image,[31] human beings can trust in the reliability of the basic process of knowing (which includes such intellectual acts as apprehension, judgment, and reasoning). All human knowledge is dependent upon God because he serves as the necessary objective foundation for man's cognitive and sensory capabilities as well as the world's built-in intelligibility. Evangelical theologian Carl F. H. Henry explains this outcome of God's coordinated creative action:

> Divine revelation is the source of truth and the human mind a created instrument for recognizing it. Human knowledge of the cosmos, as well as of other selves, rests on the ontological [relating to ultimate being] significance of reason. The Creator has fashioned a *Logos*-ordered and *nomos*-structured universe, one meshed to the categories of understanding implanted in mankind at creation.[32]

Some Christian theologians and philosophers argue that human beings even possess an innate knowledge of God (Latin: *sensus divinitatis*, "a sense of the divine"[33]) as part of being made in God's image (see chapter 10).

3. Knowledge is directly connected to God's revelatory acts.

God's general and special revelation (via the created order and through God's personal actions, events, and written words) make knowledge available. In other words, people can come to "know" through exercising their God-given rational capacities, through empirical observation (which includes science), and from understanding and reflecting upon God's unique propositional revelation—Scripture.

Ideally, the sources of general and special revelation work in a complementary fashion, providing human beings with genuine divine truth. Christian philosophers debate the specific grounds of just how humans acquire knowledge (rationalists give priority to reason whereas empiricists give priority to the five senses). Nevertheless, the Christian worldview affirms the five senses as generally reliable and that human beings have the capacity for rational thought because God serves as the necessary epistemological ground of both. Even inductive reasoning (with its probabilistic nature) can be appropriate and cogent because God serves as the foundation for all thought processes.

4. Knowledge is properly justified true belief.

Many Christian philosophers today (as well as some significant ones from the past) agree that knowledge can be rightly defined as "properly justified true belief."[34] Starting at the end of this definition and working backward explains how knowledge differs from mere opinion.

First, knowledge involves belief. It is a necessary part of knowing, for no one can *know* something unless he *believes* it. A person cannot know, for example, that Jesus Christ is Lord and not believe it. It would be absurd for a person to say that he knows Earth is round but doesn't believe it. Skeptics often want to sharply separate belief from knowledge, but it seems clear that believing is a critical part of knowing. Yet, though belief and knowledge go together, knowledge is definitely more than mere belief.

Second, a person can only know things that are true. An individual can *think* she knows something to be true but, in fact, be wrong. Or she can know of something false that is indeed false. But she can only actually and authentically *know* something if it is indeed true.

A Los Angeles Lakers fan (like this author) cannot know that his team won the NBA Championship in the 1968–1969 season, because they didn't. The Lakers lost game seven of the Finals to the Boston Celtics at the fabulous

Forum in Inglewood, California, by two points. Knowledge, therefore (no matter how devastating), is built upon the foundation of true beliefs. However, still more must be added to have genuine knowledge.

Third, a person can believe something to be true, that is in fact true, but it wouldn't constitute knowledge if it lacks *proper justification*. For example, a woman on a television game show might make a wild guess as to what 101,758,969 cubed equals. But even if she came up with the right answer it wouldn't be knowledge, because her response was just an incredibly lucky guess. Knowledge involves some form of confirmation or evidence—what philosophers call proper justification.

Most Christian philosophers accept some (often modest) form of the epistemological theory known as *foundationalism*.[35] This idea involves beliefs usually being justified based upon other more "foundational" convictions. Beliefs that stand on their own without appealing to other convictions for justification are called "properly basic beliefs."

A modest form of foundationalism suggests that beliefs are properly basic when they are either self-evident (true on the face of it), logically necessary, inescapable, or incorrigible (expressing an immediate state of consciousness).[36] There may be other beliefs as well that are basic or immediately justified (such as memories, intuitions, and even God's existence[37]). Knowledge, then, means believing what is true with proper justification.

5. Human knowledge is limited and affected by sin.

Real limitations to reasoning can be found in two important respects. First, human beings, though quite well-endowed intellectually by way of bearing God's image, are nevertheless finite creatures by nature.[38] As a result, unlike God, they have limitations with regard to knowledge and rational comprehension in the essence of their being.[39] Therefore an approach to knowledge characterized by pure rationalism (all things are discoverable through human reasoning) would be impossible. Because God is an infinite being, any interaction between him and his creatures has to involve mystery.[40]

Christian truth may range above human comprehension (for example, the doctrines of the Triune nature of God and the Incarnation). But that truth never violates the principles of reasoning, which themselves flow from God's mind. A Christian view of knowledge thus rejects both pure rationalism and irrationalism.

Second, human reason has been negatively affected by sin. The noetic (cognitive and/or belief-forming) faculties of people suffer from the effects of the fall.[41] To some degree sin impairs human intelligence and rationality. Theologians debate, however, the exact nature and extent of this negative effect upon a person's capacity to reason. Some suggest that the effects of sin are more of a moral nature (impairing the ability to discern good and evil) than of a cognitive variety.

Though sin definitely impacts human beings for the worse, it has no effect upon the laws of logic or of correct reasoning. These laws remain cognitively necessary, ontologically real, and irrefutable (see chapter 3). Even so, logic's laws alone can't bring about a proper relationship with God. For sinful individuals to comprehend and positively respond to the gospel of Christ—God's grace must soften their hearts, illumine their minds, and incline their wills to believe.[42]

6. The Christian faith involves knowledge and is compatible with reason.

While a variety of positions have been represented throughout church history regarding the proper relationship between faith and reason,[43] a broad measure of agreement shows that they are indeed compatible.[44] Historic Christianity is reasonable in four distinct ways:

First, the Christian faith affirms that there is an objective source and foundation for knowledge, reason, and rationality. That basis is found in a personal and rational God. This infinitely wise and all-knowing God created the universe to reflect a coherent order, and in his image he made man with rational capacities to discover that logical organization.

Second, Christian truth-claims do not violate the basic laws or principles of reason. Christian faith and doctrine, though they often transcend finite human comprehension, are not irrational and absurd.

Third, the Bible encourages the attainment of knowledge, wisdom, and understanding, and promotes such intellectual virtues as discernment, testing, and reflection.

Fourth, the truths of the Christian faith correspond to and are supported by such things as evidence, facts, and reason. Biblical faith (Greek: *pisteuō*, the verb "believe"; *pistis*, the noun "faith"[45]) can be defined as confident trust in a reliable source (God or Christ). Faith (or belief) is a necessary component of knowledge and reason because, as explained previously, a person must believe something in order to know it. Yet reason can be used to evaluate, confirm, and buttress faith.

Reason and faith therefore function in a complementary fashion. While reason in and of itself—apart from God's special grace—cannot cause faith, the use of reason is normally a part of a person's coming to faith and supports faith in innumerable ways. Faith is foundational to reason, and reason can evaluate or confirm faith.

In the New Testament, descriptions of faith always focus upon an object. And the trustworthy object of a person's faith is God or the Lord Jesus Christ. Even the very faith that results in salvation involves knowledge (concerning the facts surrounding the life, death, and resurrection of Jesus Christ) and discursive reasoning (as to what those facts really mean). Saving faith[46] then includes knowledge of the gospel, assent to its truth, and confident reliance upon the Lord and Savior Jesus Christ. It involves the full faculties of a human being—mind (knowledge), will (assent), and heart (trust).

Christian faith and reason also connect in the renewing of the mind.[47] This important transformation involves individuals using their cognitive faculties to the fullest extent in devotion to God. Christian philosopher and theologian Augustine of Hippo (A.D. 354–430) called this indispensable intellectual and spiritual activity "faith seeking understanding."[48]

Believers should use their God-given reason to explore the depths of their faith. They should strongly endeavor to discover the Bible's truths—stretching mental and spiritual muscles, so to speak, to apprehend (yet never fully comprehend) such doctrines as the Triune nature of God and the Incarnation of Jesus Christ. Such exercise moves a person from the initial stage of faith to the deeper stage of reflective understanding and a greater sense of God's infinite and eternal majesty. Loving God with a person's mind is part of fulfilling the overarching commandment to love and honor God with one's entire being.[49]

A Christian Perspective on History

The Christian worldview has important implications concerning the nature, direction, and purpose of historical events. Christianity, though deeply rooted in the facts of history, also makes profound projections about the future that affect human beings and the cosmos itself. Of all the world's religions, Christianity has a special relationship to history because, according to the Bible, God actually appeared in a specific time and place.

1. God is sovereign over history.

Both Jews and Christians refer to the God of the Bible as "the God of history." The Christian position asserts that an infinite, rational divine mind stands behind the historical order and gives it meaning, purpose, and order. God ordains and unfolds according to his sovereign will, the ultimate sequence of historical events.[50] Nature,[51] world history,[52] and the personal circumstances of individual people[53] (especially believers in the Lord[54]) reflect God's providential plan and purpose. History has been appropriately called "His Story," for Jesus Christ is the Lord over all human historical events.

2. God is responsible for history's beginning, direction, purpose, and completion.

History began with God's sovereign action in creation when he brought matter, energy, space, and time into existence. And unlike the repeating cycles of history commonly described in Eastern religions, the Christian view of history moves forward in a linear direction (from beginning to end without repeat). There is only one historical time-space sequence for the world and one life for human beings.[55]

God's design and plan (teleology) give history purpose, direction, and a specific goal. The whole picture unfurls according to God's providential plan—not by blind fate, chance, random natural accident, or chaos as some ancient and modern philosophies contend. It will be brought to fruition according to God's appointed timetable. (See the discussion of the doctrines of creation and providence in chapter 9.)

3. God personally entered into human history.

At the heart of the Christian worldview is the truth that God became man in the person of Jesus Christ.[56] This historical person was born under the reign of Caesar Augustus in first century A.D. in the small city of Bethlehem in Judea.[57] Jesus lived in the real world of time and space as a fully human person. After being crucified under Pontius Pilate, a first-century Roman governor,[58] he rose bodily from the dead before numerous and sundry eyewitnesses.[59] God came in the midst of human history to seek and save lost sinners.

4. Two "cities" or "kingdoms" can be identified as operative in history.

In his massive and profound book *The City of God*, Augustine told a tale of two cities—"the City of God" and "the City of Man." He used these cities to describe two systems of thought (each with definite worldview implications) that exist within and beyond human history.[60]

The City of God, "Jerusalem," has a divine origin and a heavenly or eternal destiny. Love for God characterizes its citizens, who hold a distinctively Christian value system and worldview perspective. The City of Man, "Babylon," is of human origin and has an earthly or temporal destiny. Citizens in this human city are characterized by their love of self and the present world. As a result, their value system is self-focused and earthly.

Thus, within the unfolding historical eras, there have always been two systems of ultimate allegiance.[61] While Augustine's two-cities metaphor illustrates the historical divide between church and state, it is more accurate to understand the two cites as representing two competing systems of thought or worldview perspectives. Augustine saw human affairs, like all things, as subject to the sovereign and providential plan of Almighty God. Giving the Western world its first philosophy of history, Augustine presented and defended a distinctly Christian linear view.

5. God will bring history to an apocalyptic end.

God was responsible for bringing human society and history into being and at the appointed time will bring it to an abrupt, cataclysmic, and final end. Jesus Christ will come back again, marking the final and complete victory of God over Satan and all evil forces.[62] At that time Christ the Lord will resurrect and judge all humanity—with believers enjoying God's eternal presence in heaven (beatific vision)[63] and unbelievers suffering eternal conscious punishment in hell. The exalted Jesus will reign in a kingdom with no end.

6. History unfolds in divine revelatory stages.

Five stages—the creation, fall, redemption, glorification, and new creation—reveal God's sovereign plan for the cosmos and humanity.

Creation. By using his infinite power and incalculable wisdom alone, God made all things in their totality *ex nihilo* (out of nothing). God subsequently made man in his own image and likeness.

Fall. The first humans misused their God-given freedom to rebel against their Creator by breaking his express commands.[64] This act of original sin left Adam and Eve and their progeny (all humankind) in a sinful state of separation from God and justly deserving divine wrath.

Redemption. Motivated by his infinite love and mercy, God the Father sent his Son into the world to provide an atoning sacrifice for sin. Jesus Christ suffered the wrath of God upon a Roman cross to bring about the forgiveness of sinners. His life, death, and resurrection brought about a way for sinners, through faith and repentance (made possible by the power of the Holy Spirit), to be reconciled to their holy Creator.

Glorification. Having begun with the great events of the past, Christianity projects to the future.[65] Jesus Christ's Second Coming and the apocalyptic events associated with it (resurrection and judgment) will lead to the final stage of redemption where believers are completely and permanently transformed into the image of their Lord and Savior.

New Creation. After these glorious future events, God will destroy this present universe[66] and bring forth the creation of a new heaven and a new earth.[67] A new and glorious realm without sin, pain, sorrow, and death will be made by the almighty power and infinite wisdom of God.

Thus the creation, fall, redemption, glorification, and new creation reveal the theological and historical sequences of God's plan and purpose for the ages.

Making a Difference

The Christian vision of truth, knowledge, and history stands as a polar opposite of the relativistic mindset in the world today. According to Christian theism, objective truth exists, genuine knowledge is possible, and history reflects God's sovereign will.

As revealed in Scripture, the descriptions of God, creation, providence, humanity, and values strongly contribute to this overarching Christian worldview. Each of these topics is worthy of further exploration. But first, a concise summary of the Christian position as set forth in the Apostles' Creed provides a glimpse of the biblical position's most important features.

Discussion Questions

1. According to historic Christianity, how does God serve as the necessary and objective ontological foundation for such objective realities as truth and knowledge?
2. What is the "correspondence view of truth"? How is it reflected in Scripture and in the broader Christian worldview?
3. How does the truth of Christ's unique lordship affect those who make similar claims?
4. In what specific ways is the Christian faith compatible with reason? What does it mean for Christian truth-claims to range above reason but not against it?
5. What is God's relationship to history? How does historic Christianity's view of history differ from the view held by other religions?

For Further Study

Augustine. *The City of God*. Translated by Henry Bettenson. New York: Penguin, 1984.

Groothuis, Douglas. *Truth Decay: Defending Christianity against the Challenges of Postmodernism*. Downers Grove, IL: InterVarsity, 2000.

Miller, Ed L. *God and Reason: An Invitation to Philosophical Theology*. 2nd ed. Upper Saddle River, NJ: Prentice-Hall, 1995.

Moreland, J. P., and William Lane Craig. *Philosophical Foundations for a Christian Worldview*. Downers Grove, IL: InterVarsity, 2003.

Nash, Ronald H. *The Meaning of History*. Nashville: Broadman & Holman, 1998.

6

A Soldier's Creed

Some truths are so critical that they must be repeated over and over again.

Luke Timothy Johnson, *The Creed*

Courage in the face of death—my father's example as an American combat soldier in World War II on the great and terrible battlefields of Europe fueled my desire to face my own physical battle involving ill health with bravery.

Though my dad didn't often speak of his wartime experience, the locked trunk in his bedroom closet convinced me that all of his Army-related things were sacred. On rare and special occasions he brought out his medals and ribbons and showed them to me. But I never actually saw some of the wartime papers, mementos, and keepsakes until many years later when my father passed away. He died almost forty years to the day after the war ended in Europe.

The greater significance of my father's service to his country dawned on me when I was in the eighth grade. Having been assigned a school research project, I asked my dad if we could go buy some reference books on World War II. He readily agreed and we went to a local bookstore and picked out a couple of resources.

One book was entitled The Decline and Fall of Nazi Germany and Imperial Japan *by Hans Dollinger. Upon coming home and inspecting this book, we discovered my father's photograph in two different places. My dad had been an integral part of a worldwide conflict—one of millions of American servicemen who fought against Nazi Germany. This unexpected discovery taught me that ideas have real consequences that affect everyone, even my own family. That epiphany led me on the path to asking the big questions of life—especially questions about God and history.*

My dad also taught me how his spiritual convictions helped him face the unparalleled challenges of being a combat soldier on the frontlines. He told me that he carried a small copy of the New Testament in his uniform pocket throughout his days in combat and read it whenever time and events allowed. Our family still has that government-issued copy of the Scriptures produced by the Gideons International.

He also said that the chaplain in his infantry division led soldiers in reciting the Apostles' Creed, sometimes even while they were concealed in a foxhole. The words of that creed reminded the men of historic Christianity's great truth-claims centering upon the life, death, and resurrection of their Lord and Savior Jesus Christ.

The Apostles' Creed encouraged those brave soldiers in the truth of their faith, and the ultimate Christian perspective on the world, life, and death. It reassured them that they had a reason to live and a reason to die. Likewise, as mentioned earlier, while I lay in my hospital bed, that same creed reassured me.

An Historic Christian Summary

The Christian worldview comes from a dramatic account set forth in the Bible that includes the great narrative of historic actions and events involving God and his relationship with humanity. Five stages (introduced in the previous chapter)—creation, fall, redemption, glorification, and new creation—represent Scripture's unfolding message and give shape and substance to the Christian position.

The Apostles' Creed, one of the most important statements of faith ever written, has been used for centuries to convey the distinct vision of truth and reality based on the Bible's broad revelatory content. While Scripture is the primary narrative and (for Protestant evangelical Christians at least) the supreme authority of Christian belief and practice (see chapter 7), the Apostles' Creed sets forth the essence of the Christian message in clear and concise terms. In doing so, it presents a logical and well-reasoned belief system that possesses a properly derived authority.

This simple, yet organized summation reveals the way Christians throughout the centuries have viewed God, the world, humankind, life, and the future. Millions recite the Apostles' Creed each Sunday morning because it succinctly captures the heart of the historic Christian world-and-life view in just over one hundred words.

Apostles' Creed

I believe in God, the Father almighty, creator of heaven and earth.

I believe in Jesus Christ, his only Son, our Lord, who was conceived by
the Holy Spirit and born of the virgin Mary. He suffered under Pontius Pilate, was crucified, died, and was buried; he descended to hell.
The third day he rose again from the dead. He ascended to heaven
and is seated at the right hand of God the Father almighty. From
there he will come to judge the living and the dead.

I believe in the Holy Spirit, the holy catholic church, the communion
of saints, the forgiveness of sins, the resurrection of the body, and
the life everlasting. Amen.

Understanding the history and purpose of this creedal statement, along
with some commentary about each section, reveals many details of the historic Christian worldview and supplies a model for defining and testing its
premises.

A Concise Christian Creed

Early Christians used brief scriptural declarations as creedal or proto-creedal
statements even in biblical times. For example, the simple but profound New
Testament pronouncement "Jesus is Lord!" is likely the earliest Christian creed
(see Rom. 10:9; 1 Cor. 12:3; 2 Cor. 4:5; Phil. 2:11).

Saying "Jesus is Lord" (*kyrios Iēsous*) was the New Testament Greek equivalent of saying "Jesus is Yahweh" (the Lord God).[1] The Apostles' Creed ex-
panded on 1 Corinthians 8:6: "Yet for us there is but one God, the Father,
from whom all things came and for whom we live; and there is but one Lord,
Jesus Christ, through whom all things came, and through whom we live."
Many scholars think the apostle Paul took this statement from an earlier
Jewish creed—Deuteronomy 6:4, which states, "Hear, O Israel: The Lord
our God, the Lord is one."

While no creed could convey all the fullness of God's special revelation
as found in Scripture, the Apostles' Creed focuses critical attention on Jesus
Christ, particularly upon his life, death, and resurrection. Oxford professor of
historical theology Alister E. McGrath notes: "At the center of the Christian
faith lies the person of Jesus Christ."[2]

The statements about Christ in the Apostles' Creed expand on another
early creed in 1 Corinthians 15:3–4, which Paul says he received and passed
on as of first importance: "that Christ died for our sins according to the
Scriptures, that he was buried, that he was raised on the third day according

to the Scriptures." Hence the core of the Apostles' Creed goes back to early proclamations quoted in the New Testament.

But gradually there arose a need for a more detailed summary of Christian beliefs, particularly as a corporate profession of faith in the church. By the second century, Christians developed an early Latin version of the Apostles' Creed (known as the Old Roman Creed) intended to outline the main points concerning the life, death, and resurrection of Jesus Christ. They saw this creed as a brief distillation of Christian truth, drawn from the doctrinal content of Holy Scripture itself.

Though not written by the original apostles, what came to be known as the Apostles' Creed reached its present form by the eighth century A.D.

Sacred Truth

The Apostles' Creed is the most widely accepted and frequently used statement of faith within Christendom. Its purpose is to present with clarity the historic Christian vision of what is really true. Philosopher Peter Kreeft said: "And that is the point of the creeds: truth. In fact, Primal Truth, the truth about God. That is why the words of the Creed are sacred words."[3]

The three sections of the Apostles' Creed acknowledge the three divine Persons of the Godhead (Father, Son, and Holy Spirit), who are all involved in various ways in human redemption. The first section focuses on the Father and emphasizes his work of creation. The second section concentrates on the Son and explains his work of redemption. And the third section spotlights the Holy Spirit, who plays a critical role of providing regeneration (the new birth). This view of the world, life, and death changes everything for those who take it to heart.

"I believe in God, the Father almighty, creator of heaven and earth."

Section 1 of the Apostles' Creed begins with a paramount statement about ultimate "Truth" and "Reality." The believer affirms God's existence, power, and divine action. That's always the starting place for a Christian believer—assent to the objective truth about God actually existing.

In a Christian sense, belief or faith always has God as its proper object. The believer is the subject (the "I" in the creed) and God is the true object (the truth believed).[4]

"I believe." The words "I believe" encapsulate important epistemological (ways of knowing) and worldview implications. Skepticism is clearly incompatible with the faith because the believer knows things about God, Christ, and even the future. And so is rationalism because the belief affirms

knowledge that goes beyond a person's ability to discover using unaided human reason. To believe in God in a biblical sense involves more than mere intellectual assent to his existence, important as that is. It also involves personal confidence, trust, and reliance on who and what God has revealed himself to be.

So who and what has God revealed himself to be?

The God of the Bible and historic Christianity is the Triune God. This one God exists eternally and simultaneously as three distinct (though not separate) persons—Father, Son, and Holy Spirit. God is therefore one in essence or being but three in subsistence or personhood. A philosophical way of describing the Trinity doctrine is to say that God is one personal What (essence) and three distinct Whos (persons). This essence/subsistence distinction is a fundamental point in understanding the Christian doctrine of the Trinity (see chapter 8).

"In God the Father." The first section of the Creed identifies the first person of the Godhead as "the Father." This description immediately indicates that God is no mere abstract concept, nor is he an impersonal being or power or force. Rather God is the personal, or better yet the superpersonal Father dynamically revealed in Scripture.

Understanding God as Father means thinking of God as analogous to (both like and unlike) a human father. While a man physically begets his children, God the Father is the actual source of each person's very existence and being.

The apostle Paul declared in his speech before the Athenian philosophers at the Areopagus: "And he [God] is not served by human hands, as if he needed anything, because he himself gives all men life and breath and everything else . . . 'For in him we live and move and have our being'" (Acts 17:25, 28). God is not an austere, uncaring, and distant deity, but rather to his children he is a loving Father who knows and cares and provides for them. In contrast to imperfect human fathers, God the Father has a morally perfect love for his children.

"Almighty." The Creed describes God the Father as being "almighty," which in a narrow sense refers to God's immeasurable power, but in a broader way can be taken to imply God's infinite and sovereign nature as a whole. In fact, the Greek word *pantokratora* can be interpreted either as "all-mighty" or as "ruler over all." As a result, believers recognize God as an infinite and sovereign being who has no limitations or boundaries with regard to power, space, or knowledge.

The Psalmist declares God's infinite attributes: "Great is our Lord and mighty in power; his understanding has no limit" (Ps. 147:5). And in his prayer, the Old Testament prophet Jeremiah appealed to God's complete control: "Sovereign LORD, you have made the heavens and the earth by your great power and outstretched arm. Nothing is too hard for you" (Jer.

32:17). Thus, the first words of the Creed shape the worldview of believers, reminding them of these important biblical truths—God is omnipotent (all-powerful), omnipresent (everywhere present), and omniscient (all-knowing).

Scripture also says that this God has no imperfections in character. He is a morally perfect being (completely holy, righteous, just, and wise). Moses, the great prophet of Israel, sang of God his Father: "He is the Rock, his words are perfect, and all his ways are just. A faithful God who does no wrong, upright and just is he. . . . Is he not your Father, your Creator, who made you and formed you?" (Deut. 32:4, 6). To be able to call this awesome and sovereign being "Father" instills believers with confidence and reassurance to face whatever difficulties they may encounter in life. Even frontline combat soldiers in World War II who had to confront death on a daily basis could find strength and assurance in reciting the very first line of the Creed.

"Creator of heaven and earth." The opening sentence of the Creed also highlights God the Father's work of creation as a divine accomplishment. The expression "heaven and earth" is an ancient way of attributing to God the creation of all things in their totality. In fact, the very first verse of the Bible declares this comprehensive creative act of God: "In the beginning God created the heavens and the earth" (Gen. 1:1).

Historic Christianity affirms the doctrine of creation *ex nihilo* (see chapter 9), which asserts that God created all things (both visible and invisible) from or by nothing (without the use of preexisting materials such as matter). By his infinite wisdom and incalculable power alone, God called or spoke the universe into existence (Prov. 3:19). He sustains, controls, and directs it toward his sovereign ends (Neh. 9:6).

God created both the realm that can be seen (the physical universe, "earth") as well as the realm that cannot be seen ("heaven"). Thus historic Christianity views God as the transcendent Creator and immanent Sustainer of the world. The Bible reveals that God subsequently created human beings in his expressed image (*imago Dei*, Gen. 1:26–27). As divine image bearers, human beings are spiritual, intellectual, volitional, relational, and immortal creatures (see chapter 10).

McGrath describes the practical implications of a believer's view of this created order: "The doctrine of creation allows us to feel at home in the world. It reminds us that we, like the rest of creation, were fashioned by God. We are here because God wants us to be here. We are not alone but in the very presence of the God who made and owns everything."[5]

Creation is a critical Christian doctrine for it shows God's incredible wisdom and power. Knowing that an almighty loving Father created everything tells human beings where they came from (origin) and who they really are (identity).

ANSWERS TO THE BIG QUESTIONS

A mere twelve words in the first section of the Creed summarize vital answers to some fundamental worldview questions:

Questions: Does God exist? And if so, who is he and what is he like?

Answers: Yes, God is real, and that one true God is the infinite, eternal, and sovereign King, the superpersonal Triune God uniquely revealed in the Old and New Testaments of the Bible. This God is a morally perfect being—fully and completely possessing such moral attributes as wisdom, justice, holiness, righteousness, and love. And this awesome and incomprehensible God is also a loving, caring, and faithful Father.

Questions: Who am I? Why am I here?

Answers: Each individual is a special and planned creation of God that bears his divine image. That image makes people spiritual, intellectual, volitional, relational, and immortal creatures. They possess inherent dignity and moral worth and were created by God to know, love, and serve him forever. Just as God created and sustains the world, so does this loving Father provide for all the needs of his children.

Questions: Where did the world come from and what is its purpose? And why is there order in the cosmos?

Answers: The world was eloquently crafted by a transcendent (beyond the world) Creator who is also its immanent (within the world) Sustainer. A finely tuned universe supplies humanity with a suitable place to dwell and sets the stage as a grand theater where God performs his great role as the Redeemer of lost human sinners. The created order itself testifies to God's character. The universe's beauty, design, order, and regularity reflect God's glory—his infinite wisdom, power, and sovereign nature. The continued existence of the universe reveals God's sustaining care for his creation.

The first section of the Creed ascribes an objective meaning both to the universe and to life itself—a meaning found specifically in God. McGrath elaborates: "Behind the apparently faceless universe lies a person."[6]

Human beings are not alone in this vast cosmos; rather, a transcendent and immanent Creator who redeemed humanity watches over it. The universe is not an unplanned, chance, or accidental entity. Life is not a mere fortuitous physical accident. And according to the first line of the Apostles' Creed, human beings are not the product of a blind, purposeless, and purely naturalistic evolutionary process.

Rather, human beings can discover their purpose and significance in life through knowing their Creator. The universe was created by God for human life and is the place where he intends human beings to live out their temporal destiny.

According to the Apostles' Creed, the sovereign and Triune God is the proper object of prayer, worship, and devotion. God wants his people to genuinely believe in him and in his gracious promises. That faith commitment involves assent, trust, and obedience.

"I believe in Jesus Christ": The Heart of the Apostles' Creed

The second section introduces the person of Jesus Christ as the direct object of the Christian faith and draws the believer's attention to Jesus's life, death, and resurrection. These Christological events form the core of the historic Christian belief system. They are not only the centerpiece of Christian truth-claims and the focus of corporate church worship (the events behind the celebration of such holidays as Christmas, Good Friday, and Easter) but also the essence of the Christian worldview.

Section 2a states:

I believe in Jesus Christ, his only Son, our Lord, who was conceived by the Holy Spirit and born of the virgin Mary.

Beginning with affirmation of belief in the person of God the Father, the Creed next confirms belief in God the Son. His name, Jesus, means "Savior." The title "Christ" designates him as Messiah—the one specially anointed by God to carry out the divine work of redemption (Matt. 16:16; Mark 14:61; John 20:31).

The term *Messiah* underscores that the Creed presupposes the Old Testament revelation and hope. This important Jewish title leaves no doubt that Christianity is to be understood and interpreted as the fulfillment of the Jewish religion, not as an Eastern path to enlightenment like Buddhism and Hinduism. It shows that Jesus is not another guru but the Promised One of Israel, the one specially gifted by God to save humanity. The early church accepted the Jewish belief (so offensive to the Greco-Roman civilization) that the God of Abraham, Isaac, and Jacob was the only true God. The roots of the historic Christian worldview are found in the Old Testament revelation and covenant.

The Apostles' Creed affirms the Bible's claim that Jesus is none other than the Father's "only Son" (John 1:18; Gal. 4:4), the eternally existent Son of God (John 17:4–5), the second divine person of the Holy Trinity.

Jesus is not a creature made by the Father, as so many heretical sects and modern-day cults assert, but is himself the "Lord" (Yahweh). He shares the one divine nature fully, equally, and eternally with the Father (John 1:1; 8:58; Rom. 9:5; Titus 2:13; Col. 2:9; Heb. 1:8). The New Testament Greek word for "Lord," *kyrios*, is applied to Jesus in scriptural contexts that clearly imply deity (John 20:28; Rom. 10:9–13; Phil. 2:11). Therefore the first and second members of the Godhead enjoy an eternal Father-Son relationship. The Creed acknowledges the Son as possessing the exalted status of deity.

God the Son took to himself a perfect human nature in becoming man. As the apostle John stated: "The Word became flesh and made his dwelling among us" (John 1:14).

Christ's work of redemption on behalf of humanity began with the supernatural conception of his human nature by the third member of the divine Godhead (Luke 1:35). The Holy Spirit made the Incarnation (Latin: "in the flesh") possible when he miraculously brought about the Christ child's conception in the womb of the virgin Mary. Her mention in the Creed underscores the fact that Jesus Christ possessed a full and authentic human nature, that indeed he had an earthly mother, and an ancestral lineage (Matt. 1; Luke 3).

The Apostles' Creed refutes early heretical sects that proclaimed that Jesus merely appeared to be human (for example, the docetists; see 1 John 4:1–3). As the Incarnate Son of God, Jesus Christ is indeed fully human but not solely human, for he possesses two natures, one human and one divine. The early church referred to the Incarnate Christ as the *theanthrōpos*—the "God-man." The core of Christian belief is uncovered in the identity and accomplishments of Jesus the Christ.

Section 2b goes on to say:

He [Jesus] suffered under Pontius Pilate, was crucified, died, and was buried; he descended to hell.

The Creed presumes a critical biblical truth rather than explicitly disclosing it—the sinful state of humanity.[7] According to Scripture, Adam and Eve (the first humans created by God) disobeyed God by eating the divinely forbidden fruit (Genesis 3). As a result, they suffered alienation from God and were subjected to physical and spiritual death. Man's willful departure from God took the specific form of violating his explicit commands (Rom. 2:12–14; 4:15; James 2:9–10; 1 John 3:4).

The Bible teaches in some detail about the doctrine of original sin (Pss. 51:5; 58:3; Prov. 20:9; Rom. 5:12, 18–19). It asserts that all of Adam's progeny are conceived in sin and inherit a depraved nature—a severely incapacitating force permeating the center of a person's being. Humans have violated God's law, offended him, and earned alienation. This sin nature separates man from a holy God.

Scripture defines sin as missing the mark set by God and going astray from him in active rebellion. Because the moral law revealed in the Bible is an extension of God's holy and righteous character, to break his law is a direct affront to him. In light of this offense, sin can rightly be described as anything and everything (including actions, attitudes, and nature) that is contrary to the moral character and commands of God.

The good news of the gospel message, however, is that Christ atoned for human sin. He suffered—in his own personhood—the Father's just wrath against sin while being crucified at the hands of the Romans (Rom. 3:25; 1 John 2:1–2).

The explicit mention of the Roman governor Pontius Pilate in the Creed illustrates the historical and factual nature of Christ's life, suffering, and death. He didn't live "once upon a time in a land far away"; he lived and died during a specific time period in history, in a real geographical locale, and under a specific historical authority (during the first century A.D. in Judea under the Roman rule of Pontius Pilate).

The reference to Pilate also shows that the early church viewed the Roman Empire as opposed to Christ, thus acknowledging that confessing Christ entailed a choice of "kingdoms." It also reveals that the early church focused culpability for Christ's death on the Roman authorities (worldly kingdom powers), not the Jews. Anti-Semitism has no place in the Christian worldview. The sins of humanity put Jesus Christ on the cross of Calvary.

The Apostles' Creed, therefore, clearly states that Jesus Christ "was crucified, died, and was buried." Jesus suffered crucifixion (Roman capital punishment) and died in the place of sinners, suffering on their behalf so repentant sinners could receive forgiveness and have the righteousness of Christ's perfect law-keeping applied to their account before God (2 Cor. 5:21; 1 Peter 3:18).

Jesus Christ actually expired on the cross and was subsequently buried. His body was wrapped in a burial garment and placed in the tomb of Joseph of Arimathea (Matt. 27:57–60).

Undoubtedly the most controversial part of the Creed is the brief and enigmatic statement "he descended to hell."[8] What does this mean? Why is it a part of the Creed?

The phrase was apparently historically late in becoming part of the Creed.[9] A modern version of the Creed translates the statement "he descended to the dead,"[10] meaning the grave. This is a fair translation because Scripture states that Jesus was raised from the abode of the dead (Acts 2:24, 27; Rom. 10:7; Eph. 4:9). This difficult creedal statement could simply be an attempt to underscore that Jesus actually died and was among the dead or in the world of the dead (*Sheol* or *Hades*).

The reference to "hell" could also be taken to mean that Jesus Christ suffered the wrath of God on behalf of the sinner while on the cross.[11] This controversial phrase should not be taken to mean that Jesus Christ actually went to hell (*Gehenna*, the place of fire) following his death or during the intermediate state (the time between his death and resurrection).

Section 2c of the Apostles' Creed continues with the glorious hope of the Christian worldview:

The third day he rose again from the dead.

From a historic Christian perspective, both the nature and truth of Christianity uniquely rest upon Jesus's bodily resurrection from the dead.[12] That he was raised to life three days after being executed is at the center of the gospel (doctrine) and is Christianity's central supporting truth (apologetics). According to the apostle Paul, Christianity stands or falls on Christ's resurrection: "If Christ has not been raised, our preaching is useless and so is your faith. . . . If Christ has not been raised, your faith is futile; you are still in your sins" (1 Cor. 15:14, 17).

The resurrection of Jesus carries significant theological weight. If Christ has risen from the dead then all of Christianity's truth-claims are indeed true. Jesus's identity, mission, and message rest on the truth of his resurrection. The entire New Testament was written in light of Christ's bodily victory over death, and each book bears witness to its veracity. In fact, the essential function of the apostles was to witness to the truth of the resurrection (Acts 1:22; 1 Cor. 9:1).

According to Scripture, this resurrection was *not* merely a coming back from the dead—a resuscitation or near-death experience. Nor was it something akin to the Eastern principle of reincarnation or transmigration. Rather, Jesus rose to a new type of human life—eternal life with a transformed, glorified physical body that is no longer subject to weakness, pain, sickness, or death. In his resurrection, Jesus Christ fully and completely defeated death forever.

This event impacts human beings who trust in Jesus as their risen Lord and Savior in two significant ways. First, Christ's resurrection is the answer to mankind's greatest predicament—being stalked by death. Fear and the existential angst over death is a paramount issue that every person must face alone. Even a famous rock-and-roll song proclaims the inevitability of death: "No one here gets out alive now."[13]

For believers the resurrection of Jesus provides hope, purpose, meaning, and confidence in the presence of death (John 11:25–26; Rom. 14:7–8). Second, Christ's resurrection is the pledge and paradigm for the future bodily resurrection of all believers (1 Cor. 6:14; 15:20; Phil. 3:21; Col. 1:18; 1 Thess. 4:14). Because he rose, believers will also rise. Even physical death cannot defeat the believer who trusts in the risen Lord.

The Creed illustrates the necessary link between human faith or belief and the salvation found in Jesus Christ. The New Testament words for "faith" and "believe" (Greek: *pistis*, the noun; *pisteuō*, the verb) carry rich meaning. To have biblical faith in Jesus Christ for salvation includes (1) a genuine (factual and historical) *knowledge* of the gospel events, namely, Jesus's life, death, and resurrection; (2) a personal *assent* to the truth and importance of those events; and (3) a confident *trust* in the object of that faith (the risen Lord Jesus Christ). Faith, in a biblical context, is therefore not separated from authentic human knowledge of truth, reality, and history (see chapter 5).

Section 2d adds yet another tenet:

He ascended to heaven and is seated at the right hand of God the Father almighty.

After forty days of appearances in his resurrected bodily state, Jesus left his followers and Earth's domain and ascended back to God the Father in heaven (Luke 24:51; Acts 1:9). The ascension marks the Son's return to the glorious state he left to humbly submit to the work of redemption (Phil. 2:5–11). Choosing an act of humiliation, the royal and heavenly Son of God condescended to an earthly human level to redeem humankind. In the process of atoning for sin, Jesus suffered separation from his Father. Upon their reunion, Jesus once again enjoyed the personal intimacy, glory, and divine majesty he had shared with his Father before the world began (John 17:5).

Having perfectly finished his work as the suffering servant on Earth (Isa. 53), Jesus began his ongoing work in heaven as intercessor or mediator (1 Tim. 2:5; Heb. 4:14–16). Being at the "right hand of God the Father" means that Christ has an exalted position of unparalleled status, power, influence, and authority. Evangelical theologian J. I. Packer remarks: "To sit on such a throne, as the Grand Vizier in the Persian court used to do, is to occupy the position of executive ruler on the monarch's behalf."[14]

Jesus serves as his people's great High Priest (Heb. 7:23–28), specifically praying for them and their needs as well as representing their position and case before the Father. From heaven, as the God-man, he empathizes with the plight of human beings and, along with the Father, he sends the Holy Spirit (John 16:7–14) to enrich the lives of his people and equip them for his kingdom (Eph. 4:8–12).

Whether on Earth as the Redeemer or in heaven as the High Priest, Jesus Christ is the believer's special and powerful divine ally. His death on the cross and prayers of intercession in heaven are directly responsible for salvation. Christian believers have a high priest who experientially understands (empathizes, not merely sympathizes) what it is like to live on Earth and face life's challenges.

Section 2e supplies additional details:

From there he will come to judge the living and the dead.

Having addressed Christ's great redemptive actions and events of the past, the Apostles' Creed now focuses on the apocalyptic events of the future. While Christianity is rooted in history, it nevertheless projects forward. Jesus came the first time in humility as the Lamb of God who takes away the sin of the world (John 1:29). But at his Second Coming he will return as the sovereign King, Ruler, and Judge of all creation (Acts 17:31; 2 Thess. 1:7–10; Heb. 9:27–28).

The return of Christ will bring an end to human history and life as we know it in this world. The Lord Jesus Christ will come back to this earth—personally, bodily, and visibly—to establish his glorious reign in a kingdom with no end. Everyone alive at that time will publicly witness his power, authority, and glory. As the sovereign Lord, Jesus will resurrect and judge all humanity. These incredible actions will testify to Christ's divine status.

As the Creed declares, Jesus functions as the final judge of humanity because he is God. Those who have rejected God and his gracious work of redemption will face God's just wrath because of their sins (John 3:36).

Believers will also face God's judgment, but fortunately they already know the verdict. The debt for the believer's sin was paid when Jesus Christ suffered and died on the cross of Calvary. That's why the apostle Paul so confidently and boldly informs Christians of two crucial resulting facts:

> Therefore, since we have been justified through faith, we have peace with God through our Lord Jesus Christ.
>
> Romans 5:1

and

> Therefore, there is now no condemnation for those who are in Christ Jesus.
>
> Romans 8:1

To use a wordplay, the cross is the crux (Latin for "cross" but English for "essential point") of the Christian faith. Jesus's sacrifice purchased the salvation that ensures reconciliation with the Father for all who repent and believe the good news of the gospel.

The New Testament doctrine of justification by faith addresses both the matter of a person's sins as well as the matter of God's righteousness. Having a saving relationship with Christ involves what the Protestant Reformer Martin Luther called the "great exchange." This exchange is one of both lives and destinies.

Jesus took on the nature of humankind. Though he himself did not sin, he represented the life of a sinner and bore the sins of the world. As a result, he suffered the shameful death of a criminal on a cross. Ironically, by embracing this atonement through faith, human beings receive Christ's life—perfect in holiness and obedience to God and his Law. In other words, the Righteous One (Christ) bore the destiny of the many unrighteous ones (human beings) in facing divine condemnation. The unrighteous ones (human beings) therefore gain the destiny of the holy and obedient one (Christ)—the riches of eternal life with God. And that's good news indeed!

Scripture clarifies this exchange of judgment:

> God made him who had no sin to be sin for us, so that in him we might become the righteousness of God.
>
> 2 Corinthians 5:21

> For Christ died for sins once for all, the righteous for the unrighteous, to bring you to God.
>
> 1 Peter 3:18

ANSWERS TO THE BIG QUESTIONS

The second section of the Apostles' Creed also answers some essential worldview questions:

Questions: What is humankind's basic problem? What consequences result from that fundamental predicament?

Answers: All human beings are sinners by nature, having inherited that condition from Adam, the first human person made by God. For that reason moral corruption is pervasive in the lives of all people—affecting their thoughts, words, and deeds. This sinful condition results in specific acts that break God's moral law, offend him, and leave humankind deserving of his just punishment. As a result, individuals face both physical and spiritual death (divine wrath). Human sin has also caused people to be estranged among themselves, apart from their Creator, and has led to a variety of selfish and evil actions against others.

Questions: What is the prescribed remedy for humankind's universal ailment? How can man's problem be solved?

Answers: The solution to the problem of sin, death, and divine punishment is found uniquely in the person of Jesus Christ. Through his perfect life, sacrificial death, and bodily resurrection from the grave, human beings can find forgiveness of their sins and can be restored to peaceful fellowship with God. This salvation comes to the repentant sinner by God's grace alone, through faith alone, in Christ alone (Eph. 2:8–9; Titus 3:5).

Questions: How should I then live? What should be the greatest motivating factor in my life?

Answers: In light of God's gracious gift of salvation offered in Jesus Christ, those who wish to hold a biblical worldview must attempt to live a life filled with gratitude to God for his unmerited favor and love. A desire to love God motivates that life because he first loved the sinner. Genuine faith in Christ cannot help but manifest itself in love for God and for one's fellow man.

The Christian life is, however, a process of growing in loving obedience to God and is never perfect or complete in this life. It must be emphasized that believers are justified or forgiven sinners, but they still sin and must regularly confess their sin and seek repentance before God (1 John 1:8–10).

The doctrine of justification reveals that God declares individual sinners righteous because of their union with Christ through faith (changing each sinner's status before God). The life of being set apart for God's purposes (sanctification) is a cooperative venture with God whereby his grace slowly but steadily transforms the believer's inner character. The doctrine of sanctification reveals that God actually begins making the believer righteous in character (changing the sinner's state before God).

Questions: What awaits a believer in death? What does the future hold for unbelievers?

Answers: Those who have received Christ's offer of life through the gospel will go to be with the Lord upon their death (2 Cor. 5:8; Phil. 1:21–24). This intermediate state in Christ's presence will be a disembodied one awaiting resurrection. Upon the glorious Second Coming of Christ, all believers will be given immortal and incorruptible bodies. Evil, suffering, and death will be eliminated.

The redeemed of Christ will enjoy companionship with God and all believers, along with the eternal blessings of heaven. Those who have rejected God and his forgiveness in Christ will face eternal, conscious torment in hell (Matt. 25:32–33, 46; Rev. 14:11; 20:10, 15), which is eternal separation from the life of God (2 Thess. 1:8–9).

"I believe in the Holy Spirit . . ."

The third section of the Creed proclaims this resurrection and more:

I believe in the Holy Spirit, the holy catholic church, the communion of saints, the forgiveness of sins, the resurrection of the body, and the life everlasting. Amen.

"I believe in the Holy Spirit." The final section of the Creed begins by formally introducing the Third Person of the Holy Trinity—the Holy Spirit. Redemption involves all three members of the Godhead. The Holy Spirit is not a mere power or force as some non-Christian sects teach. Instead Scripture shows him to be a genuine person by the attributes, works, and titles ascribed to him (Acts 13:4; 1 Cor. 2:10–11; Eph. 4:30; see also chapter 8).

Fully God, the Holy Spirit is, in fact, an equal person with the Father and the Son. They share the one divine nature and together perform divine works (Gen. 1:2; John 14:26; Acts 5:3–4; Rom. 8:11). Scripture refers to the Spirit as the Counselor or Paraclete (one who comes alongside to help) sent by the Father and the Son (John 14:16–17a, 26; 15:26; 16:7) to carry out critical tasks in the work of redemption.

Directly involved in salvation, the Holy Spirit convicts people of sin (John 16:8–11), regenerates souls (Titus 3:5), and indwells believers (1 Cor. 6:19). The Spirit of God was intimately involved in the life and ministry of Jesus Christ (including Christ's conception, miracles, and resurrection).

Belief in the doctrine of the Holy Spirit as expressed in the Apostles' Creed sets the Christian worldview apart from all other worldview perspectives. For example, spirituality is not a matter of human beings exploring an impersonal realm of the spirit and lifting themselves up into higher planes of consciousness (as in Eastern mysticism). Rather the person of the Holy Spirit illuminates and transforms ordinary people.

"The holy catholic church, the communion of saints." The Apostles' Creed states two closely connected concepts back to back—"the holy catholic church" and the "communion of saints." To place one's faith in Jesus Christ means that a person becomes part of a historic Christian community, the church. Only one church is built upon the foundation of Jesus Christ (Col. 1:18), though many denominations and traditions exist as part of that one invisible church.

That church is "holy" because members are called out by God (sanctified), and the church is "catholic" in the sense of being universal or whole. The word *catholic*, when spelled with a lowercase *c*, means universal and is not a specific reference to the Roman Catholic Church. Membership in the historic Christian church makes each believer part of the "communion of saints." This association not only ties believers today with believers from the past, but also unites them in one locale with believers all around the globe. McGrath explains:

The "church" is not a static building but a dynamic pilgrim people who are constantly moving on in faith and obedience. It includes those who have gone ahead of us and those who will follow. It is a great fellowship of faith, spanning the ages and the continents.[15]

"The forgiveness of sins." The Creed again highlights the importance in the historic Christian faith of being delivered from guilt. Through Christ's crucifixion, suffering, and death, God's just wrath against sin is satisfied and appeased. That death on the cross extended both divine grace and mercy to sinners. Grace gives what one does not deserve (forgiveness and righteousness), while mercy does not give what one does deserve (the just wrath of God). Christianity is a religion characterized by the importance of redemption (being forgiven and reconciled through Christ).

"The resurrection of the body, and the life everlasting." The last two truths affirmed in the Creed again look to the future in terms of the Christian vision of reality. God plans to resurrect physical bodies in the future state. Heavenly bodies will be like Christ's resurrected body, free from all stains of sin.

In their new bodies people will enjoy what the Creed calls "life everlasting." This phrase means that individuals will not only live forever, but will also dwell with God in a perfect state of intimacy. The resurrection of the body entails that the eternal future awaiting the redeemed is not a ghostly existence but involves eternal life in the new heavens and new earth as glorified, perfected human beings (Rev. 21:1–4).

"Amen." The Apostles' Creed closes with this single word, meaning that the creed is both a prayer and a confession of faith.[16] It ties together doctrine and spiritual devotion. When Christians recite the Creed they affirm their faith in God (Father, Son, and Holy Spirit). They also affirm their deepest conviction in the truth of the historic Christian world-and-life view.

ANSWERS TO THE BIG QUESTIONS

The third section of the Apostles' Creed supplies additional answers to important questions:

Questions: Where do I belong in this world? And what will happen to me when I die?

Answers: To know Jesus Christ as Lord and Savior is to belong to the kingdom of God, where there are no loners. Believers are members of Christ's church, which is his body and of which he is the living head. In the world to come each believer will be part of the communion of saints—living and reigning with God and his people forever and ever in

the eternal city of God. People were created by God and
redeemed by God and will enjoy his intimate presence in
a kingdom that will never end.

Questions: What is the hope of the believer in looking to the future
reality? What will Jesus Christ do at his Second Coming?

Answers: The glorious Second Coming of Christ gives each
believer hope for the future. When Jesus returns he
will bring an end to human history, raise the dead,
judge humanity, reward his followers, and usher in the
eternal kingdom of God where his people will enjoy life
everlasting.

A Creed Worth Living and Dying For

The concise summary of the historic Christian worldview in the Apostles'
Creed has offered comfort and hope to soldiers, terminally ill patients, and
people just living everyday life. The belief system expressed by its statements
contains the central message of the faith—one that never ceases to strengthen
and encourage those who commit the Creed to memory and recite it often
with conviction.

The next chapter explores the Christian worldview by looking more specifically at the Scripture from which the Apostles' Creed was drawn.

Discussion Questions

1. Why should the study of the past be especially important to the Christian? Of what value is historical theology and church history?
2. What contemporary problems in the Christian church might be helped
   by a serious study of the content of the Apostles' Creed?
3. What is the specific relationship of historic creeds to Scripture in terms
   of inspiration and authority?
4. What worldview issues does the Apostles' Creed highlight?
5. How does the Apostles' Creed illustrate the centrality of Jesus Christ
   in the Christian faith?

For Further Study

Bray, Gerald. *Creeds, Councils, and Christ.* Ross-shire, UK: Mentor, 1984.

Ecumenical Creeds and Reformed Confessions. Grand Rapids: CRC Publications,
1988.

Kelly, J. N. D. *Early Christian Creeds*. London: Harlow, 1972.

McGrath, Alister E. *I Believe: Understanding and Applying the Apostles' Creed*. Grand Rapids: Zondervan, 1991.

Packer, J. I. *Concise Theology: A Guide to Historic Christian Beliefs*. Wheaton, IL: Tyndale, 1993.

7

GOD'S WRITTEN
WORD—SCRIPTURE

Whenever the Bible prescribes the content of our belief (doctrine) or the pattern of our living (ethics) or records actual events (history), it speaks the truth.

Bruce Milne, *Know the Truth*

*O*ne thing that made my hospital stay far worse than it might have been was having my head ache so bad that I couldn't read. Not for an entire month did I read a single book. That hadn't happened since my intellectually apathetic high school days. Dutch Renaissance scholar and theologian Desiderius Erasmus once said, "When I get a little money, I buy books. And if there is any left over, I buy food." How much I would have preferred books to the food the hospital wanted me to eat.

My obsession with books began with my conversion to Christianity. I was a sophomore in college when I sensed that my mind really mattered in my relationship with the Lord. So I began a serious pursuit of the "life of the mind." Today I have a personal library of somewhere between three and four thousand books. And I've taught courses to help others develop good reading skills and comprehension.

I encourage my students to study the esteemed educator and philosopher Mortimer J. Adler's outstanding works on reading to develop their skills. Adler helped pioneer a classical approach to education through the reading of the great books *of Western civilization.[1] But in his estimation only a small percentage of books qualify as great.*

A genuinely great book can be identified, says Adler, when it can be read and read again and yet continues to challenge the reader to grow in wisdom and understanding:

> *Your impression of increased understanding on your previous reading was not false. The book truly lifted you then. But now, even though you have become wiser and more knowledgeable, it can lift you again. And it will go on doing this until you die.[2]*

As for me, I need great books, especially the greatest book of all. Not only does the Bible supply the ultimate answers to life, but it is often the source and inspiration for other literary masterpieces. If I could never read any of them again, I might as well be dead.

The Greatest of the Great Books

Christians claim that the Bible exceeds all books in providing endless wisdom and understanding about life, the human condition, and the world. Jews and Christians throughout the centuries have concurred that no matter how many times it's read, Scripture continues to uplift, challenge, instruct, and convict at the deepest levels of the human mind and soul. Previous reading and studying of the sacred text is never invalidated by the latest encounter, but each new reading increases spiritual, moral, and intellectual insight. The Bible is the definitive world-and-life view source for the believer.

Clearly something unique and creative is found in its text, something not found in other books—even other religious books. This dynamic cannot be equaled by church tradition, creeds, or other ecclesiastical statements. That special something, according to the Bible, is divine inspiration (2 Tim. 3:15–17). When Christians read its words, they sense the authority and hear the voice of God.

The Definitive Christian Worldview Text

Because holy books illuminate their respective religions, one may wonder about the significance of the Bible in terms of authority and Christian belief. The three historic branches of Christendom (Roman Catholicism, Eastern Orthodoxy, and Protestantism) basically agree concerning the revelatory nature, canonical extent,[3] and divine inspiration of the Bible; nevertheless, these theological traditions disagree vigorously on the authoritative place and role that Scripture properly plays within the faith.

A brief explanation and defense of the historic Protestant evangelical position on Scripture shows it to be the most viable.[4] Exploring in brief the nature of the biblical revelation, its canonicity, and inspiration explains why Christians consider the Bible to be so trustworthy. This summary helps answer questions of the Bible's inerrancy and introduces proper principles for its interpretation. Also, an explanation and justification for the Protestant principle of *sola Scriptura* (Scripture as the supreme doctrinal authority) sheds light on the controversial issue of Scripture's authority. This theological exploration demonstrates the foundational and necessary role that the Bible plays within the broader Christian theistic world-and-life view.

Scripture and Revelation

People have fundamental and necessary questions about God as part of any worldview: Just how does anyone know that there is indeed a God? And if God does exist, who is he, and what can be known about his being and character? How does God relate to the universe? What does he require of humankind? And what path should be taken by human beings to encounter God?

Historic Christianity provides the answers to these critical queries in the doctrine of revelation.[5] Unlike other religions, the God of the Bible did not leave his creatures to grope in the dark wondering about his existence, character, and wishes. Christianity is a faith built upon the truths of divine revelation. This foundational principle has direct worldview implications for it sets Christianity apart from other belief systems such as secularism (atheism, agnosticism), deism, and pantheism—all of which deny the existence of divine revelation.

In Christian theology, revelation refers to God's personal self-disclosure to his creatures. He took the initiative and actively and decisively revealed himself in two ways: through general revelation (the knowledge of God that comes via the created order) and special revelation (the knowledge of God that comes via redemptive history).

General Revelation

God's existence, power, wisdom, majesty, and glory are made known in a general way to all people at all times in all places through the created order. That includes nature (see Ps. 19:1–4; Rom. 1:18–21), history (Dan. 2:21; Acts 17:26), and the inner human conscience (Gen. 1:26–27; Rom. 2:11–16).

This disclosure takes two distinct forms. First, external, which consists of the created order or nature (manifesting God's work as the caring transcendent Creator of the world) and God's providential ordering of the universe including history (manifesting God's work as the sovereign Sustainer of the world). Second, internal, consisting of both an innate sense or consciousness of God and the moral law of conscience in the heart of the human person.

Special Revelation

God's more specific self-disclosure comes in and through his great redemptive acts, events, and words (see John 20:31; 2 Tim. 3:15–17; Heb. 1:1–4). It comes at special times and in special places. This detailed unveiling occurs in two stages. First, God manifested himself through his covenant people such as the Hebrew patriarchs, prophets, and kings (as recorded and interpreted by the prophets in the Old Testament).

Second, God's revelation culminated decisively in the Incarnation of Jesus Christ—the God-man whose life, death, and resurrection were recorded and interpreted by the apostles in the New Testament. Biblically speaking, the agent of all revelation is the divine Logos—the eternal Word and Son who "gives light to every man" (John 1:9).

Two-Books Theory

Protestant theologians sometimes call this dual view of revelation the "two-books theory." God is the author of both the figurative book of nature (God's world) and the literal book of Scripture (God's written Word).

The Belgic Confession (a Reformed confession of 1561) uses this two-book metaphor under the heading "The Means by Which We Know God":

> We know him by two means: First, by the creation, preservation, and government of the universe, since that universe is before our eyes like a beautiful book in which all creatures, great and small, are as letters to make us ponder the invisible things of God. . . . Second, he makes himself known to us more openly by his holy and divine Word, as much as we need in this life, for his glory and for the salvation of his own.[6]

In this second book (the Bible), the infinite God condescends and makes himself known propositionally (in words and statements that people understand) for the very purpose of salvation. This propositional revelation is special—that is, given to a special people (first Israel, then the church) at special times and places.

The two forms of revelation from the same infinitely perfect God mutually reinforce and complement one another. The biblical worldview considers all truth to be God's truth. Human interpretations of the two sources

---

Does It Make Sense to Believe the Bible Is a Revelation from God?

Historic Christianity considers the Bible to be the propositional Word of God. The following list offers six reasons why it is intellectually credible to believe the Bible is God's actual revelation to man.[7]

1. Unlike most other religious books, the Bible is uniquely connected to history. Therefore, many of its central claims are open to historical investigation (verification/falsification).

2. To some degree, a number of the scriptural accounts (though certainly not all) have been corroborated or supported by extrabiblical historical sources and archaeological evidence.

3. The bibliographic evidence (manuscript abundance, authenticity, and integrity) on the part of the Bible far surpasses all other ancient literary works, secular and religious.

4. Though written in antiquity, the Bible presents a cosmology (a singular beginning to all matter, energy, time, and space) that matches well with the prevailing views of modern science.

5. The Bible appeals to the fulfillment of prophecy and to miracles to substantiate its claims. Both areas can be evaluated in terms of their historical accuracy and explanatory power and scope.

6. The Bible presents a realistic view of human beings (their nature, predicament, and resolution) and offers a world-and-life view that is rational, viable, and existentially fulfilling for humanity.

---

of revelation may indeed conflict, but not when properly understood and correctly applied.

Scripture instructs its readers to take the message of general revelation seriously (Psalm 19; Romans 1). And the created order illustrates the need for the specificity and completeness of special revelation's message. In other words, general revelation points toward special revelation and provides a rational context for accepting it. Ultimately divine revelation is one unit. It is appropriate to distinguish between its two forms, but they should never be separated from each other.

Some critically important truths in general revelation are not explicitly spelled out in special revelation (including many mathematical, logical, and scientific principles). However, in all matters addressed by the Bible (the essence of special revelation having been embodied in Scripture), this verbal revelation should be considered final and supreme. (See the section on Scripture's authority later in this chapter.) This revelatory priority is granted because of the Bible's specificity, its unique propositional nature, and its self-authenticating nature.

God's written Word speaks in a way that creation cannot. Scripture, through the work of the Holy Spirit, can correct man's misinterpretation of general revelation. In this way, the Bible correlates and unifies the whole revelation of God. Because of this coherence, the full importance of general revelation can be affirmed while also embracing the unique authority and divine inspiration of Scripture.

Scripture and Inspiration

The biblical authors (prophets and apostles) were aware that they were speaking and subsequently writing the words of God (see Exod. 34:27; Deut. 18:18; 1 Cor. 2:12–13; 1 Thess. 2:13; 1 Peter 1:11–12). Some of the apostles of Jesus even placed their New Testament writings on par with the Old Testament (see 1 Tim. 5:18b, which quotes Luke 10:7 and Deut. 25:4 together; 2 Peter 3:16; Rev. 22:18–19), which they recognized as sacred Scripture (Rom. 3:1–2).

The biblical doctrine of inspiration is exemplified by the apostle Paul's statement, "All Scripture is God-breathed" (2 Tim. 3:16). The Greek word *theopneustos*, used to describe Scripture, implies that it is the product of the creative breath of God, not unlike how God produced the universe and the first human being.[8]

In addition, the apostle Peter declares that "no prophecy of Scripture came about by the prophet's own interpretation. . . . But men spoke from God as they were carried along by the Holy Spirit" (2 Peter 1:20–21). The inspiration of the Bible may therefore be defined as the divine act whereby God superintended human authors to ensure their writings reflected his intended revelation.

God nevertheless produced the authorized text while using the genuine contributions of human authors (confluent inspiration). They brought their backgrounds, educations, vocabularies, and styles to the writing task but God produced the inspired Scripture through them (see 2 Tim. 3:16; 2 Peter 1:19–21). Theologian Bruce Milne notes, "The words used were consciously the free composition of the authors and at the same time the very Word of God."[9]

This divine inspiration extended not only to the precise wording (verbal inspiration) chosen by the authors but also to the whole Bible itself (plenary inspiration). Theologian Louis Berkhof provides an explanation for how God inspired the biblical authors: "The Holy Spirit illumined their minds, aided their memory, prompted them to write, repressed the influence of sin on their writings, and guided them in the expression of their thoughts even to the choice of their words."[10] The Bible, though written by human beings, is nonetheless the inspired Word of God because of the Holy Spirit's unique power and supervision.

Scripture and Inerrancy

Scripture's divine inspiration implies the doctrine of biblical inerrancy (Ps. 18:30; 119:89). The Chicago Statement on Biblical Inerrancy sets forth the doctrine this way:

> Holy Scripture, being God's own Word, written by men prepared and superintended by his Spirit, is of infallible divine authority in all matters upon which it touches. . . .
>
> Being wholly and verbally God-given, Scripture is without error or fault in all its teaching, no less in what it states about God's acts in creation, about the events of world history, and about its own literary origins under God, than in its witness to God's saving grace in individual lives.[11]

God's absolutely trustworthy nature and moral integrity (John 17:3; Rom. 3:4) and his direct supervision of the original autographs (2 Tim. 3:16; 2 Peter 1:19–21) resulted in scriptural text that—when correctly understood and properly interpreted—is free of all error (historically, scientifically, morally, and spiritually).

Theologian John Jefferson Davis notes: "All Scripture is the direct product of the omnipotent and omniscient God who is not subject to error."[12] Jesus Christ himself taught that Scripture came from the mouth of God and is therefore error free (Matt. 5:17–18; John 10:35). As a result, evangelical Protestants view the doctrine of biblical inerrancy as a necessary implication.

Scripture and Interpretation

As written propositional revelation, the Scriptures must be responsibly and objectively interpreted. This science is known as hermeneutics.[13]

Historic Protestantism has cautioned that Scripture must be approached and interpreted based upon sound hermeneutical principles. To do so, Protestant evangelicals use the historical-grammatical method. Discovering a text's original meaning and intent requires a credible interpreter to carefully (1) examine the grammar, (2) determine the genre of literature being used, (3) investigate the text's cultural and historical setting, and (4) study both the immediate and wider contexts affecting the given passage.

Accurate biblical interpretation also involves allowing Scripture to interpret Scripture. A passage must be analyzed in light of other passages on the same theme. Clearer, later, and more complete texts illumine earlier and more obscure ones. For example, the earlier Old Testament is explained in light of the later New Testament.

Scripture and Canonicity

Biblical canonicity[14] also builds upon the principle of biblical inspiration. Because the prophets and apostles recognized that what they said and wrote was the inspired Word of God, the sacred documents were placed in an exclusive collection that became known as the canon of Scripture. Derived from the Greek word *kanōn*, the canon refers to a rule, standard, or measuring rod. These "Writings" or "Scripture" (Latin *scriptura*, Greek *graphē*) became the standard by which acceptable belief and practice were judged.

The basic facts surrounding the Old and New Testament canons can be summarized as follows.

OLD TESTAMENT

A part of the ancient Palestinian collection,[15] the thirty-nine books of the Old Testament canon were originally written primarily in Hebrew, though some parts were drafted in Aramaic. This canonical collection was established by the covenant people of Israel (Rom. 3:1–2; 9:4–5). Jesus viewed the Old Testament texts as his Bible—divinely composed in preparation for his coming into the world (Incarnation). And he taught his followers to discover him in its pages (Luke 24:44).

Jesus confirmed the authenticity of this canon and even called attention to its threefold Jewish divisions: "the Law of Moses, the Prophets and the Psalms" (Luke 24:44). Christ considered the entire Old Testament as coming directly from the mouth of the Lord (Matt. 4:4; cf. Deut. 8:3). Likewise, the apostle Paul viewed these texts as the very words of God almighty (Rom. 3:1–2). Generally accepted by Jewish tradition, the Jewish Council of Jamnia[16] (A.D. 90) formally confirmed this Hebrew canon. Warnings against additions and omissions to these books are found within the Old Testament itself.[17]

The Protestant evangelical tradition, like the Jewish tradition, does not accept the apocryphal writings[18] as part of the Old Testament canon. Jesus and his disciples never quoted from them. And at certain points these writings are even at odds with sound biblical doctrine. However, some Protestant groups find historical and even some ethical value in the apocryphal books.

NEW TESTAMENT

The New Testament canon[19] of twenty-seven books was all written in Greek and classified into five categories: Gospels, historical accounts (Acts), Pauline Epistles, General Epistles, and apocalyptic literature (Revelation).[20] The apostles recognized early on that their writings were inspired by the Holy Spirit and considered them on par with the Old Testament. Though a few books were questioned for a time (for example, Hebrews, 2 Peter, 2 and 3 John, Jude, and Revelation), later church councils (Hippo, A.D. 393; Carthage, A.D. 397) recognized the inherent authority of all twenty-seven books.

> ### Thought Box: The "Other" Gospels
>
> In addition to the four canonical Gospels (Matthew, Mark, Luke, John), numerous other alleged "Gospels" (some of which were Gnostic) were circulated in the first several centuries of the Christian era.[21] However, these alternative pseudepigraphal writings—the Gospel of Mary, Gospel of Thomas, Gospel of Judas, Gospel of Peter, Gospel of Philip, and others—clearly failed the criteria set forth for inclusion into the New Testament canon (see earlier in this chapter).
>
> These writings could not be tied to the original apostles or their associates in terms of authorship. Rather they emerged long after the apostolic era and, in fact, taught doctrines the apostles themselves condemned. (Among other things Gnostic teachings categorically denied the Christian doctrines of creation and the Incarnation, the latter being a test of orthodoxy according to the apostles; see 1 John 4:1–3.)
>
> These writings were thus excluded from the New Testament canon because they could not be historically and doctrinally connected to Jesus's apostles. These reasons, not some type of spiritual conspiracy or politically based agenda (as alleged in Dan Brown's book *The DaVinci Code*), led the historic Christian community to reject them.

The early church embraced these particular writings and rejected others based primarily upon the issue of apostolicity. New Testament scholar F. F. Bruce identifies this and other major criteria for canonical selection:[22]

- apostolic authority (written by an apostle or a close associate)
- antiquity (emerging from the apostolic era)
- orthodoxy (fidelity to apostolic doctrine)
- catholicity (universal church acceptance)

These qualities caused the church to recognize, rather than declare, the inherent inspiration and authority of the New Testament canon. Bruce comments:

> The New Testament canon was not demarcated by the arbitrary decree of any Church Council. When at last a Church Council—the Synod of Hippo in A.D. 393—listed the twenty-seven books of the New Testament, it did not confer upon them any authority which they did not already possess, but simply recorded their previously established canonicity.[23]

Orthodox Christians believe that the Holy Spirit inspired the writings of the New Testament books and controlled the historical process of canonical selection. However, Protestant evangelicals insist that the church only recognized and received the canon of Scripture. The church did not and, in fact, could not stand above Scripture and authoritatively define or create the canon.

Milne concludes, "In the final analysis only God can be an adequate witness to himself."[24] In other words, Scripture is the Word of God because the Holy Spirit says so, not because the church says so. Each canonical book of Scripture was inspired the day it was written. It didn't somehow become inspired the day the church recognized it as canonical.

Scripture and Authority

The authority of Scripture in evangelical Protestant thinking is embodied in the theological principle known as *sola Scriptura*.[25] Evangelical theologian and apologist Robert M. Bowman Jr. offers this working definition:

> Scripture, which is by definition the only written Word of God, is the only publicly accessible, visible infallible verbal expression of God's truth in the world; only those truths about God and our saving relationship with him, which are clearly taught in Scripture or shown to follow from the teaching of Scripture, may be required of Christians to believe.[26]

The Historic Protestant Principle of *Sola Scriptura*

The watchword of the Reformation of the sixteenth century was *sola Scriptura*, which means that Scripture is the absolute standard of doctrine and the final court of appeals in all matters of faith and practice for the church and the individual Christian. Scripture can appropriately serve as the supreme and final Christian authority because it is the only infallible, written Word of God publicly accessible to the church.

Various confessional statements written in the Reformation era make the position of Scripture's supreme authority clearly evident. Evangelical statements of faith still reflect that status today.

The Belgic Confession (a popular Reformed statement of faith written in 1561), article 7, says:

> We believe that this Holy Scripture contains the will of God completely and that everything one must believe to be saved is sufficiently taught in it. . . . For since it is forbidden to add to or subtract from the Word of God, this plainly demonstrates that the teaching is perfect and complete in all respects.[27]

The thirty-nine Articles of the Church of England (a historic Anglican statement of faith written in 1571) states:

Holy Scripture containeth all things necessary to salvation: so that whatsoever is not read therein, nor may be proved thereby, is not to be required of any man, that it should be believed as an article of the Faith, or be thought requisite or necessary to salvation.[28]

The Formula of Concord (a popular Lutheran statement of faith written in 1577), article 1, says:

We believe, teach, and confess that the sole rule and standard according to which all dogmas together with [all] teachers should be estimated and judged are the prophetic and apostolic Scriptures of the Old and of the New Testament alone.[29]

The Westminster Confession of Faith (a popular Presbyterian statement of faith written in 1647), chapter 1, section 10, puts it this way:

The supreme judge by which all controversies of religion are to be determined, and all decrees of councils, opinions of ancient writers, doctrines of men, and private spirits, are to be examined, and in whose sentence we are to rest, can be no other but the Holy Spirit speaking in the Scripture.[30]

The Chicago Statement on Biblical Inerrancy (a consensus written in 1978 that is representative of theologically conservative American evangelicals from various denominations), articles 1 and 2, states:

We affirm that the Holy Scriptures are to be received as the authoritative Word of God.
    We deny that the Scriptures receive their authority from the Church, tradition, or any other human source.
    We affirm that the Scriptures are the supreme written norm by which God binds the conscience, and that the authority of the Church is subordinate to that of Scripture.
    We deny that Church creeds, councils, or declarations have authority greater than or equal to the authority of the Bible.[31]

What *Sola Scriptura* Means

Three important theological implications of the principle of *sola Scriptura* are the authority, sufficiency, and clarity of Scripture.

The authority of Scripture. For the Christian worldview, the right to give commands, enforce proper obedience, and make final or ultimate decisions resides with God. However, Christian theology views divine authority as a chain from God to man. The absolute authority is God, or more specifically the Triune God who has revealed himself—his authority and revelation are complementary. God's revealed Word carries this immeasurable clout.

God has made himself known in various ways, but his greatest and clearest self-disclosure is found in the Incarnation of the eternal *Logos*—the Living Word, Jesus Christ (John 1:1, 14). The God-man, Jesus, as the living head of the church (Eph. 1:22–23), is the imperial authority for the church and the individual believer. However, Christ delegated his authority to his apostles, who—through the inspiration of the Holy Spirit—recorded the written Word.[32] As an infallible record of God's self-revelation, the Bible maintains dominion because it perpetuates Christ's personal oversight. When Scripture speaks, God speaks.

The Bible is the only objectively written Word of God and, upon the death of the apostles, the only publicly accessible apostolic authority. Neither Scripture nor the clear consensus of Christian church history equates so-called apostolic oral tradition (or any other extrabiblical source) with God's written Word.[33] Nor does either teach that any successors of the apostles (ecclesiastical officials) will have an equal or greater directive.[34] In fact, the Christian church's authority is derived from submitting to the divine influence found in the apostolic writings (Scripture).

The sufficiency of Scripture. The Bible conveys all that the church and the individual believer could ever need to experience a redemptive relationship with God through faith in Jesus Christ and to live a God-honoring life. The apostle Paul explicitly told his associate Timothy that Scripture is "able to make you wise for salvation through faith in Christ Jesus" (2 Tim. 3:15). The written Word is also "useful for teaching, rebuking, correcting and training in righteousness, so that the man of God may be thoroughly equipped for every good work" (2 Tim. 3:16–17).

Scripture is enough to make the believer complete in both belief (faith) and practice (life). Because of its supreme adequacy, a Christian is not required to believe or practice anything of a theological or moral nature not found in, or implied within, the Bible's pages.

Further evidence for Scripture's complete sufficiency is found in its prohibitions against adding or taking anything away.[35] Virtually all cults and heretical sects place extrabiblical writings on par with the Bible's text (for example, *The Book of Mormon* or *Science and Health with Key to the Scriptures*). Even other branches of Christendom (Roman Catholicism, Eastern Orthodoxy) assert that certain forms of ecclesiastical tradition possess an authority virtually equal to that of Scripture.[36] But such practices violate the commands of Scripture itself.

The clarity of Scripture. *Sola Scriptura* also affirms the essential clarity (or perspicuity) of the Bible. The written Word clearly communicates what is necessary for knowing God, experiencing salvation, and living the Christian life.[37] All people can, by God's grace, understand the presentation of the gospel message explained in this great book.

Its perspicuity does not mean that every passage is equally clear, nor that scholarly study is not needed, but this quality does signify that the essential message of salvation is plainly revealed within its pages. And because not all Scripture is equally clear, hermeneutically speaking the less clear parts are meant to be interpreted in light of the clearer parts (Scripture interprets Scripture).

The Bible is not an obscure book, written to mystify, but rather it was written to be understood—especially its central message (the gospel)—by the masses. An appreciation for Scripture's authority, sufficiency, and clarity provides insight into the overall Christian worldview. Proponents of this position look to the Bible to understand what God requires them to believe and how he wants them to live (see figure).

Implications of Divine Revelation

Revelation
(Divine Unveiling: God's personal self-disclosure)

Two Books Theory
(example: The Belgic Confession, Article 2)

General Revelation	**Special Revelation**
(figurative book of nature)	(literal book of Scripture)
Ps. 19:1–4; Rom. 1:18–21	2 Tim. 3:15–17; 2 Pet. 1:20–21

Biblical Inspiration
Holy Spirit superintends the writing of Scripture
Theopneustos: God-breathed Word
verbal/plenary/confluent inspiration

Biblical Interpretation
(Historical-Grammatical Method)

Implications of Scripture's Inspiration

Inerrancy	**Authority**	**Canonicity**
(without error)	(*sola Scriptura*)	(exclusive collection)
historically, scientifically,	final court of appeals in	based upon apostolicity:
morally, and spiritually	faith and practice	recognition not declaration

What* sola Scriptura *does not mean. Because this foundational Protestant principle guides many Christians in terms of their beliefs and practices, frequent misunderstandings of *sola Scriptura* necessitate clarification of five points about what it does not mean:[38]

1. *Sola Scriptura* does not mean that other authorities besides Scripture can't be appropriately recognized by the church. Creeds, tradition, consensus of the church, and human reason all provide valuable judgment. However, they are subordinate to the supreme and final authority of Scripture.
2. *Sola Scriptura* does not repudiate the usefulness of tradition in particular as a subordinate norm in theology. It may be quite acceptable to allow tradition to play a secondary (or derivative) role in the formulation of doctrine (for example, the ecumenical creeds of Christendom).
3. *Sola Scriptura* does not repudiate the church fathers or church history overall. The great leaders and teachers in the history of the church have provided invaluable instruction in theology, but (as those same individuals have often remarked) their views must be appropriately evaluated in light of the supreme theological norm—Scripture. Examples from church history can still provide a secondary form of spiritual guidance for Christians.
4. *Sola Scriptura* does not mean that all truth is found in the Bible or can only be found there. Certainly all truth is indeed God's truth. Information found outside Scripture (in general revelation, tradition, and so forth) can be genuinely true and may actually correct misunderstandings of Scripture. However, alleged truths that contradict Scripture are not genuinely true.
5. *Sola Scriptura* does not deny that the Word of God was initially in oral form. When the apostles were living, they spoke and wrote with divine authority as the Holy Spirit worked through them. However, upon their deaths, the only reliable and accessible apostolic source is found in the Bible.

Objections to *Sola Scriptura*

The authority of Scripture holds supreme importance in a Christian worldview, especially for Protestant evangelicals who believe that their faith and the way they live depend upon Scripture. Other branches of Christendom and skeptics sometimes raise objections to this crucial distinction.[39] They suggest that this principle is incoherent or unworkable. Responses to seven common objections explain how *sola Scriptura* impacts Christian theology and the larger world-and-life view.

Objection #1: Scripture itself does not teach the principle of *sola Scriptura*; therefore, this principle is self-defeating.

Response: The doctrine of *sola Scriptura* need not be taught formally and explicitly. It may be implicit in Scripture and inferred logically. Scripture explicitly states its inspiration in 2 Timothy 3:15–17 (discussed previously) and its sufficiency is implied there as well. This passage contains the essence of *sola Scriptura*, revealing that Scripture is able to make a person wise unto salvation. And it includes the inherent ability to make a person complete in belief and practice.

Scripture has no authoritative peer. While the apostle Paul's reference in verse 16—to Scripture being "God-breathed"—specifically applies to the Old Testament, the apostles viewed the New Testament as having the same inspiration and authority (1 Tim. 5:18 [Deut. 25:4 and Luke 10:7]; 2 Peter 3:16). They mention no other apostolic authority on par with Scripture. Bowman notes:

> The New Testament writings produced at the end of the New Testament period direct Christians to test teachings by *remembering* the words of the prophets (OT) and apostles (NT), not by accessing the words of living prophets, apostles, or other supposedly inspired teachers (Hebrews 2:2–4; 2 Peter 2:1; 3:2; Jude 3–4, 17).[40]

Scriptural warnings such as "do not go beyond what is written" (1 Cor. 4:6) and prohibitions against adding or subtracting text (Rev. 22:18–19) buttress the principle that Scripture stands unique and sufficient in its authority.

Christ held Scripture in highest esteem. The strongest scriptural argument for *sola Scriptura*, however, is found in how the Lord Jesus Christ himself viewed and used Scripture. A careful study of the Gospels reveals that he held Scripture in the highest regard. Jesus said: "The Scriptures cannot be broken" (John 10:35); "Your word is truth" (John 17:17); "Not the smallest letter, not the least stroke of a pen, will by any means disappear from the Law" (Matt. 5:18); and "It is easier for heaven and earth to disappear than for the least stroke of a pen to drop out of the Law" (Luke 16:17).

Christ appealed to Scripture as a final authority. Jesus even asserted that greatness in heaven will be measured by obedience to Scripture (Matt. 5:19) while judgment will be measured out by the same standard (Luke 16:29–31; John 5:45–47). He used Scripture as the final court of appeal in every theological and moral matter under dispute. When disputing with the Pharisees on their high view of tradition, he proclaimed: "Thus you nullify the word of God by your tradition that you have handed down" (Mark 7:13).

Because Scripture came from God, Jesus considered it binding and supreme, while tradition was clearly discretionary and subordinate. Whether tradition was acceptable depended on God's written Word. This recognition by Christ of God's Word as the supreme authority supplies powerful evidence for the principle of *sola Scriptura*.

When Jesus was tested by the Sadducees concerning the resurrection, he retorted, "You are in error because you do not know the Scriptures" (Matt. 22:29). When confronted with the devil's temptations, he responded three times with the phrase, "It is written," followed by specific citations (Matt. 4:4–10). In this context Jesus corrects Satan's misuse of Scripture. Theologian J. I. Packer says of Jesus: "He treats arguments from Scripture as having clinching force."[41]

Christ deferred to Scripture. Jesus based his ethical teaching upon the sacred text and deferred to its authority in his Messianic ministry.[42] His very destiny was tied to biblical text: "The Son of Man will go just as it is written about him" (Matt. 26:24). "This is what is written: The Christ will suffer and rise from the dead on the third day " (Luke 24:46). Even while dying on the cross Jesus quoted Scripture (see Matt. 27:45, cf. Ps. 22:1). His entire life, death, and resurrection seemed to be arranged according to the phrase "the Scriptures must be fulfilled" (see Matt. 26:56; Luke 4:21; 22:37).

Clearly, Christ accepted Scripture as the supreme authority and subjected himself to it.[43] Jesus did not place himself above Scripture and judge it; instead he obeyed God's Word completely. A follower of Christ can do no less. A genuinely biblical worldview requires Scripture to be the supreme authority.

> **Objection #2:** The earliest Christians didn't have the complete New Testament. Therefore, references to Scripture by Jesus and his apostles apply only to the Old Testament.
>
> **Response:** This objection fails for four reasons. First, the early church had the living apostles to teach them. Though the inscripturation process took some time, immediacy wasn't an issue because the apostles were still living. And the written New Testament circulated among the churches early in the first century.
>
> Second, Christ promised to send the Holy Spirit who would guide his apostles "into all truth" (John 16:13), as well as "remind" them of everything Christ said (John 14:26). In this way Jesus put his stamp of approval on the New Testament yet to come (prospectively), as he had done for the previously written Old Testament (retrospectively).[44]
>
> Third, considering his identity, the words of Jesus (Gospels) would carry at least the same authority as the words of the Old Testament prophets.
>
> Fourth, Christ's apostles, who were promised Spirit-guided illumination and total recall, placed their writings on par with the Old Testament.

The apostolic witness to Scripture claims it is inspired, infallible, and authoritative.[45]

Objection #3: The Roman Catholic Church wrote, canonized, and interpreted Scripture. The Bible cannot be greater than its cause—the Church.

Response: First, the claim that the church produced the Bible is wrong. (Note: Protestant scholars typically view the early church as catholic but not Roman). The church did not exist officially when the prophets and patriarchs wrote the Old Testament books. And the church accepted the Old Testament canon on the authority of Jesus Christ's personal testimony. As an institution, the church did not produce the New Testament writings either. The apostles and their close associates (initial leaders of the church at large) wrote those books under the Holy Spirit's direct inspiration.

Though the early church preceded the apostolic writings, it was the gospel message preached—later recorded and expounded in those writings—that by divine grace produced the church. This progression can be described as:

$$\text{Gospel} \longrightarrow \text{Church} \longrightarrow \text{New Testament}$$

The New Testament books became a permanent, infallible record of an oral message. Because Scripture is identified with the preached gospel, it is authoritative. The church (made up of gospel-believing communities) submits to the Word (gospel) which created it. Scripture derives no authority from the church; the authority of Scripture is inherent because the text is the very words of God (Rom. 3:2; 2 Tim. 3:16).

The early church did not *create* Scripture. The church merely *received* Scripture and recognized its inherent authority. God determined the canon by inspiring certain books and then guided the church to recognize and receive them.

The true church derives authority from rightly understanding and applying Scripture. The purpose of Scripture is to bear witness to Christ, who himself bears witness to the integrity and authority of Scripture: "You diligently study the Scriptures. . . . These are the Scriptures that testify about me" (John 5:39).

Objection #4: Oral apostolic tradition is mentioned in Scripture (see 1 Cor. 11:2; 2 Thess. 2:15; 3:6; 2 Tim. 2:2) and granted divine authority alongside the apostolic writings.

Response: While living, the apostles could express their authoritative statements either orally or in writing, for they were hand-selected, authoritative spokespersons for the Lord Jesus Christ. This apostolic authority in both forms must have been tremendously helpful as the early church emerged in the first century. It's reasonable to conclude that the oral communication of the apostles was no different in content than their writings.

However, upon the apostles' deaths, the only way to confirm whether a particular so-called extrabiblical (apostolic) tradition is in accord with what the apostles taught and believed is to rely upon the permanent written Word (Scripture). Not all such claims were historically authentic and factually true even in apostolic times.[46]

In this regard to oral tradition, Bowman makes this point:

> Nowhere in the New Testament is it stated or implied that the church was commissioned to transmit to future generations oral traditions teaching doctrines or practices *not found anywhere in the Bible*—much less any guarantee that they would do so *infallibly*.[47]

Ancient church traditions may serve as a type of noninspired subordinate norm in theology, but they possess a derivative and ministerial function only. However, such church tradition often suffers from being contradictory, biblically inconsistent, and even nebulous in nature.

Objection #5: *Sola Scriptura* is an unhistorical position. Nobody believed in it before the sixteenth century. *Sola Scriptura* was therefore a theological innovation of the Protestant Reformers.

Response: Because the doctrine of *sola Scriptura* is derived from Scripture (see response to objection #1 above), it is not a sixteenth-century innovation. *Sola Scriptura* did not appear as a fully developed and consistent theological position until the time of the Protestant Reformation, but the foundations for the position appeared much earlier in church history. Historical theologian Richard A. Muller explains:

> The views of the Reformers developed out of a debate in the late medieval theology over the relation of Scripture and tradition, one party viewing the two as coequal norms, the other party viewing Scripture as the absolute and therefore prior norm, but allowing tradition a derivative but important secondary role in doctrinal statement. The Reformers and the Protestant orthodox held the latter view, on the assumption that tradition was a useful guide, that the trinitarian and christological statements of Nicaea, Constantinople, and Chalcedon were expressions of biblical truth, and that the great teachers of the church provided valuable instruction in theology that always needed to be evaluated in the light of Scripture.[48]

Other historical theologians, such as Reinhold Seeberg and J. N. D. Kelly, cite a number of early church fathers as believing Scripture to be the absolute authority as a doctrinal norm.[49] Debates over the exact relationship between Scripture and church tradition took place long before the Protestant Reformers came along. In fact, some of the most powerful quotations concerning biblical authority can be drawn from two of the greatest Catholic thinkers in history, Augustine and Thomas Aquinas.

Augustine of Hippo (354–430) said:

[I]t is to the canonical Scriptures alone that I am bound to yield such implicit subjection as to follow their teaching, without admitting the slightest suspicion that in them any mistake or any statement intended to mislead could find a place.[50]

This Mediator . . . has besides produced the Scripture which is called canonical, which has paramount authority, and to which we yield assent in all matters of which we ought not to be ignorant, and yet cannot know of ourselves.[51]

[T]here is a distinct boundary line separating all productions subsequent to apostolic times from the authoritative canonical books of the Old and New Testaments. . . . In the innumerable books that have been written latterly we may sometimes find the same truth as in Scripture, but there is not the same authority. Scripture has a sacredness peculiar to itself.[52]

Thomas Aquinas (1225–1274) stated:

We believe the prophets and apostles because the Lord has been their witness by performing miracles. . . . And we believe the successors of the apostles and prophets only in so far as they tell us those things which the apostles and prophets have left in their writings.[53]

Thomas even affirms Augustine's exalted view of Scripture by citing the greatest of the church fathers:

In this sense St. Augustine wrote to St. Jerome: "Only to those books or writings which are called canonical have I learnt to pay such honour that I firmly believe that none of their authors have erred in composing them. Other authors, however, I read to such effect that, no matter what holiness and learning they display, I do not hold what they say to be true because those were their sentiments."[54]

Objection #6: Private interpretation leads to denominationalism. *Sola Scriptura* is therefore unworkable as an authoritative principle.

Response: Roman Catholic apologists in particular bring this major objection against *sola Scriptura*. Simply stated, if the Bible is so clear, why are there so many denominations within Protestantism?

The first point is that not all denominational splits are scandalous. Whole-sale departures from historic Christianity by theological liberalism must be opposed. When historic churches deny the very essence of the faith (the creeds), then division is obligatory.

Evangelical theologian J. I. Packer gives a concise and forceful answer to this objection:

> To the traditional Roman Catholic complaint that Protestant biblicism produces endless divisions in the church, the appropriate reply is twofold: firstly, the really deep divisions have been caused not by those who maintained *sola Scriptura*, but by those, Roman Catholic and Protestant alike, who reject it; second, when adherents of *sola Scriptura* have split from each other the cause has been sin rather than Protestant biblicism, for in conventional terms the issues in debate have not been of the first magnitude.[55]

Packer goes on to identify six concerns that divide Protestants: (1) God's sovereignty and man's freedom, (2) the Lord's Supper, (3) ecclesiology (church order), (4) church/state issues, (5) baptism, and (6) eschatology (last things).[56]

One explanation for the differences on secondary issues is that diverse groups use a variety of hermeneutical approaches. Another factor is that no one has all of the spiritual and scholarly gifts and abilities to rightly interpret every detail of Scripture. It should also be noted that Catholicism, regardless of its Teaching Magisterium[57] (teaching office or authority) and its claim to infallibility, has as much diversity as Protestantism.[58] And it must be remembered that the East-West (Orthodoxy-Catholicism) church schism of 1054 severely divided the church five centuries before the Reformation.

Objection #7: The original biblical manuscripts did not contain a table of contents to designate exactly which books were canonical and which were not. Therefore Protestants relied upon Roman Catholic tradition in order to even produce the canon of Scripture. This dilemma is self-defeating for the principle of *sola Scriptura*.

Response: The process that the Christian community went through in deciding which books should be included in the canon is open to historical investigation. It seems unreasonable that a Protestant must rely upon Catholic tradition (as some type of revelation) to objectively investigate this historical process. The canonical debate is not part of what Catholics consider "apostolic tradition."

Protestant Christians can warrant knowledge of the canon on the objective internal evidences of the biblical texts. Those books that (1) profess to be Scripture or are acknowledged so by other such books, (2) are authentic (written by the persons to whom they are attributed), and (3) have some objective evidence supporting the claim that they are part of the inspired canon, belong in the canon.

In practical terms, Protestants accept the Old Testament as canon because Jesus, whose inspiration is evident, did so. And, Protestants accept the New Testament books as canon because it can be verified that Jesus's apostles and their associates produced them with his authorization.

Catholic apologists admit the ecclesiastical process that resulted in the biblical canon was long and drawn out. But this assertion seems inconsistent with their claim that the Pope possesses the gift of infallibility. Why were there so many different lists and such strong disagreement about certain books? For example, even the great patristic scholars Augustine and Jerome differed over the canon. Why didn't the pope at the time, as the Vicar of Christ on Earth, simply intervene with the definitive list and settle the issue quickly and permanently? Could it be that in the early church the Bishop of Rome wasn't recognized as having that power?

It is a mistake to assert that the early church determined or created the canon of Scripture. Rather the early church recognized the inherent inspiration in the apostolic writings. In other words, an ecclesiastical pronouncement did not inspire scriptural writings; instead the pronouncement followed what had always been considered inspired revelation. When were the canonical books inspired? Not at the Councils of Hippo (A.D. 393) or Carthage (A.D. 397). Each book was inspired the day it was written. Clearly the inspiration of Scripture preceded the pronouncements of councils some 300 years later.

The divine inspiration and authority of Scripture is self-authenticating ("God-breathed," 2 Tim. 3:15–16). The church cannot function as the one who confirms Scripture's authority (determining the canon), for only God can attest to the truth of his holy Word. Therefore, an unofficial (but decisive) list of canonical books, namely the self-authenticating books written by the apostles or their associates, emerges. Their inspiration identifies the books as canonical. The Holy Spirit speaking in Scripture provides the final confirmation that a book is canonical, not the church's later recognition of that fact.

Scripture and Worldview

The Bible is the Christian's definitive worldview text. It reveals what is to be believed and how the believer is to live. Because it is the inspired Word of God, Scripture is inerrant, sufficient, and the supreme and final authority for the church and the individual Christian. The greatest of all of history's great books, the Bible can illumine the mind with truth, soften the hardest heart, and direct the soul toward life eternal.

128 Exploring the Christian Worldview

With this foundation for the inspiration and authority of Scripture set, the historic Christian view of God builds upon it, as can be seen in the next chapter.

Discussion Questions

1. How do general and special revelation differ? In what way does special revelation have presuppositional priority?
2. What is the "two-books theory" of revelation? Is all truth really God's truth? Why?
3. What is the connection between the doctrines of biblical inspiration and biblical inerrancy?
4. What criteria did the church follow in accepting or rejecting books into the New Testament canon?
5. What does the Protestant principle of *sola Scriptura* imply about Scripture? How can the principle of *sola Scriptura* be misunderstood and misapplied? How would you support the principle of *sola Scriptura* from Scripture itself?

For Further Study

Archer, Gleason L. *Encyclopedia of Bible Difficulties*. Grand Rapids: Zondervan, 1982.

Bruce, F. F. *The Canon of Scripture*. Downers Grove, IL: InterVarsity, 1988.

Carson, D. A., and Douglas J. Moo. *An Introduction to the New Testament*. 2nd ed. Grand Rapids: Zondervan, 2005.

Davis, John Jefferson. *Foundations of Evangelical Theology*. Grand Rapids: Baker, 1984.

Geisler, Norman L., and William E. Nix. *A General Introduction to the Bible*. Rev. ed. Chicago: Moody, 1986.

Geisler, Norman L., ed. *Inerrancy*. Grand Rapids: Zondervan, 1980.

Kitchen, K. A. *On the Reliability of the Old Testament*. Grand Rapids: Eerdmans, 2003.

8

THE HISTORIC
CHRISTIAN VIEW OF GOD

The most important element of any worldview is what it says or does not say about God.

Ronald H. Nash, Worldviews in Conflict

*A*s an instructor of philosophy and theology, I've always enjoyed thinking about, discussing, and debating the attributes of God. However, my life-threatening illness caused my theology to become very personal and practical. Instead of rigorous debate, I desperately needed comfort and security. I longed for consolation and true peace of mind and soul.

I needed to find rest in God and be reassured of his love and concern for me. Over the many sleepless nights of my health crisis accompanied by constant pain and anxiety, I leaned heavily on my basic doctrinal beliefs and called out to the Lord in prayerful searching.

Scripture reminded me that he is an infinite being with no limitations to power, space, and knowledge. So, to the best of my ability I reflected upon these great truths:

- *As an all-powerful being, God is greater than all my problems, and my relationship with him extends beyond any present painful and confusing circumstances.*
- *Because God is not limited by space, the truth that God is always near— nearer, in fact, than my own breath, and closer even than the beat of my heart—comforted me.*
- *God also knows all things, giving me assurance that he knew all about my vulnerable condition. Concentrating on the truth that God indeed knows exactly what I need at every moment made a tremendous difference.*

These revealed doctrines were no longer just philosophical and theological principles. They had become the truths that allowed me to endure with hope, with purpose, and with courage.

A God Worth Trusting

The central component of any worldview is its concept of God. *Theology* (taken from the two Greek words *theos*, "God"; and *logos*, "word" or "study") can be defined as "rational discourse about God." The study of theology should help a person to think and talk intelligently about God.

The Christian theistic worldview therefore centers upon the distinct, majestic, and sovereign God revealed in the Bible.[1] This historic view of God is unique and mysterious, yet rooted in the personal experiences of God's people and in the unfolding, objective events of human history. The true and living God who created all things and who sustains that creation by his infinite power and wisdom cannot be fully comprehended by finite creatures. Thus God's self-disclosure (revelation) is crucial if human beings are to have a genuine and meaningful understanding of him and of his will.

This eternal and morally perfect divine being—though one God—is nonetheless Triune in nature. First unveiled in the Hebrew Scriptures of the Old Testament, this same God made a dynamic and decisive appearance in the historical person of Jesus Christ.

The New Testament embodies the truth of that revelation. Through his perfect life, sacrificial death, and bodily resurrection from the dead, Jesus Christ—the God-man—secured salvation for all who repent of their sin and believe the gospel message of redemption. After Jesus's death and resurrection, the Father and the Son gave the gift of the Holy Spirit to be with, teach, guide, and abide in believers forever.

God's Triune nature, the Incarnation of Jesus Christ, and the person and nature of the Holy Spirit are critical doctrines in understanding the distinctive Christian view of theology. The unique attributes of the biblical God distinguish him from other religious worldview perspectives.

The Triune God: Father, Son, and Holy Spirit

Christian theism affirms the existence of an infinite, eternal, unchanging, and tripersonal spiritual God. This Being is the transcendent Creator and immanent Sustainer of the world (see chapter 9) and is therefore the sovereign Ruler over all things. Historic Christianity therefore affirms a special Trinitarian form of monotheism (Tri-unity: three persons are the one God).

The doctrine of the Trinity[2] reflects the Christian belief that God eternally and simultaneously exists as three distinct and distinguishable (though not separate) persons: Father, Son, and Holy Spirit. As theologian J. I. Packer notes: "God is not only *he* but also *they*."[3]

Not a mere convention of man or of the church, the Bible itself reveals a God who possesses plurality of personhood within the one divine essence (Trinitarian monotheism). The one true God has forever been, is now, and shall ever subsist as three distinct persons. None of them came into being or became divine at a given moment in time. God is thus one in essence or being but three in personhood or subsistence.

The three distinct persons, though distinguishable from each other, all share equally the one divine essence and are thus the one God. Because there is no subordination or inferiority of essence or nature among the members of the Trinity, the three persons are coequal in nature, attributes, and glory. The Trinity sets the Christian concept of God apart from all other alternative views including even other monotheistic concepts.

The Trinity's Biblical Basis

Though some people challenge the idea of biblical support for the Triune nature of God, six simple statements show how this doctrine is derived from Scripture:[4]

1. ***There is only one true God*** (Deut. 6:4; Isa. 43:10; John 17:3; Gal. 3:20).

> For there is one God and one mediator between God and men, the man Christ Jesus.
>
> 1 Timothy 2:5

2. *The Father is called or referred to as God* (Ps. 89:26; Eph. 4:6; Col. 1:2–3; 2 Peter 1:17).

> On him [Christ] God the Father has placed his seal of approval.
>
> John 6:27

3. *The Son (Jesus Christ) is called or referred to as God* (John 1:1; Phil. 2:6; Col. 2:9; Titus 2:13; Heb. 1:8).

> Thomas said to him [Jesus Christ], "My Lord and my God."
>
> John 20:28

4. *The Holy Spirit is called or referred to (or granted the status) as God* (Gen. 1:2; John 14:26; Acts 13:2, 4; Rom. 8:11; Eph. 4:30).

> Then Peter said, "Ananias, how is it that Satan has so filled your heart that you have lied to the Holy Spirit. . . . You have not lied to men but to God."
>
> Acts 5:3–4

5. *The Father, Son, and Holy Spirit are distinct persons and can be distinguished from one another (the Father is not the Son; the Father is not the Holy Spirit; and the Son is not the Holy Spirit)* (Matt. 28:19; Luke 3:22; John 15:26; 16:13–15; 2 Cor. 13:14).

> As soon as Jesus [second person] was baptized, he went up out of the water. At that moment heaven was opened, and he saw the Spirit of God [third person] descending like a dove and lighting on him. And a voice from heaven [first person] said, "This is my Son, whom I love; with him I am well pleased."
>
> Matthew 3:16–17

6. *The three persons (Father or God; and Son or Christ or Lord; and Holy Spirit or Spirit) are frequently listed together in a triadic pattern of unity and equality* (Rom. 15:16, 30; 1 Cor 12:4–6; 2 Cor. 1:21–22; 3:3 Gal. 4:6; Eph. 2:18; 4:4–6; 2 Thess. 2:13–14; Rev. 1:4–6).

> Peter, an apostle of Jesus Christ,
>   To God's elect . . . chosen according to the foreknowledge of God the *Father*, through the sanctifying work of the *Spirit*, for obedience to *Jesus Christ* and sprinkling by his blood.
>
> 1 Peter 1:1–2, emphasis added

An additional consideration. The logical inference drawn from these six biblical statements is that because there is only one true God, and because three distinct persons are all called God, then those three distinguishable persons mentioned in unity and equality must be the one divine entity. Therefore, the one God subsists as three distinct and distinguishable (but not separate) persons: God the Father, God the Son, and God the Holy Spirit.

Thus, the Trinity doctrine is derived directly from the content of Scripture. Though the apostles of Jesus were Jewish monotheists who believed strictly in one God, they nevertheless recognized that two other persons (the Son and the Holy Spirit) were spoken of as God. All three persons possessed the qualities and prerogatives of deity. The apostles therefore modified traditional Jewish monotheism in light of the revelation concerning the Son (Jesus Christ) and the Holy Spirit.

What the Trinity Doctrine Is Not

Because the Trinity doctrine is often misunderstood and misrepresented,[5] it is important to understand what this principle does *not* teach or imply. In addition, how Christianity's Triune God differs from other religious and worldview conceptions of God needs to be considered.

The three "persons" in the Godhead should not be understood to imply three different beings or gods, for this would wrongly divide the one divine essence (monotheism). Orthodox Trinitarianism rejects belief in more than one or many gods (polytheism) in general and belief in three different gods (tritheism) in particular. Trinitarian monotheism, therefore, stands at odds with the various forms of dualism (two foundational deities) and the polytheism[6] found in ancient and Eastern religions (Shintoism, popular Hinduism, and animism). Other polytheistic expressions such as in the Church of Jesus Christ of Latter Day Saints (Mormonism) can be found primarily in the Western world.[7]

The unity of God's nature (monotheism) should not be emphasized at the expense or exclusion of the plurality of personhood found within God's single essence. Orthodox Trinitarianism therefore rejects radical or extreme forms of monotheism that make God a solitary person. Types of these more extreme unitarian religious systems are found in the ancient heresy of Monarchianism[8] as well as in the traditional monotheistic religions of Judaism, Islam, and Unitarianism.[9] They also appear in the more philosophical system known as deism.[10]

Because the Triune God of the Bible is superpersonal (more than personal), religions that view God as impersonal (less than personal)—such as some versions of Buddhism, Hinduism, and the New Age movement—are ruled out. God's superpersonal existence also eliminates those rare forms of religion that tend to be atheistic in their core beliefs, such as Theravada Buddhism and Jainism.[11]

The three persons in the Godhead should not be thought of as mere modes or expressions of existence (a single divine person changing roles, titles, or manifestations). Rather, these three persons are eternally and simultaneously distinct from each other. Orthodox Trinitarianism, therefore, rejects all forms of modalism that blend or confound the persons by defining them as mere modes of existence such as found in the contemporary United Pentecostal Church (sometimes referred to as Oneness or Jesus Only pentecostals).[12]

The Trinity doctrine does not teach that the persons within the Godhead came into existence or progressively became divine at a given moment in time. God is an eternally Triune being. Orthodox Trinitarianism, therefore, rejects all Arian-like religions (such as Jehovah's Witnesses, Christadelphians, and the Iglesia ni Cristo) that make the Son a creature and deny the Holy Spirit's personality and deity.[13] Mormonism's progression-to-godhood teaching is likewise rejected on this basis.

The three persons of the Trinity should not be understood as three parts, fractions, or emanations of God. Each person is fully and completely divine and equally and simultaneously possesses all of God's being. The dualistic emanations of God found in the ancient religions of Zoroastrianism and Manichaeism are at odds with historic Christianity.[14] Orthodox Trinitarianism, therefore, rejects any and all views that diminish the deity of each particular person of the Trinity.

The Trinity doctrine should not be understood to imply a subordination or inferiority of essence among the three persons. The members of the Trinity are qualitatively equal in attributes, nature, and glory. While Scripture reveals subordination among the divine persons in terms of position or role (for example the Father glorifies the Son, the Son submits to the Father, the Holy Spirit proceeds from the Father and Son), there exists absolutely no subordination of essence or nature. Orthodox Trinitarianism, therefore, rejects any and all views that teach a subordination of essence among the three members.

Each member of the Trinity is recognized as a divine person who possesses the prerogatives and attributes of deity. Table 8.1 shows a biblical outline of their names, characteristics, and actions.

Christology: Jesus Christ—God Incarnate

The person of Jesus Christ is at the very core of the Christian faith. Therefore understanding his identity and nature is crucial for embracing this belief system. Scripture presents Jesus of Nazareth as none other than God Incarnate.

Table 8.1
One God—Three Divine Persons
(One What, Three Whos)

Name and Position in the Godhead	Also Called	Qualities of Deity	Works of Deity
The first person of the Godhead: **The Father**	*God* (John 17:3; 1 Cor. 8:6; 2 Cor. 1:3; Eph. 1:3; 4:6; Col. 1:2–3; 1 Peter 1:2–3; 2 Peter 1:17) *Lord/Yahweh* (Gen. 2:4; Exod. 3:15–18; Deut. 6:4; 2 Sam. 7:22; Isa. 64:8)	*Self-existence* (Acts 17:25) *Immutability* (James 1:17) *Omnipresence* (Jer. 23:23–24) *Omniscience* (Isa. 40:28) *Omnipotence* (Jer. 32:17)	*Creation* (Gen. 2:7) *Salvation* (Isa. 45:21) *Incarnation* (Heb. 10:5) *Resurrection* (Acts 2:32) *Judgment* (Eccles. 12:14)
The second person of the Godhead: **The Son**	*God* (John 1:1, 18; 20:28; Rom. 9:5; Titus 2:13; Heb. 1:8; 2 Peter 1:1) *Lord/Yahweh* (Rom. 10:9–13; 1 Cor. 8:5–6; 12:3; Phil. 2:9–11; 1 Peter 2:3; 3:15)	*Self-existence* (John 5:26) *Immutability* (Heb. 13:8) *Omnipresence* (Matt. 28:20) *Omniscience* (Col. 2:3) *Omnipotence* (Col. 1:16–17)	*Creation* (John 1:3; Heb. 1:10) *Salvation* (Rom. 10:12–13) *Incarnation* (Heb. 2:14) *Resurrection* (John 2:19) *Judgment* (John 5:22)
The third person of the Godhead: **The Holy Spirit**	*God* (Acts 5:3–4) *Lord/Yahweh* (2 Cor. 3:17)	*Self-existence* (Rom. 8:2) *Immutability* (2 Cor. 3:18) *Omnipresence* (Ps. 139:7) *Omniscience* (1 Cor. 2:10–11) *Omnipotence* (Gen. 1:2)	*Creation* (Gen. 1:2) *Salvation* (Titus 3:5–7) *Incarnation* (Luke 1:35) *Resurrection* (Rom. 1:4) *Judgment* (John 16:7–8)

The biblical doctrine of the Incarnation[15] teaches that the eternal Logos (or Word), the second person of the Trinity, took unto himself a genuine human nature without in any way diminishing his divinity. Jesus, one undivided person, nevertheless has both a divine nature and a human nature. Those two natures were united in the historical person of Jesus Christ, making him the divine-human person: fully God and fully man.

As the *theanthrōpos* (God-man), Jesus Christ is therefore "two Whats" (a divine "what" [or nature] and a human "what" [or nature]) and "one Who" (a single "person" or "self"). As God Incarnate, Jesus retained all of his divine attributes through his divine nature, and yet through his human nature was fully human. Like the Trinity, the doctrine of the Incarnation separates Christianity from all other religions.

Explicit Passages

Challenges by various groups to the biblical basis for the orthodox doctrine of the Incarnation require explanations from Scripture. Several explicit passages that reveal the truth of Jesus Christ as God Incarnate are worth exploring in more detail:[16]

The Word became flesh and made his dwelling among us.

John 1:14

John's Gospel explicitly teaches that the Word (the preexistent Son), who both was with God and was himself God,[17] became incarnate as a man. God the Son always had a divine nature, but at his incarnation he took a real human nature and became henceforth both God and man. Viewing Jesus as God "in-fleshed" or incarnate distinguished historic Christianity from the incipient Gnosticism, which taught that God could not become flesh because matter was inherently evil. Religious groups today perpetuate Gnostic-like views in the mind-science sects and the New Age movement.[18]

Regarding his Son, who as to his human nature was a descendent of David, and who through the Spirit of holiness was declared with power to be the Son of God by his resurrection from the dead: Jesus Christ our Lord.

Romans 1:3–4

The apostle Paul mentions both Jesus's human nature and his divine nature. Jesus's humanity is recognized through his ancestry—he was a descendent of Israel's King David with the royal Messianic lineage.[19] His divine nature as the Son of God, however, becomes evident through his miraculous resurrection from the dead. Thus, Jesus is the *Christ* (Greek for "Messiah") and the *Lord*.

From them [the Jews and/or the patriarchs] is traced the human ancestry of Christ, who is God over all.

Romans 9:5

Again Paul distinguishes both Jesus's humanity and his deity. His human nature is tied to his Jewish lineage and his divine nature makes him "God over all." Contextually, this reference to "God over all" appropriately applies to the person of Christ and is not a separate doxological reference to God.

Your attitude should be the same as that of Christ Jesus:

> Who, being in very nature God,
>   did not consider equality with God something to be grasped,
> but made himself nothing,
>   taking the very nature of a servant,
>   being made in human likeness.
>
> Philippians 2:5–6

This passage speaks of Jesus Christ as possessing the very metaphysical nature or form of God (*en morphē theou*) in his preexistent state. He had the same essence as God and thus was God. However, though he possessed the nature and prerogatives of deity, Jesus didn't insist upon clinging to his lofty status and surroundings but instead humbled himself as a servant and took on a fully human nature. Thus, he was the God-man.

> For in Christ all the fullness of Deity lives in bodily form.
>
> Colossians 2:9

God's total essence resides in union with the body of Jesus Christ and this passage from Colossians makes that unequivocally clear. In context, the apostle Paul responds directly to the heresy that categorically denied that Christ had come in the flesh (ideas anticipating Gnosticism). This verse, along with those discussed above, illustrates that the doctrine of the Incarnation was clearly a central feature of Paul's preaching and teaching.

> This is how you can recognize the Spirit of God: Every spirit that acknowledges that Jesus Christ has come in the flesh is from God.
>
> 1 John 4:2

The apostle John also responds to heretics that deny the real humanity of Christ by asserting that true Christian doctrine must include the Incarnation. In fact, John makes "God in the flesh" the true test of Christian orthodoxy (correct belief).

All religious sects, both ancient and contemporary, that deny Jesus's deity and humanity are outside the historic Christian communion of belief. The apostles of Jesus took doctrine and doctrinal disputes seriously, and their example should be followed today.

While Christ's deity was addressed under the discussion of the Trinity, table 8.2 shows the biblical support for his genuine human nature.[20]

Table 8.2
The True Humanity of Christ

Jesus Christ's Genuine Human Nature	New Testament Support
His birth:	
Born of a woman	Matthew 1:25; Luke 2:7; Galatians 4:4
Had family ancestors	Matthew 1:1–17; Luke 3:23–38
Called a man:	
Before his resurrection	John 8:40; Acts 2:22; 1 Corinthians 15:21; Philippians 2:7–8
After his resurrection	Acts 17:31; 1 Corinthians 15:47; 1 Timothy 2:5; Hebrews 2:14
Human life:	
Underwent normal human growth and development	Luke 2:40–52; Hebrews 5:8
Subject to authentic physical limitations:	
Hunger	Matthew 21:18
Thirst	John 19:28
Fatigue	John 4:6
Need for sleep	Matthew 8:24
Sweat	Luke 22:44
Temptation	Matthew 4:1–11
Lack of knowledge	Mark 5:30–32; 13:32
Experienced pain and death	Mark 14:33–36; Luke 17:25; 22:63; 23:33; John 19:30

What the Incarnation Is Not

To prevent confusion and misunderstandings concerning this critical doctrine requires an explanation of how the Incarnation should *not* be understood.[21]

Though Jesus has two distinct natures (one divine and one human), he should not *be thought of as two persons.* The union of these natures is found in the one person of Jesus Christ. The Incarnation involves a unity of personhood and a duality of natures. Historic Christianity rejected the Nestorian heresy that taught that there were two separate persons in Christ.

Though Jesus is one person, his two natures did not *blend together to form one hybrid (divine-human) nature.* These two natures are distinct and retain their own attributes or qualities and are thus not mixed together. Historic Christianity rejected the Eutychian heresy that viewed Christ as having a single undifferentiated nature (also known as Monophysitism: one nature).

Table 8.3
Jesus Christ: "Who Do the People Say I Am?"

Baha'i Faith	One of many manifestations of God
Hinduism	One of many divine avatars of Brahman
Islam	One of many merely human religious prophets of Allah
Jehovah's Witnesses	A spirit creature who became a perfect man (and is now a spirit creature again)
Judaism	A merely human religious rabbi or blasphemer
Liberal theology	A merely human social reformer
Mormonism	The first of God's spirit children to become a god
New Age movement	One of many mystical gurus with a divine consciousness
Secularism	A mythical religious figure
UFO religions	An extraterrestrial visitor to earth

Jesus is not *a semi-divine or merely Godlike creature.* Through his divine nature, Jesus Christ is God the Son, the second person of the Holy Trinity. He shares the one divine essence completely and equally with the Father and the Holy Spirit. Historic Christianity rejected the influential Arian heresy that viewed Jesus merely as a Godlike creature and thus as clearly subordinate in essence to God.

Jesus should not *be thought of as only quasi-human.* His human nature makes Jesus completely human, possessing all the essential attributes of a genuine human being, yet without sin. Historic Christianity rejected the heresy of Docetism (a type of early Gnosticism) that denied the true humanity of Christ.

The person of Jesus should not *be thought of as anything other than the God-man.* The properties or attributes of both natures are properly established in the one, single person of Jesus Christ. (For example, through his divine nature he knows all things while simultaneously through his human nature he may lack knowledge.) The two natures "coinhere" or interpenetrate in perfect union so that the human is never without the divine nor the divine without the human, yet the natures do not mix or mingle.

Worldview Implications

If it is true that Jesus Christ is the one and only God Incarnate (God in the flesh: a single person fully God and fully man), then contradictory views of his identity must be false ("A" cannot equal "A" and equal "non-A," see table 8.3).[22]

Christ's Lordship and Worldview Thinking

The lordship of Jesus Christ[23] is a critical truth in Christian theology and crucial to the Christian world-and-life view. The earliest of Christian creeds, "Jesus is Lord," (Greek: *kyrios Iēsous*; Rom. 10:9–10; Phil. 2:11) actually affirms Jesus's unique oneness with the self-existent Lord God almighty. This declaration, which according to Scripture can only genuinely take place by the Holy Spirit's enabling,[24] uses the personal name of Israel's God—Yahweh.

New Testament writers, like other Jews of the first century, used "Lord" (*kyrios*) in place of the name Yahweh, often inferring that name's meaning in context by calling Jesus "Lord" (see Rom. 10:11–13; Phil. 2:9–10). The lordship of Christ therefore implies that Jesus is Yahweh and is thus recognized as Creator,[25] Sustainer,[26] and sovereign Ruler over all things.[27]

Christ's unique claim to be the Lord means he possesses the prerogatives of deity and can engage in those actions reserved exclusively for God. Christ forgave sins,[28] received worship,[29] claimed power over life and death,[30] and claimed the authority to judge humanity.[31] According to the Old Testament, only God can perform such actions.

To proclaim "Jesus is Lord" not only acknowledges his deity but also grants him absolute supremacy in and over all things,[32] including the physical universe, the unseen spiritual realm, human history, the church, and one's individual life and death.[33] Jesus's lordship does not mean that he is one Lord among many, but rather he is Lord to the *exclusion* of all others who make such claims (including pagan deities, Rome's Caesar, secular authorities, and Satan: see Rom. 10:12–13; 1 Tim. 6:15).

The Christian church corporately and believers individually are called to submit every area of life to Christ's lordship. Everyone and everything is ultimately accountable to Jesus Christ. Dutch theologian and politician Abraham Kuyper (1837–1920) proclaimed: "[T]here is not a square inch in the whole domain of our human existence over which Christ, who is Sovereign over *all*, does not cry: 'Mine!'"[34]

It is the universal and absolute lordship of Jesus Christ that motivates Christians to think in worldview categories. The obvious and monumental question is: How does Christ's lordship impact the world, culture, the church, and each believer's life? An orthodox Christology (Jesus as Messiah, Savior, and Lord) compels people to think in worldview terms. That's why the conceptual development of the Christian worldview has been initiated and carried forth by those who embrace and greatly value Christ's role of King and Ruler.[35]

Pneumatology: The Person, Nature, and Work of the Holy Spirit

The Bible speaks of the Holy Spirit (Hebrew: *rûaḥ haqōdeš*, from *rûaḥ*, "breath, spirit, violent wind," and *qōdeš*, "holy"; Greek: *pneuma hagion*) as a divine person. In addition to the deity of the Holy Spirit[36] discussed in the section on the Trinity doctrine, table 8.4 shows scriptural support for the Holy Spirit as an authentic person.

The Holy Spirit, the Incarnate Christ, and the Father are God in three persons—one What and three Whos. Focusing on the characteristics of this one God dramatically impacts the way believers see life and the world.

A Systematic Approach to God's Attributes

While Christian theologians classify God's attributes in different ways,[37] there is no perfect or universally accepted method. However, two categories—*incommunicable* and *communicable*—can be a useful way of thinking about his characteristics.

Incommunicable attributes are those qualities of God not shared with human beings or those far more difficult to find in, or associate with, humanity. In contrast, God's communicable attributes are shared with humans, or are at least more easily associated with them. Because of the *imago Dei*,[38] humans are like God but certainly not identical in nature to him (see chapter 10).

This categorical distinction may be the most common method of classifying God's attributes used by theologians. However, there are difficulties associated with thinking about God in this way. The problem is that no divine attribute is completely incommunicable (without some trace in man, if only analogously). And no divine attribute is completely communicable (at best each can only be found in humans in a limited and/or imperfect way). For this reason, evangelical theologians also sometimes differ over whether a certain attribute is communicable or incommunicable. Perhaps it would be better to see these categories as overlapping at certain points.

Mystery always accompanies the creature's effort to think and speak about the Creator. Nevertheless this method of classification—even with its imprecision—is meaningful and serves an instructive purpose in Christian theology. A final point is that every divine attribute qualifies every other attribute. For example, God is not only infinite, eternal, and unchanging, but he is also infinite, eternal, and unchanging in his love, in his wisdom, in his justice, and so forth. These principles are helpful to keep in mind while examining Scripture to see what it says about God's perfect qualities and characteristics.

God's Incommunicable Attributes

Some divine characteristics[39] are metaphysical in nature and illustrate just how the Creator is separate from the human beings he created. God alone possesses these attributes.

Table 8.4
The Holy Spirit: A Divine Person

Authentic Personhood	Biblical Support
Personal Faculties:	
Mind/intelligence	Romans 8:27
Thought/knowledge	1 Corinthians 2:11
Will/deliberation	1 Corinthians 12:11
Emotion/feelings	Ephesians 4:30
Moral Qualities:	
Holiness	John 16:7–8
Wisdom	Isaiah 11:2
Love	Romans 5:5
Faith	2 Corinthians 4:13
Personal Communication:	
Teaches	Luke 12:12
Speaks	Acts 13:2
Commissions	Acts 13:4
Intercedes	Romans 8:26
Guides	John 16:13
Relational Traits:	
Obeyed	Acts 10:19–20
Called upon	Ezekiel 37:9
Reverenced	Psalm 51:11
Lied to	Acts 5:3
Resisted	Acts 7:51
Blasphemed	Matthew 12:31
Insulted	Hebrews 10:29
Grieved	Ephesians 4:30
Works in Salvation:	
Convicts people of sin	John 16:8
Reveals Christ	John 15:26
Regenerates hearts	Titus 3:5
Baptizes believers into Christ	Acts 1:5
Indwells the believer	1 Corinthians 6:19
Enables persons to confess Christ as Lord	1 Corinthians 12:3
Empowers the believer's witness	Acts 6:9–10
Helps the believer to pray	Romans 8:26
Develops fruit in the believer	Galatians 5:22–23

Self-Existent (Independent, Aseity)

God does not need nor does he depend upon anything outside himself (such as the creation) for his continued existence. Unlike all creatures, the source of God's eternal or everlasting existence is found within himself (self-sufficiency). As the only uncreated and uncaused being, everything else (the entire created order) depends upon his creative and sustaining power. This absolute independence places God in a different category of being than man.

The Creator is qualitatively different than the creature and is a necessary being (God must exist or cannot *not* exist). J. I. Packer contrasts God's existence with that of man: "He exists in a different way from us: we, his creatures, exist in a dependent, derived, finite, fragile way, but our Maker exists in an eternal, self-sustaining, necessary way."[40] Scripture clearly reveals God's self-existence or aseity.[41]

> And he [God] is not served by human hands, as if he needed anything, because he himself gives all men life and breath and everything else.
>
> Acts 17:25

Worldview implication. Because God alone is the ground of all life, any philosophy that attributes the ultimate life principle to the impersonal and accidental forces of nature such as matter, time, and chance (Darwinian evolution[42]) is both a false and blasphemous claim. Further, a philosophy that places ultimate value upon human beings (secular humanism) rather than upon God should likewise be rejected as false.

Christian worldview assurance. Because God is self-sufficient and cannot cease to exist, he will always be there.

Immutable (Constant)

God is unchanging with regard to his being, attributes, purpose, and promises. This unchangeableness does not mean that God is static or immobile or that he is detached, unconcerned or indifferent to the condition of his creatures. Rather God is eternally active and experiences something analogous to passionate emotion[43] as is consistent with his infinite, perfect, and unchanging moral character.

Instances in Scripture where God appears to change his mind or expresses regret (Genesis 6; Exodus 32; 1 Samuel 15; Isaiah 38; Jonah 3) should be understood as anthropomorphic expressions of God's attitude toward a given situation (for example, displeasure at sin). In reality these examples reflect man's change with respect to God rather than the reverse. God's constancy is clearly shown in the Bible.[44]

Every good and perfect gift is from above, coming down from the Father of the heavenly lights, who does not change like shifting shadows.

James 1:17

Worldview implication. Because God is immutable in his being, attributes, purpose, and promises, then philosophical and religious systems that view God as changing (process theology, panentheism) should be rejected as false. The Mormon doctrine of progression from the human state to the divine state should also be regarded as false.

Christian worldview assurance. God's unchanging nature and character means that his promises remain forever sure.

Eternal (Unlimited by Time)

With no beginning or end, God (who transcends time) has no temporal limitations. Some classical Christian theologians believed that God does not experience a succession of moments in his being and therefore exists in an infinite present without past or future (God is timeless).

While some present-day theologians continue to hold to the classical view, others believe that eternity should be understood as an endless duration of time over which God has always existed (God is everlasting). Regardless of which of these two views a person accepts, Christian orthodoxy affirms that God sees all time and events with equal vividness. He also acts in time without time changing or limiting his being in any respect. God stands as the Creator of time itself.[45] His eternality is clearly reflected in Scripture.[46]

Now to the King eternal, immortal, invisible, the only God, be honor and glory for ever and ever. Amen.

1 Timothy 1:17

Worldview implication. Because God is infinitely perfect with regard to time, all philosophies and religions that view God as finite and limited in terms of time (finite godism) must be considered false.

Christian worldview assurance. Unlimited by time means that God perfectly knows each individual's future.

Simple (Unified)

God is a unique and uncompounded being without divisions, parts, or disparate elements within the one divine nature. The three persons within the Godhead share fully and equally the one unified divine essence. Every attribute of God found in Scripture is fully characteristic of all God's being. Wayne Grudem notes: "The doctrine of the unity of God should caution us against attempting to single out any one attribute of God as more important than all the others."[47] The Bible makes this simplicity known.[48]

> Hear, O Israel: the LORD our God, the LORD is one.
>
> Deuteronomy 6:4

Worldview implication. God's unified nature rules out all those religions that confound and complicate God's essence (dualism, polytheism, tritheism).

Christian worldview assurance. The unity of God's being reminds the believer to be single-minded in devotion to God.

Spiritual (Invisible, Incorporeal)

An infinite being of pure spirit, God is without a body or material parts and is by nature invisible to the physical eye and imperceptible by the rest of man's senses. God's total divine essence has not and cannot be seen. Scripture clearly reflects this divine attribute.[49]

> God is spirit, and his worshippers must worship in spirit and in truth.
>
> John 4:24

Worldview implication. Because God is an infinite invisible spirit, all religions that speak of God as having a body (animism,[50] folk religions,[51] Mormonism) must be regarded as false.

Christian worldview assurance. God's pure spiritual nature reminds the believer that most of the meaningful things in life are invisible.

Omnipotent (All-Powerful)

God is an infinite, all-powerful being, and nothing can frustrate his sovereign will or purpose. He can do all things that are consistent with his character and nature. However, God cannot engage in irrational or immoral acts, for these actions would violate his rational and ethical nature.[52] God can thus do that which is humanly impossible (for example, raise the dead), but he cannot do that which is impossible by definition or logic (for example, create a square circle). Many Bible texts confirm God's omnipotence.[53]

> Sovereign LORD, you have made the heavens and the earth by your great power and outstretched arm. Nothing is too hard for you.
>
> Jeremiah 32:17

Worldview implication. Because God is infinitely powerful, all philosophies and religions that view him as finite and limited (finite godism) must be considered false.

Christian worldview assurance. God being all-powerful reminds the believer that the Creator is greater than all life's problems.

Omnipresent (Everywhere Present)

With no spatial limitations or boundaries, God is an infinite being. His entire being is present everywhere throughout the created order—at every point throughout all space, although space itself cannot contain him.[54] God is the Creator of space, time, matter, and energy.[55] The Bible clearly demonstrates his omnipresence.[56]

> God did this [orchestrated life on Earth] so that men would seek him and perhaps reach out for him and find him, though he is not far from each one of us.
>
> Acts 17:27

Worldview implication. Because God's omnipresence implies his immanence (God is within the world), all religions and philosophies that deny God's presence in the world (deism) should be regarded as false.

Christian worldview assurance. God being everywhere present reminds the believer that God is always near.

Omniscient (All-Knowing)

God, as an infinite being, has a perfect and complete knowledge of all things. This knowledge includes the past, the present, and the future[57] as well as what is possible[58] and what is actual.[59] He has a complete awareness of himself[60] and of human beings.[61] Unlike the creature, God's knowledge is immediate and direct[62] so that his knowledge does not grow or change. His omniscience is clearly reflected in Scripture.[63]

> Nothing in all creation is hidden from God's sight. Everything is uncovered and laid bare before the eyes of him to whom we must give account.
>
> Hebrews 4:13

Worldview implication. Because God is infinite in knowledge, all religions and philosophies that limit his knowledge (open theism, finite godism) are regarded as false.

Christian worldview assurance. Because God knows all things, he knows exactly what each person needs.

Additional Characteristics Implied by Incommunicable Attributes

God's divine attributes often signify other characteristics. These qualities are manifested in God's relationship to the created order and to human beings.

Though some of them are addressed in greater detail under the discussion of the doctrines of creation and providence (see chapter 9), a brief description is worth noting here.

Transcendent (Above and Beyond the Created Order)

God exists outside of the created order and rules over it. He is distinct in nature from the cosmos. His transcendence is closely connected to his work as Creator.[64]

> The God who made the world and everything in it is the Lord of heaven and earth and does not live in temples built by hands.
>
> Acts 17:24

Worldview implication. God's transcendence rules out worldviews that consider the universe as part of God's being or body (pantheism, panentheism, animism).

Christian worldview assurance. God's transcendence reminds the believer that God oversees the world.

Immanent (Present within the Created Order)

Though transcendent, God is present and active in the world he created.[65] (God is distinct in being from creation but geographically present within it.) His immanence is closely connected to his omnipresence and work as providential Sustainer.

> "Do not I fill heaven and earth?"
>   declares the LORD.
>
> Jeremiah 23:24

Worldview implication. God's immanence rules out worldviews that consider God as being exclusively transcendent (deism).

Christian worldview assurance. God's immanence reminds the believer that God is in the world.

Sovereign (Absolute Controller)

God is the supreme Ruler of all things, absolute and independent of any authority outside himself.[66] His sovereignty is closely tied to his omnipotence and to his work as Creator and Sustainer (see chapter 9).

The LORD has established his throne in heaven,
and his kingdom rules over all.

Psalm 103:19

Worldview implication. God's sovereignty rules out all worldviews that consider him as limited and lacking in control over the world (panentheism, open theism, finite godism).

Christian worldview assurance. God's sovereignty assures the believer that God is in control of all things.

Wisdom

All God's decisions, goals, and actions are right and bring about the greatest ultimate result.[67] God's wisdom is closely tied to his omniscience and to his work as Creator.

Oh, the depth of the riches of the wisdom and knowledge of God!
How unsearchable his judgments,
and his paths beyond tracing out!

Romans 11:33

Worldview implication. God's infinite wisdom rules out all worldviews that consider God as limited in knowledge or flawed in decision-making (panentheism, open theism, finite godism).

Christian worldview assurance. God's perfect wisdom assures his people that he always knows what is best for them.

Incomprehensible (Beyond Human Comprehension)

Finite creatures cannot completely fathom God's infinite nature.[68] This lack of understanding does not imply that God is somehow unintelligible or contradictory. His incomprehensibility is closely tied to his omniscience and wisdom.

As the heavens are higher than the earth,
so are my ways higher than your ways
and my thoughts than your thoughts.

Isaiah 55:9

Worldview implication. God's incomprehensibility rules out all worldviews that view God as comprehensible to the finite mind of man (rationalism, deism).

Christian worldview assurance. God's incomprehensibility reminds the believer that mystery always accompanies a relationship with God.

God's Communicable Attributes

Some divine attributes are moral in nature and are reflected in the creature to some degree. These reflections of God's moral perfection in humanity set the biblical God apart from all other religious and philosophical views in which God is less than morally perfect (Hinduism, Buddhism, the gods of the ancient Near East, Greco-Roman deities, basic and folk religions, etc.). God's moral attributes can be divided into three basic categories: he is perfectly just, true, and good.

Perfectly Just

God's moral perfection is reflected in his just nature (moral rectitude and fairness). His just character thus shapes God's holiness, righteousness, and wrath.

Holy. God is a majestic and morally perfect being—utterly set apart from all evil, sin, vice, and impurity.[69]

> Holy, holy, holy is the LORD Almighty;
>   the whole earth is full of his glory.
>
> Isaiah 6:3

Righteous. All of God's judgments, commandments, and actions are perfectly right, just, and equitable.[70]

> Righteousness and justice are the foundation of your throne.
>
> Psalm 89:14

Wrathful. Perfect holiness and justice require God to express his intense displeasure at anything that runs contrary to his character, will, and commands.[71]

> The wrath of God is being revealed from heaven against all the godlessness and wickedness of men who suppress the truth by their wickedness.
>
> Romans 1:18

Christian worldview assurance. God's perfectly just character reminds believers that God takes sin seriously.

Perfectly True

God is truth and thus his nature reflects perfect veracity. His trustworthy character is reflected in his genuine, faithful, and truthful ways.

Genuine. God is perfectly authentic, sincere, and true in his character, promises, commands, and relationships.[72]

> Now this is eternal life: that they may know you, the only true God, and Jesus Christ, whom you have sent.
>
> John 17:3

Faithful. God is perfectly reliable, loyal, and trustworthy in his character, commands, promises, and relationships.[73]

> If we are faithless,
>   he will remain faithful,
>   for he cannot deny himself.
>
> 2 Timothy 2:13

Truthful. God's character, words, and actions carry an absolute veracity.[74]

> Jesus answered, "I am the way and the truth and the life."
>
> John 14:6

Christian worldview assurance. The true God is totally trustworthy.

Perfectly Good

God is generous and benevolent in his treatment of his creatures. This fundamental goodness is reflected in his love, grace, and mercy.

Loving. Perfect affection and unswerving commitment characterize God's love toward his children. He gives of himself sacrificially to meet all their needs.[75]

> This is love: not that we loved God, but that he loved us and sent his Son as an atoning sacrifice for our sins.
>
> 1 John 4:10

Gracious. God's perfect unmerited favor, love, and kindness is manifested in his granting sinners what they do not deserve, namely the forgiveness of their sins.[76]

> For the grace of God that brings salvation has appeared to all men.
>
> Titus 2:11

Merciful. God's moral goodness is manifested in his remission of punishment and in his desire to relieve misery due to sin.[77]

> He saved us, not because of righteous things we have done, but because of his mercy.
>
> Titus 3:5

Christian worldview assurance. God's perfectly good character assures believers that God is on their side.

God's attributes can be categorized as being incommunicable or communicable. The incommunicable qualities illustrate the stark contrast between God and man (reflecting the Creator-creature distinction, see chapter 9). The communicable qualities are those divine characteristics that are reflected to some degree in man (via the *imago Dei*, see chapter 10).

God: The Defining Lens

How a person sees God deeply shapes that person's world-and-life view. The Bible presents God as an infinite, eternal, immutable, and tripersonal Spirit. This basic overview of God leads to consideration of his work as the transcendent Creator and immanent Sustainer of the created order. The next chapter addresses the doctrines of creation and providence.

Discussion Questions

1. How would you defend the Trinity doctrine using Scripture? What major points would you present? Just how is the Trinity a logical inference drawn from Scripture? Explain the reasoning process.
2. Can you explain how the orthodox Trinitarian view differs from both tritheism and modalism? Can you name contemporary examples of the ancient heresies of tritheism and modalism?
3. Give a clear, concise, and correct definition for the Christian doctrine of the Incarnation. How does the historic Christian view of the Incarnation differ from the ancient heresies of Gnosticism and Arianism? Can you name contemporary examples of Gnostic and Arian-like belief systems?
4. On what scriptural basis would you support the orthodox view of the Holy Spirit as a divine person?
5. What is the difference between incommunicable and communicable divine attributes? Are there problems with this theological distinction?

How do these attributes affect your view of God? Do they provide intellectual challenge or comfort?

For Further Study

Bowman, Robert M. Jr. *Why You Should Believe in the Trinity: An Answer to Jehovah's Witnesses*. Grand Rapids: Baker, 1989.

Bray, Gerald. *The Doctrine of God*. Downers Grove, IL: InterVarsity, 1993.

Harris, Murray J. *3 Crucial Questions about Jesus*. Grand Rapids: Baker, 1994.

Nash, Ronald H. *The Concept of God: An Exploration of Contemporary Difficulties with the Attributes of God*. Grand Rapids: Zondervan, 1983.

Reymond, Robert L. *Jesus, Divine Messiah: The New Testament Witness*. Phillipsburg, NJ: P & R Publishing, 1990.

Rhodes, Ron. *Christ before the Manger: The Life and Times of the Preincarnate Christ*. Eugene, OR: Wipf and Stock, 2002.

Warfield, Benjamin B. *The Person and Work of Christ*. Ed. Samuel G. Craig. Phillipsburg, NJ: P & R Publishing, 1950.

9

God's World— Creation and Providence

Creation is that work of the triune God by which he called all things that exist, both material and spiritual, into existence out of nonexistence.

Bruce Milne, *Know the Truth*

*T*he initial assessment was cancer in my lungs and brain. Several doctors thought the disease had already reached stage four—usually terminal. Many of my friends and family came to visit and left wondering if they'd see me again— alive. When my children stood by my bedside, I wondered how much longer they would have a father.

Slogging through a swamp full of pain and deep concern—no secure anchor provided me a place to rest. "God help me!" I pleaded.

My favorite hymn, Martin Luther's "A Mighty Fortress Is Our God," came to mind. God alone was my rock and my fortress, the one in whom I could find refuge. I asked him to supply the strength and the courage I needed so desperately.

That evening when my pastor came to visit, he reminded me that these events were under God's complete and providential control. The outcome of my condition would be exactly what God had foreordained for my life. And he told me that God was definitely not punishing me for my sins because the Lord Jesus Christ had already atoned for all of them on the cross. Jesus was *my Lord and Savior, my High Priest in heaven who was interceding for me before the Father. In effect, my pastor reminded me that, as Creator, God is sovereign in all things, and I belonged to him through faith in Jesus Christ. Then we prayed together.*

Afterward, my life's verse came clearly to my then shaky memory: "And we know that in all things God works for the good of those who love him, who have been called according to his purpose" (Rom. 8:28). My Creator was indeed my rock and my fortress; he provided me with a secure place to rest in the midst of this great storm (Ps. 18:2).

The biblical truths of God's sovereignty and providence were then and are today a source of great comfort to me. I rejoice in the truth that the Lord of creation and redemption is in complete control of all things, especially when life's circumstances become painful and difficult to understand.

Two Christian Worldview Truths

God's sovereign actions and providential ordering in creation supply two foundational truths for the historic Christian perspective. These two critical doctrines—of creation *ex nihilo* (creation out of nothing) and God's providence (his unique act of sustaining and guiding his creation)—reveal his character and care and provide an anchor of truth that cannot be moved. Examining the various aspects of creation and providence tests the historic Christian worldview against alternative positions and competing religious belief systems.

The Doctrine of Creation

Throughout Christian history, the concept of biblical creation has been highly esteemed for three basic reasons: First, creation is a foundational truth. It addresses the big questions of life, such as: Where did I come from? Who am I? Where did the universe come from? Why is the world an orderly cosmos rather than chaos? (See chapters 1 and 6.)

All adequate worldviews must answer these crucial questions in order to provide meaning, purpose, and significance for both the world and for humankind. Creation touches upon questions concerning ultimate truth and reality—issues foundational to a world-and-life view.

Second, the doctrine of biblical creation affects other areas of biblical thinking. For example, God's action as Redeemer presupposes his action as Creator (Isa. 44:24). A God who made the world and exercises complete sovereign control over it can also guarantee his people's salvation and destiny. The God of the Bible is known as the Creator-Redeemer (Acts 17:24–31).

The biblical concept of creation also greatly impacts regard for human life (see chapter 10). Man's distinguishing characteristic—being made in the image and likeness of God (Gen. 1:26–27)—gives humankind special value and dignity.

This pattern shows how biblical creation powerfully impacts other areas of Christian thought. It demonstrates that the historic Christian worldview is unified and coherent.

Third, the doctrine of creation helps set Christianity and the historic Christian worldview apart from other religions and worldviews. As demonstrated later in this chapter, God's unique relationship to the universe highlights his astonishing attributes. For example, God has no limitations or boundaries with regard to time, space, and knowledge.

Throughout history, some of the very best arguments for God's existence and for the truth of Christianity have appealed to various aspects of the doctrine of biblical creation. The ancient Nicene Creed begins with this great truth: "We believe in one God, the Father almighty, maker of heaven and earth, of all things visible and invisible." Other Protestant confessions of faith prominently mention and discuss different aspects of this principle as well (see also chapter 6 for the Apostles' Creed).[1]

From Beginning to End

The very first verse in Genesis begins with God's creation of all things. Many references to God's involvement occur in that book's early chapters. But this prominent biblical truth[2] also appears in every major area or division of Scripture. In the Old Testament, creation is addressed in the Pentateuch, in the Major Prophets, and in the Wisdom Literature. Some of the most important discussions of this doctrine can be found in Job, Psalms, and Isaiah.[3]

The concept of creation receives prominence in the New Testament as well. The first verse of John's Gospel takes readers back to the moment before everything began (Greek: *en archē*, "in the beginning"). This text introduces the preexistent "Word" (or *Logos* in Greek), Jesus Christ. Before his incarnation as the God-man, Jesus was with God the Father in the beginning. Jesus shared the same divine nature with his Father (John 1:1) and was directly involved in the formation of all things (1:3).

Creation is mentioned in every major part of the New Testament, including the Gospels, Acts, the Pauline and General Epistles, and even the book of Revelation. Several of the most important references can be found in the books of Romans, 1 Corinthians, Colossians, and Hebrews.[4]

The Triune Creator

According to Scripture, each person within the divine Godhead was involved in the work of creation. While God the Father initiated the act (1 Cor.

8:6; Eph. 4:6), nevertheless God the Son (John 1:3; Col. 1:15–17; Heb. 1:2, 10–12) and God the Holy Spirit (Gen. 1:2; Ps. 104:30) served as his divine coagents. Thus, the Triune God created all things.

When one member of the Godhead is involved in a work, then in some way all three members participate.[5] However, clear examples demonstrate that sometimes one member of the Trinity is recognized as the primary agent in performing a given work. For instance, the Father is the compelling force behind creation, whereas the Son plays this role in redemption, and the Holy Spirit performs this function in human beings who experience regeneration (the new birth).

Evangelical theologian Millard J. Erickson explains further: "It appears from Scripture that it was the Father who brought the created universe into existence. But it was the Spirit and the Son who fashioned it, who carried out the details of the design. While the creation is *from* the Father, it is *through* the Son and *by* the Holy Spirit."[6]

Chief Distinctives of Creation Theology

The historic Christian understanding of creation includes two predominant distinctives: the doctrine of creation *ex nihilo*[7] and the origination of the first human beings—Adam and Eve. Chapter 10 examines the subject of man being made in the expressed image of God, so this topic receives only a brief discussion here. Instead, more detail is supplied for the concept of creation *ex nihilo*. Understanding this critical truth-claim and exploring some of its biblical support draws out important theological, apologetic, and worldview implications.

What Is Creation Ex Nihilo *and Is It Scriptural?*

Historical theologian Richard A. Muller defines the Latin term *ex nihilo* as a reference "to the divine creation of the world *not* of preexistent, and therefore eternal, materials, but out of nothing."[8] This doctrine teaches that there was originally nothing but God (an infinite, eternal, and tripersonal spirit). By means of his incalculable wisdom and infinite power, God alone brought the universe (all matter, energy, time, and space) into existence from nothing (not from any preexistent physical reality such as matter and its connected realities).

To clarify further, creation *ex nihilo* means that God created out of or from nothing, therefore *nothing* should not be understood as being an actual *something*. In other words, *nothing* is not itself an entity; it is literally *no thing*. Creation out of nothing means that God spoke or called all things (material and spiritual) into existence out of nonexistence. The implication is that all of creation had a singular beginning and is completely dependent upon God for coming into being and for its continued existence.

This doctrine is implicit in several passages of Scripture. Appropriately enough, the very first verse of the Bible begins with creation *ex nihilo*: "In the beginning God created the heavens and the earth" (Gen. 1:1). This verse implies a singular beginning or actual origination to creation; the universe has not always existed. The expression "the heavens and the earth" reveals that God created everything in its *totality* or that God created the *sum total of reality*.[9]

A passage from the Wisdom Literature of the Old Testament follows suit informing readers that merely "by wisdom the LORD laid the earth's foundation, by understanding he set the heavens in place" (Prov. 3:19). There's no mention of any preexisting materials in God's creative actions.

The Psalmist declares: "Before the mountains were born or you brought forth the earth and the world, from everlasting to everlasting you are God" (Ps. 90:2). Therefore only God is eternal or everlasting; the created order is not, for it had a distinct beginning from nonexistence.

A word aptly spoken. The Psalms proclaim that God spoke or commanded and the created order came forth: "By the word of the LORD were the heavens made, their starry host by the breath of his mouth" (Ps. 33:6). "Let them praise the name of the LORD, for he commanded, and they were created" (Ps. 148:5).

Further support for creation *ex nihilo* comes from the New Testament, where the apostle John states that through the preincarnate Jesus Christ "all things were made; without him nothing was made that has been made" (John 1:3). Jesus Christ, who shares the one divine nature with the Father and the Holy Spirit (Trinitarian monotheism), is identified as taking part in the work of creation. John also identified Jesus Christ as the *Logos* or "Word" who brings about the created order.

The author of Hebrews recognized Jesus Christ as the Creator as well by stating that he was the one "through whom he [God the Father] made the universe" (Heb. 1:2). And the apostle Paul added support for the doctrine of creation out of nothing by asserting that it is God who "calls things that are not as though they were" (Rom. 4:17). This passage certainly signifies God's capacity to create in an *ex nihilo* fashion. Paul also identified Jesus Christ as the Creator, noting that he created "all things," including "things in heaven and on earth" as well as things that are "visible and invisible" (Col. 1:16).

Two passages from Acts underscore the biblical precept that God is the absolute Creator of all. In one passage, the early Christians addressed God in prayer as follows: "Sovereign Lord, . . . you made the heaven and the earth and the sea, and everything in them" (Acts 4:24). In the other, Paul told the ancient Greek philosophers in Athens, "The God who made the world and everything in it is the Lord of heaven and earth. . . . 'For in him we live and move and have our being'" (Acts 17:24, 28). These passages specifically say that God created "everything." Scripture further reveals that God not only created matter, energy, and space, but also *time* itself by stating that he and his divine decrees concerning salvation existed before time began (2 Tim. 1:9; Titus 1:2).

The writer of Hebrews even provided what some Christian theologians believe to be an *explicit* statement[10] about creation *ex nihilo*. It says: "By faith we understand that the universe was formed at God's command, so that what is seen was not made out of what was visible" (Heb. 11:3). This verse conveys the central thrust of the doctrine of creation out of nothing. And there is no reason to think the writer of Hebrews would have had an invisible preexistent reality or entity in mind when he used the words "what was visible."

Philosophers Paul Copan and William Lane Craig note: "The author of Hebrews is not making a metaphysical point about different types of matter (visible versus invisible) or that God created out of invisible matter rather than visible."[11] The preferable understanding of this verse is that it speaks of God creating out of nonexistence, or creation *ex nihilo*.

In numerous places the New Testament refers specifically to the universe as having a beginning, using such expressions as "the beginning of the world" (Matt. 24:21) or "since the creation of the world" (Rom. 1:20).[12] In light of this evidence, Copan and Craig conclude: "The biblical data are not ambiguous, as some contend; indeed, creation *ex nihilo* is the most reasonable inference to make in light of biblical texts."[13]

Profound theological implications. The Bible claims God didn't create the universe out of preexisting materials (such as matter and its constituent realities), but neither did he make the world out of his own being. Scripture asserts that God alone is infinite, eternal, and independent—while all of creation is finite, temporal, and contingent (matter, energy, space, and time are not eternal but results from the Word of God's power).

Creation *ex nihilo* not only teaches that the universe had a singular beginning but also that the created order is continually dependent upon God's sustaining power. Upon creating the world, the sovereign God continues to uphold, preserve, and direct his creation (Acts 17:28; Col. 1:17; Heb. 1:3). This divine action is addressed in more detail under the doctrine of providence.

The Bible therefore reveals God as the transcendent Creator and immanent Sustainer of all things. This wondrous intervention into his creation, to which the doctrine of divine providence attests, rules out the deistic view of God that sees the divine as wholly transcendent (creating, but not intervening or providentially upholding the universe).

A profound practical implication of the doctrine of creation *ex nihilo* is that only the sovereign Creator (who is also our benevolent Redeemer) deserves worship, adoration, and devotion, but a denial of creation *ex nihilo* implies that matter is eternal and constitutes a challenge to God's independence and sovereignty. Scripture explicitly warns its adherents not to fall prey to idolatry by engaging in the false worship of the world or of particular things in the world.[14]

While not a proper object of worship—because it was created by God—the universe possesses objective meaning, purpose, and significance. And these characteristics are all the more true of human beings made in the expressed image and likeness of God[15] and who will live even after the present creation ceases to exist.[16]

An important qualification of God's creation out of *nothing* is that this concept only applies to God's initial creation of the universe. For example, God's subsequent creation of the animals (Gen. 2:19) and of humankind (Gen. 2:7) involved the use of preexisting materials (namely "the dust of the ground").

Consequently, creation *ex nihilo* means:

1. The universe had an absolute origination (coming into being).
2. The universe had an absolute beginning (start in time).
3. God solely initiated or caused the creation.
4. At the point of creation, the universe became a distinct temporal entity.
5. While the universe is an independent reality from God, it nonetheless is continually dependent upon God's intervening and sustaining power for its continued existence.
6. Nothing other than God has an eternal, independent ontological status.

Conversely, creation *ex nihilo* does not mean:

1. That the universe was created either in God or out of God's being. (Nor does it mean the universe was part of God or emanated from God.)
2. The universe was made of preexisting materials such as matter.
3. God created the world out of a nothing that was an actual "something."
4. God wound up the universe so it could then run on its own power.

What Does Creation Ex Nihilo Reveal about God?

The following points can be drawn about God from his act of creating the world out of nothing.

First, God did not *need* to create the universe, for he was in no way desperate or incomplete in personhood or being. Within the Godhead, three eternally distinct (but not separate) persons live in loving community with each other. Theologian Cornelius Plantinga explains:

> The persons within God exalt each other, commune with each other, defer to one another. Each person, so to speak, makes room for the other two. . . . From eternity God has had a communal life and didn't need to create a world to get one. Nothing internal or external to God compelled him to create.[17]

This eternal community of fellowship among the three members of the Trinity solves philosophical problems for which unitarian concepts of God have no answer. For example, arguably the greatest of the church fathers, Augustine (A.D. 354–430), explained in his monumental work *De Trinitate* (*On the Trinity*) that only a God who has plurality within unity can adequately account for his love and for the use of his divine mind. If God were a single solitary person (such as in Islam or Unitarianism), then before creation he had no one to love. Moreover, he could not distinguish between the knower and the known (a requisite of self-knowledge).

In this way, the Trinity becomes quite practical. Because human beings are created in the image of the fully relational Triune God, concepts such as love and institutions such as family and community take on a new and critical dimension. Redemption in Christ is adoption into the family of God.[18]

Creation was thus a totally free act of God, an expression of the divine will (which stands in contrast to pantheism's divine emanation view). The universe is not eternal, but neither was it an accident. Copan and Craig assert that "creation out of nothing expresses, among other things, the unhindered freedom, sovereignty, and graciousness of God."[19] It is obvious from Scripture that God took enormous delight in his creation of all things.

Second, God's creation of the universe out of nothing is consistent with God's *aseity*,[20] or the concept that he is a self-existent and necessary being. Because God created all existing entities, and he himself is an eternal and everlasting being who is completely self-sufficient, God is therefore an absolute being who cannot *not* exist. As the transcendent Creator and immanent Sustainer of the universe, the Bible's God is the sovereign Lord of all. And he has exhibited his infinite power and wisdom by creating all things out of nothing.

Critical Worldview Implications

Profound theological and philosophical implications of the biblical doctrine for creation of something out of nothing set historic Christianity apart from alternative worldview perspectives. Fifteen points follow logically when the biblical doctrine of creation *ex nihilo* is affirmed as true:

1. **The universe is not an extension or emanation of God's essence or being.** Thus, pantheism (the Eastern mystical view that all is God and

God is all) and panentheism (the view that God is in the world but more than the world) must be rejected as false.[21]

2. **God created a universe with a distinct existence of its own (though always dependent upon God's power for its continuance).** Therefore, metaphysical views that assert monism, the belief that all reality is one or that reality is a seamless garment, must be rejected as false. These include various forms of Eastern mysticism, which affirms that everything is divine; idealism, the belief that everything is mind and/or idea; and metaphysical naturalism or physicalism, the belief that everything is physical or material (see chapters 12–14).[22]

3. **The world is a distinct reality that cannot rightly be denied.** As a result religions and worldviews that view the physical universe as an illusion or as only apparently real (such as Vedanta Hinduism, Buddhism, Sikhism, Gnosticism, Christian Science, and other mind-science religions) must be rejected as false (see chapter 14).[23]

4. **The world is a finite and contingent creation of God and therefore not a proper object of worship.** Thus, religious systems that engage in this type of devotion and deification (such as animism, popular polytheism, and folk religion) should be rejected as false.[24]

5. **Matter was created by God and is therefore not eternal (nor the sole reality).** Therefore, philosophies that affirm the eternity of matter, whether dualistic (considering matter and god as eternal) or materialistic (believing that everything is reducible to, or explainable in terms of, matter), should be rejected as false.[25]

6. **The universe is not self-sufficient, self-explanatory, or self-sustaining.** Whereas the universe is not self-caused and did not pop into existence as the result of a quantum accident, a worldview that asserts such things (like metaphysical naturalism—nature is the sole reality) must be regarded as false.[26]

7. **Everything has value and meaning as implied by the doctrine of creation *ex nihilo*.** Therefore, philosophies that discount value and meaning in life and in the world (such as nihilism) must be rejected as false.[27]

8. **The natural, material, and physical universe was created by a supernatural, personal divine agent.** As a result methodological naturalism (which accepts only natural scientific explanations for things) must be rejected as false.[28]

9. **God's creation of the world from nothing demonstrates his complete power and control over all things (his sovereign lordship).** Thus, any religious philosophy that denies God's sovereignty (such as finite godism, process theology, and open theism) must be rejected as false.[29]

10. **God is both transcendent and immanent.** Therefore, religious systems that view God as being wholly transcendent (such as deism and Islam) must be rejected as false.[30]

11. **God not only created the universe, but also continually sustains its existence.** Worldviews that consider God as merely winding up the universe so that it then became self-sustaining (such as deism) must be rejected as false.

12. **God created all things, not out of need or desperation but as an act of divine freedom (given the Triune nature of the Christian God).** Religions that view God as a single solitary person (such as Islam and other unitarian conceptions of God) should be rejected as ontologically inadequate.

13. **God made the universe as a very good creation.** Therefore religious philosophies that affirm an eternal and intrinsic evil as a metaphysical part of the universe (such as Manichaeism, Gnosticism, and Zoroastrianism) must be rejected as false.[31]

14. **A creation out of nothing excludes any preexistent or chaotic contingent entities.** Thus any religion that affirms this view (such as Mormonism) must be rejected as false.[32]

15. **The world was created by God with rich natural and living resources to be used wisely by human beings for the purpose of sustaining and enhancing human lives.** Radical environmental views (that fail to recognize mankind's proper role of dominion over nature) should be rejected as false.

What Are the Apologetic Implications of Creation Ex Nihilo?

The truly profound apologetic implication of creation *ex nihilo* is found in the field of modern cosmology. According to prevailing scientific theory, the universe had a singular beginning about 14 billion years ago. All matter, energy, time, and space exploded into existence (in a carefully controlled and fine-tuned manner) from nothing (no preexisting materials). This basic big bang cosmological model, embraced by the vast majority of research scientists because it has withstood extensive scientific testing, uniquely corresponds to the biblical teaching concerning creation *ex nihilo*. A book written a couple thousand years ago contains a view of cosmology that probatively corresponds to the latest and best scientific findings.

German mathematician and philosopher Gottfried Wilhelm Leibniz (1646–1716) asked the ultimate cosmological question: "Why is there something rather than nothing?"[33] This question seems even more provocative given the strong scientific evidence for the actual start of the universe (e.g., the basic big bang cosmological model, second law of thermodynamics).

In the beginning. Because the best science evidence supports the idea that the universe came into existence a finite period of time ago, it is difficult to escape the simple but profound reasoning of the kalam cosmological argument:

Whatever begins to exist has a cause for its coming into being.

The universe began to exist.

Therefore, the universe has a cause for its coming into being.[34]

Skeptics sometimes object to this reasoning—which favors God's existence as a cause of the universe—by suggesting that there are naturalistic scientific explanations for the universe's sudden emergence into being from nothing. One purported idea is that the universe mysteriously popped into existence through some kind of exotic and highly speculative quantum fluctuation[35] (inferred from the principle of quantum indeterminacy where virtual particles allegedly emerge from a quantum mechanical vacuum). However, this view is no longer in vogue among leading scientists because of its nontestable, speculative nature. In addition, this quantum vacuum from which the basic components of the universe are said to have sprung is obviously not *nothing*. Therefore this naturalistic theory cannot legitimately claim to have discovered an uncaused emergence of the universe.

A second exotic, quasi-scientific option is to conclude that there are actually multiple universes (sometimes called multiverse[36]). This position suggests that an eternal mechanism of physics may actually pop universes into existence one after another. This provocative view, however, is also not based upon any direct observable data, but instead appears to be largely built on speculation. As a nonfalsifiable hypothesis, this view doesn't offer a viable challenge to the notion that the universe had a beginning. One also wonders what might cause multiple universes.

In response to some of the skeptical claims raised against a world created by God, Copan and Craig observe that "some scientists will resort to the most outlandish speculations rather than entertain the simpler metaphysical idea of a personal Creator."[37]

Upon reflection, however, it is not surprising that a person staunchly committed to a purely naturalistic worldview (having ruled out the supernatural *a priori*) would pursue such speculative and exotic theories as quantum fluctuation and the multiverse. Naturalistic explanations, no matter how speculative and improbable, are the only possibility for a committed naturalist (see chapter 12).

Yet for the person willing to follow the evidence wherever it may lead, it remains eminently reasonable to conclude that if the universe had a specific beginning, then it must have had a cause. In this case, the cause must be a transcendent causal agent. The biblical teaching of creation *ex nihilo* is uniquely compatible with what is now the best established scientific theory concerning cosmology. The Bible's sovereign Lord declares his mighty deeds in creation and in redemption: "This is what the LORD says—your redeemer, who formed you in the womb: I am the LORD, who has made all things, who alone stretched out the heavens, who spread out the earth by myself" (Isa. 44:24).

Beyond what the eye can see. Though Scripture isn't explicit concerning the sequence or timing of creation, it describes both the material and spiritual realms, referred to as the "visible and invisible" (Col. 1:16). The spiritual sphere includes heaven and those beings that inhabit the spiritual realm—angels, principalities, powers, and Satan himself.

Angels are personal creatures, pure spiritual beings who are invisible. Some angels are good, holy, and elect of God, whereas others are fallen, evil, and reprobate. Satan held a powerful and prestigious position in heaven before his fall because of pride.[38] Upon his fall, Satan became an agent of evil and the enemy of God.[39] These scriptural realities (both good and bad angels) were not only created by God, but they remain under his sovereign control.[40]

Creation of Adam and Eve

According to Scripture, God created the first human beings in a special, direct, and personal way.[41] Adam and Eve were not the product of myth and legend but were actual historical persons created by God. Those who embrace the position of theistic evolution[42] raise concern in this regard, for they appear to deny the historical and factual nature of Adam and Eve's existence.

Theistic evolution takes many forms but generally holds that God used natural evolutionary processes to bring about life on Earth, culminating in the appearance of human beings. Advocates of this position typically propose that God directly initiated the creative process (origin of the universe) but afterward worked solely through natural processes to give rise to humanity. Some advocates of this position suggest that God may have intervened to create the first life form or to give a living creature (possibly a hominid or bipedal primate) a soul or spirit, thus ensuring the appearance of the first man. Many who hold this position interpret the early chapters of Genesis as figurative, archetypal, or mythological in nature.

The problem with this view is that Scripture affirms that God repeatedly and directly intervened in the creative process to create, for example, the first members of each kind of living thing (Genesis 1–2). This biblical position leads to the clear rejection of macroevolution.

Because the Bible states that God created Adam and Eve directly, the early chapters of Genesis reflect a reliable historical narrative. Theistic evolution appears to be at odds with this important biblical truth.

God exquisitely designed a universe in which man can live, thrive, rule, and fulfill his created purpose. He also gave human beings all the necessary intellectual abilities in order to live such a life. Because human beings are made in God's expressed image they possess special meaning, value, and significance. For more on the meaning of the *imago Dei* (image of God) and mankind's fall into sin, see chapter 10.

Why Did God Create?

The physical realm displays God's sheer delight in creating; why else would he create a universe that contains hundreds of millions of galaxies? In manufacturing an exquisite home for humanity he spared no expense. There, his creatures can play out their destiny on a stage, as the drama of God's redemption of fallen human beings, in and through the person of Jesus Christ, unfolds. So with a clear desire to promote the welfare of human beings (especially those who are his very own), God created for the primary purpose of manifesting his glory. In the book of Isaiah, Yahweh reveals this intent, especially for humans as those "whom I created for my glory, whom I formed and made" (Isa. 43:7). Erickson explains further: "Humans alone are capable of obeying God consciously and willingly, and thus glorify God most fully."[43]

All of creation testifies to God's awesome majesty. King David proclaimed: "The heavens declare the glory of God; the skies proclaim the work of his hands" (Ps. 19:1). The last book of the Bible summarizes an appropriate response to God's wondrous work of creation *ex nihilo*: "You are worthy, our Lord and God, to receive glory and honor and power, for you created all things, and by your will they were created and have their being" (Rev. 4:11).

The Importance of Providence

The doctrines of creation and providence are closely connected.[44] God not only called the universe into existence from nothing, but also has been continually involved with all of creation since its inception. He reveals himself as both transcendent above creation and immanent in his workings within it. Evangelical theologian John Jefferson Davis defines the doctrine of providence this way: "Providence is that sovereign activity of God whereby he sustains, preserves, and governs all his creatures, and guides all events toward their appointed ends."[45]

The Creator actively and continually sustains the universe and is thus never idle. His supernatural power keeps the created order in place and all his creatures alive. If God removed his providential hand, all of existence would tumble back into nonexistence.

God can and does intervene in the created order through natural means to maintain natural properties, and through supernatural means to go beyond the natural properties. Created things certainly have natures and properties, but they depend upon God for their continued existence and for their given causal powers. God has a purpose for all things in creation, and he sovereignly governs and directs all things in accord with his purposes.

The doctrine of providence is usually divided into three theological categories: divine preservation, concurrence, and government.[46]

Preservation

God continuously upholds (Greek: *pherō*, "carry" or "bear") all things in their existence and sustains the natural properties of those created things.[47] The apostle Paul identifies Jesus Christ as personally active in this work of preservation—steadfastly maintaining all creation in being and in action. "He [Christ] is before all things, and in him all things hold together" (Col. 1:17).

Concurrence

God continuously cooperates with the created order and causes his creatures to act in precisely the manner that they do, though people nevertheless remain responsible for their actions.[48] Real secondary causes are at work in the world (for example, nature and human effort), but they do not operate apart from God's power at work in his creation and creatures. Paul describes how God stimulates the actions of his people: "For it is God who works in you to will and to act according to his good purpose" (Phil. 2:13).

Government

As the supreme authority of all things, God continually directs the course of all actions and events toward accomplishing his sovereign purposes.[49] His providential will reigns over all things including the events of nature and the choices of human beings. Paul describes God's overruling plan: "In him we were also chosen, having been predestined according to the plan of him who works out everything in conformity with the purpose of his will" (Eph. 1:11).

Scripture reveals God's all-encompassing[50] authority:

- God sovereignly controls the entire universe.[51] "The LORD has established his throne in heaven, and his kingdom rules over all" (Ps. 103:19).
- God sovereignly controls the natural events of the world.[52] "The LORD does whatever pleases him, in the heavens and on the earth, in the seas and all their depths" (Ps. 135:6).
- God sovereignly controls the events of world history.[53] "Dominion belongs to the LORD and he rules over the nations" (Ps. 22:28).

- God sovereignly controls a human being's birth, life, and death.[54] "All the days ordained for me were written in your book before one of them came to be" (Ps. 139:16).

- God sovereignly controls the details of a person's life.[55] "And even the very hairs of your head are all numbered. So don't be afraid" (Matt. 10:30–31).

- God sovereignly controls all the needs of his people.[56] "And my God will meet all your needs according to his glorious riches in Christ Jesus" (Phil. 4:19).

- God sovereignly controls the answers to his people's prayers.[57] "And will not God bring about justice for his chosen ones, who cry out to him day and night?" (Luke 18:7).

The doctrine of providence goes hand-in-hand with the doctrine of creation. God's deliberate attention and ongoing actions underscore his sovereign rule over all heaven and Earth. This intimate involvement with the time-space world has critical implications for the Christian position.

Worldview Implications

The doctrine of divine providence validates the concept that people aren't at the mercy of arbitrary, impersonal forces such as luck, fate, or chance. Rather, God clearly holds all human affairs in his hand and is working all things together for good for his people (Rom. 8:28). Providence can be a great source of comfort, assurance, and security when God's people inevitably face difficult times. This belief that God has all things firmly in hand should lead to devotion, commitment, gratitude, and loyalty. Erickson explains:

> Providence in certain ways is central to the conduct of the Christian life. It means that we are able to live in the assurance that God is present and active in our lives. We are in his care and can therefore face the future confidently, knowing that things are not happening merely by chance. We can pray, knowing that God hears and acts upon our prayers. We can face danger, knowing that he is not unaware and uninvolved.[58]

The doctrine of providence should not be taken as a basis for human laxity, indifference, or apathy. Rather, the Bible teaches both that God is sovereign and that human beings are morally responsible agents. Sometimes these paradoxical truths are taught in the very same verse (see Luke 22:22; Acts 2:23).

People still bear real responsibility for their actions. Yet God's providential actions guarantee genuine meaning, purpose, and significance in the world and in life. While divine providence is mysterious to finite creatures, recognition of this truth should produce a deep sense of humility and thankfulness.

God's actions in providentially guiding his creation supply a solid foundation for science. Given God's work as transcendent Creator and immanent Sustainer of the universe, order, regularity, and uniformity in nature can be expected and accounted for. In fact, the deep belief in such things as creation *ex nihilo* and continued divine providence led early theological naturalists (scientists) to pursue scientific research. This effort led to the birth and flourishing of science in Christian Europe during the seventeenth century.[59]

What about Divine Providence and the Existence of Evil?

Providential involvement in all events (both good and evil) raises questions about God's relationship to evil.[60] Divine concurrence (a point of God's providence) makes evil actions and events possible. However, God does not commit evil (Ps. 5:4) and he does not coerce any creature to participate in such acts (James 1:13).

God is not ultimately accountable for the moral evil that takes place among the creatures he has made. Though the issue of evil to some degree remains a mystery, nevertheless God's relationship to it can be inferred from Scripture:[61]

1. God permits evil for his sovereign purposes (Gen. 50:20; Job 1:1–12).
2. God uses evil (and/or calamity and disaster) to punish the evil actions of his creatures (Ps. 81:11–12; Rom. 1:26–32).
3. God uses evil (and/or calamity and disaster) to test and discipline those whom he loves (Matt. 4:1–11; Heb. 12:4–14).
4. God always brings good out of evil. This goodness is especially true for those who belong to God through faith (Gen. 50:20; Acts 2:23; Rom. 8:28).
5. God has defeated the powers of evil in and through the life, death, and resurrection of Jesus Christ (Eph. 1:21; Col. 2:15).
6. God will redeem his people from the power and presence of evil completely in the future (Rev. 21:4–5).

Creator and Sustainer

The doctrines of creation and providence clearly set the Christian theistic worldview apart from other worldviews and other religious systems. The sovereign God of the Bible has created all things and he sustains, controls, and directs them all toward his appointed ends.

Grudem sums up these doctrines and draws the appropriate bottom line: "Who could make all of this? Who could make it out of nothing? Who could sustain it day after day for endless years? Such infinite power, such intricate skill, is completely beyond our comprehension. When we meditate on it, we give glory to God."[62]

The same God who created everything out of nothing and oversees the physical realm also created humankind. The comprehensive Christian worldview has much to say about the identity of human beings—their origin, purpose, and worth. The biblical concept of man is explored in the next chapter.

Discussion Questions

1. Why is the doctrine of creation so important to historic Christianity and to the broader Christian theistic worldview? How is this importance reflected?
2. How does God's role as Redeemer presuppose his role as Creator? How are the doctrines of creation and redemption connected in Scripture?
3. What does creation *ex nihilo* mean and how is it supported from Scripture?
4. What does creation *ex nihilo* say about creation and about God's nature?
5. In terms of the doctrine of providence, what do the terms *preservation*, *concurrence*, and *government* mean with regard to God and his creation? What does the doctrine of providence imply for living the Christian life?

For Further Study

Berkhof, Louis. *Systematic Theology*. New combined ed. Grand Rapids: Eerdmans, 1996.

Copan, Paul, and William Lane Craig. *Creation Out of Nothing: A Biblical, Philosophical, and Scientific Exploration*. Grand Rapids: Baker, 2004.

Grudem, Wayne. *Systematic Theology: An Introduction to Biblical Theology*. Grand Rapids: Zondervan, 1994. Chapters 15–16.

Milne, Bruce. *Know the Truth: A Handbook of Christian Belief*. Downers Grove, IL: InterVarsity, 1982.

Ross, Hugh. *The Creator and the Cosmos: How the Greatest Scientific Discoveries of the Century Reveal God*. 3rd ed. Colorado Springs: NavPress, 2001.

10

THE HISTORIC CHRISTIAN VIEW OF MAN

It is impossible for anyone who understands the distinction between difference in degree and difference in kind to assert, in the face of available evidence, that man differs only in degree from the animals.

Mortimer J. Adler, *The Difference of Man and the Difference It Makes*

*C*onfronted with the possible prognosis of an early death, I wondered about the kind of life I'd lived. Had I pursued the really important things? What about my devotion to the Lord? Had I loved and nurtured my family sufficiently? Did my life make a difference? Was I a person of deep moral character?

Of all the world's creatures, human beings seem to need—if not crave—a specific meaning and purpose to their lives. In fact, this search for enduring significance is one of the defining characteristics of the species known as Homo sapiens. *Even the ability to reflect upon life while standing in death's shadow is a unique aspect of being human.*

For me it was most critical to discover meaning and purpose in my suffering. The thought that such intense pain was gratuitous would have been intolerable and caused despair. I needed to make sense of the enigma of suffering and how it related to the context of my life.

While in the hospital I often felt weak, vulnerable—even naked. Not just physically and psychologically, but at times even spiritually. I desperately needed to know that my suffering and my life as a whole had deep and enduring meaning. As a man, I needed both a reason to live and a reason to die.

The Makings of a Man

What is man? What makes human beings so different from the rest of the creatures on Earth? A person's thoughts on the origin, nature, and characteristics of humanity (anthropology) are a critical part of any worldview.

Philosopher William Hasker notes, "Surely one of the acid tests for a world view is whether it is able to provide a consistent, coherent, and acceptable account of the nature of humanity."[1]

According to the Bible, man's central defining characteristic is that of divine image-bearer. Human beings are created in the expressed "image of God" (Latin: *imago Dei*, pronounced ih-MAH-go day).

For a biblical worldview, what Scripture reveals about humanity's creation and the implications of being made in God's image impacts every aspect of the way a Christian sees himself and lives life. The effects of both the fall and redemption on this image are critical components of the historic Christian position.

Imago Dei: A Reflection of God

The Bible reveals that of all God's creatures, *only man* was created in the expressed image of God. While Scripture mentions the *imago Dei* several times,[2] Genesis 1:26–27 is the most important text that describes this vital doctrine:

> Then God said, "Let us make man in our image, in our likeness, and let them rule over the fish of the sea and the birds of the air, over the livestock, over all the earth, and over all the creatures that move along the ground."
>
> > So God created man in his own image,
> > in the image of God he created him;
> > male and female he created them.

A careful examination of this passage reveals that Hebrew references to "image" (*ṣelem*) and "likeness" (*dĕmût*) convey the idea of an object similar to or representative of something else, but not identical to it.[3] Further, the words *image* and *likeness* should not be understood as referring to two different things but rather as interchangeable terms that reflect a Hebrew form of synonymous parallelism.[4] The New Testament Greek word for image (*eikōn*) conveys virtually the same meaning as the Hebrew. Both languages indicate that God created humans to be similar to himself, but certainly not identical to himself. Therefore from a biblical perspective, human beings are in some sense both *like* and *unlike* the God who made them.

But what exactly does it mean for man to be *like* God? Three qualifications must be made before examining this question further. First, Scripture contains no formal or explicit explanation as to what the image of God is or of its exact meaning. A definition for *imago Dei* must come from drawing proper inferences from the biblical text, hopefully buttressed with careful reflection about the state of the human condition.

Second, a comprehensive understanding of the *imago Dei*'s meaning simply isn't possible, because it would require an exhaustive understanding of God's nature (as well as a complete understanding of the nature of man).[5] Finite creatures by definition cannot comprehend or fully fathom the infinite nature of God; therefore, by necessity people are faced with limited knowledge and mystery.

Third, throughout church history a variety of positions on the exact meaning of the divine image have been taken by different theological traditions. For example, Catholics and Lutherans as well as Reformed and Arminian Christians each define the image somewhat differently or at least emphasize different aspects.[6] The various strands of Christian theology are certainly not monolithic in every detail of theology.

Nevertheless, while acknowledging these three important considerations, it's still possible to present a basic biblical description of the meaning of the *imago Dei*. Inferences drawn from Scripture and careful philosophical reflection about the nature of human beings bring forth a common Christian position.

Some theologians emphasize man's personality in suggesting how people are most like God. Evangelical theologian Millard Erickson says, "The image is the powers of personality which make man, like God, a being capable of interacting with other persons, of thinking and reflecting, and of willing freely."[7] To some degree man mirrors God and in certain respects even represents God.

Many evangelical theologians comfortably distinguish between the *natural image* and the *moral image*.[8] The broader of the two, the natural image, includes constituent aspects of man's created nature—his spiritual, intellectual, volitional, relational, immortal, and powerful capacities. The moral nature involves a more restricted sense of God's image based on man's *original* knowledge, righteousness, and holiness. Adam and Eve in the Garden of Eden possessed these latter qualities before their fall into sin. The extent to which the image of God was affected by Adam's rebellion against God is a question of great importance for understanding humanity's makeup and its moral and spiritual condition today.

The Natural Image

Man's created nature appears to include at least six endowments or gifts:[9]

1. Human beings are spiritual. Although people are material creatures, their human nature includes two aspects—physical and spiritual. Having a soul or spirit makes humans a genuine union of both spiritual and material natures, in other words a "whole person."

Genesis 2:7 alludes to this union by describing man as a "living being." Possessing a distinctive spiritual nature gives individuals the ability to know and relate to God through prayer, worship, repentance, and so forth. Inherent spiritual needs include a tremendous desire for a relationship with the Creator. Man's creatureliness makes that need for companionship his most basic necessity.

2. Human beings are personal, self-conscious, and rational. People possess a mind, will, and emotions. They are uniquely capable of grasping thought, knowledge, and truth (propositional and nonpropositional), especially truth about God.

Theologian Cornelius Plantinga captures the provocative thought of John Calvin on this point: "Calvin understood that God created human beings to hunt and gather truth, and that, as a matter of fact, the capacity for doing so amounts to one feature of the image of God in them (Col. 3:10)."[10] Though humans are capable of rational thought, emotion also plays an important role in their lives. People are uniquely capable of feeling, expressing, and even evaluating their emotional responses.

3. Human beings are volitional. Individuals possess free agency, making them capable of authentic deliberation and choice. Ultimately they are morally accountable to God for those choices. Humans are the only creatures aware of the moral spheres in life and are responsible for their actions.

4. Human beings are relational. People are capable of unique and profound interpersonal communication and relations with other humans and with God. A distinctive feature of human nature appears to be the inherent need to interact with others. While various animal species demonstrate community interaction to some degree, human beings communicate amongst themselves and with God on a much deeper level.

5. Human beings are immortal. People possess a God-given or derived immortality.[11] Humans are unique among all physical creatures in facing an eternal destiny either with God (redemption) or apart from him (damnation).

6. Human beings are powerful. People exercise dominion (control, custodianship, power) over the natural order and over Earth's living and nonliving natural resources. This environmental dominion is possible principally because of humanity's intellectual capacities.

Man's distinguishing characteristic is that he bears the image of God. This natural image illustrates six distinct ways in which man differs from Earth's other creatures. Human beings possess spiritual, personal, self-conscious, and rational components. Similar to God they are volitional, relational, immortal, and powerful—unlike any other creatures.

The Moral Image

As originally created, Adam possessed direct knowledge of God and an inherent righteousness and holiness.[12] This moral image was evident during Adam's time in the Garden of Eden prior to his fall into sin.[13]

Theologian Charles Hodge notes the importance of being made in God's image and, in a certain sense, being made on God's level: "He [man] belongs to the same order of being as God himself, and is therefore capable of communion with his Maker."[14] It is being made in God's image that elevates man to God's plane and makes it possible for human beings to know God at all.

Though angels have a unique relationship and access to God and are themselves pure spirit (without physical bodies), even they are not described as divine image-bearers. Some theologians think humans bear that privilege because "image" means a physical representative and the angels are not physical. And though animals were made by God out of the dust of the ground like humans, neither do they possess the distinctive divine image.

Dutch theologian Herman Bavinck marks the distinction: "All creatures reveal traces of God, but only man is the image of God."[15] Humanity alone is described as the crown of God's creation—the pinnacle of God's creative activity (Ps. 8:5–8).

Like and Unlike God

Biblical anthropology reveals that human beings are "created persons."[16] This view of man is, of course, paradoxical—for being a creature implies that man is absolutely dependent upon God. Yet being a person means that man possesses a relative independence (autonomy) from God.

The Bible, without explaining it, sets man's *personhood* (like God) and *creatureliness* (unlike God) side by side as compatible truths, introducing a scriptural mystery. God's power, wisdom, and ability to create eludes the human ability to comprehend.[17] However, according to the historic Christian worldview, truths of divine revelation may range above reason but not against it. Using reason can help unravel some of the mystery of how humans can be like God, yet *not* like him at the same time. Exploring his communicable and incommunicable characteristics sets forth some important distinctions in the Christian position.

Like His Father

God created human beings with the ability to understand and imitate, at least to some degree, his *communicable* attributes (seen in the natural and moral nature of the *imago Dei*). These characteristics belong to humanity, though in a significantly limited way. Like God, people are moral beings. They display knowledge, wisdom, goodness, love, holiness, justice, and truthfulness.

These attributes in humans, however, differ in degree from those found in God. In him the same characteristics are unlimited and perfect. This difference makes people fundamentally distinct in their creaturehood.

Unlike His Father

Contrastingly, God's divinity makes him differ in kind from people. His *incommunicable* attributes (see chapter 8) separate God completely from his creatures, a demarcation known as the Creator-creature distinction. These qualities consist of such metaphysical characteristics as self-existence (independence), immutability (unchanging), infinity (without limitation), and eternality (timelessness).

The *Imago Dei* and the Fall

Though human beings were created to reflect God's image, when Adam disobeyed God[18] all subsequent humanity inherited sinfulness, guilt, moral corruption, and both physical and spiritual death.[19] In a state of rebellion, individuals suffer from a totally depraved nature that keeps them alienated from a holy and just God. This depravity, while not making man completely evil, nevertheless corrupts his entire being including his mind, will, body, and spirit.[20] But to what extent does this condition affect the *imago Dei*? Did sin completely erase God's image from humankind?

Man's *original* knowledge, righteousness, and holiness—the moral image necessary for man to have a relationship with God—were eradicated by the fall. Once sin infected humanity, all human beings became unrighteous law-breakers separated from God.[21]

However, the natural image—though indeed tarnished and obscured—was not completely lost. As a popular saying indicates, the natural image was "effaced but not erased." After the fall, human beings remain God's image-bearers,[22] yet in the state of sin, people are certainly less like God than they were before.

With humanity's original righteousness gone, even the capacities of man's natural image became out of sync.[23] To some degree, sin's impact disordered them.[24] Human beings became morally and spiritually obtuse, their noetic (cognitive and/or belief-forming) faculties dulled.

Biblical scholars and apologists disagree as to the exact nature and extent of the fall's noetic effects on man. They question whether the category of sinful effects is moral (affecting the ethical nature of man) or cognitive (affecting the intellectual nature of man) or both. And they deliberate as to the extent—is it partial or total? Regardless, it appears that the closer an individual comes to acknowledging God and accepting moral accountability before him (the spiritual and moral spheres of life), the more sin seems to affect spiritual judgment and perspective.

The total depravity of human beings makes it impossible to live a God-pleasing life. Consequently, sinful people must depend upon God's saving grace to have a relationship with him and experience salvation (see chapter 6).

The *Imago Dei* and Redemption

While the moral image was entirely lost because of the fall, Scripture declares that a saving relationship with Jesus Christ can restore it. The apostle Paul stated that through God's grace believers can "put on the new self, which is being renewed in knowledge in the image of its Creator" (Col. 3:10), "transformed into his likeness" (2 Cor. 3:18), and "conformed to the likeness of his Son" (Rom. 8:29). God the Holy Spirit progressively restores in the believer the moral image of Jesus Christ through the lifelong process of sanctification (being made righteous in character).

The Bible declares that when Jesus Christ returns to Earth at his Second Coming, "we shall be like him, for we shall see him as he is" (1 John 3:2). In other words, human beings will undergo a complete transformation of character that will result in genuine Christlike beings (glorification). Finally, humankind will be set free from sin's devastating effects.

According to the New Testament, the fullest expression of God's image is not seen in humanity either before or after the fall, or even in redemption. Rather this image is found—complete and total—in the person of Jesus Christ. Scripture speaks of the God-man, Jesus, as "the image and glory of God" (1 Cor. 11:7), the one "who is the image of God" (2 Cor. 4:4), "the image of the invisible God" (Col. 1:15), and the Son who is "the radiance of God's glory and the exact representation of his being" (Heb. 1:3). To view and understand God's image correctly and fully one must look to the person of the Incarnate Christ.

God's perfect image in Jesus ties together two Christian truths—the *imago Dei* and the Incarnation.[25] While it would seem difficult if not impossible for

God to take the form of a creature with little resemblance to himself (such as an animal), making humans in the divine image at creation foreshadowed and facilitated God's decisive entrance into the world as the God-man. [26]

Reformed theologian Anthony Hoekema explains that "it was only because man had been created in the image of God that the Second Person of the Trinity could assume human nature."[27] God made man in his own image because all along he planned to become one at the Incarnation, even before the creation of the world, in order to redeem lost sinners.[28] That's why Jesus told his disciples that to see the Son was to see the perfect image of the Father.[29]

The *Imago Dei* and Humanitarian Implications

Though marred by sin, all people—believer and nonbeliever, male and female alike—reflect the image of God. This foundational biblical teaching launches the Christian view that each individual possesses inherent dignity, moral worth, and genuine eternal value. Evangelical theologian John Jefferson Davis states: "God's creation is immense, but man, as the crown of creation, has a dignity and grandeur that surpasses that of the cosmos."[30] Humanity's unique worth is directly tied to being made in God's special image.

The *imago Dei* lays the foundation for the sacredness of human life. This image makes human life unrepeatable and worthy of reverence. All people—regardless of race, sex, class, age, standing, health, appearance, or other distinctions—deserve respect and dignified treatment as the crown of creation.[31]

With this image in mind, the historical Christian position embraces the strong biblical prohibitions against slander and slurs. New Testament author James asserts: "With the tongue we praise our Lord and Father, and with it we curse men, who have been made in God's likeness" (James 3:9). Praising God and then cursing the people made in his image is morally inconsistent and sinful.

Similarly, the biblical prohibition against murder and the corresponding mandate for capital punishment are directly based upon man being made in God's image. After the great divine judgment of the flood, Noah was told: "Whoever sheds the blood of man, by man shall his blood be shed; for in the image of God has God made man" (Gen. 9:6). Murder is reprehensible not only because it steals the very life of the individual—and thus robs family, friends, and society—but also because it assaults God in whose image the victim was made.[32]

Hoekema clarifies how human murder offends God: "To touch the image of God is to touch God himself; to kill the image of God is to do violence to God himself."[33]

According to Scripture, the murderer's heinous action causes him to forfeit his own right to life (a right which is not absolute) and become subject to retributive justice, "life for life" (Exod. 21:23). The punishment must match the crime.[34] In the New Testament, God grants state authorities the right to implement the death penalty (Rom. 13:1–5). This action signifies a willingness to carry out the ultimate punishment in order to protect people, especially the innocent. From a biblical perspective, capital punishment serves both as a retributive form of punishment and as a viable deterrent to humans committing acts of murder.[35]

Human beings derive value and worth from being made in the image of the true and living God. Life is valuable because of its Creator's ultimate value.

Human Purpose, Significance, and Meaning

As creatures made in God's image, individuals can find fulfillment only through an intimate relationship with their Creator. Sinners separated from him—and therefore out of sync with his intentions—experience a real existential angst and a deep sense of estrangement from God, from others, and from themselves. A human's true knowledge of self can only be discovered in and through knowing God.

Reformer John Calvin says: "True and sound wisdom consists of two parts: the knowledge of God; and of ourselves."[36] Man is incomplete, unexplained, and even obsolete without reference to God his Creator.

The Presbyterian confessional statement known as the Westminster Shorter Catechism (1647) begins with the ultimate existential inquiry: "What is the chief end of man?"[37] The catechism's answer replies: "Man's chief end is to glorify God, and to enjoy him forever."[38] Apart from God, man cannot fulfill his function and purpose in life, for he was specifically created to know, love, and serve his Creator.

Christian thinker Augustine of Hippo (A.D. 354–430) in his classic work the *Confessions* conveys to God this prayer: "Man is one of your creatures, Lord, and his instinct is to praise you. . . . The thought of you stirs him so deeply that he cannot be content unless he praises you, because you made us for yourself and our hearts find no peace until they rest in you."[39]

Augustine, a wayward soul for the first half of his life, illustrates this truth by reflecting about his own misspent youth: "But my sin was this, that I looked for pleasure, beauty, and truth not in him but in myself and his other creatures, and the search led me instead to pain, confusion, and error."[40] Many people, just like Augustine, occupy their life with various diversions (sports, hedonism, romance, the pursuit of affluence, drugs, and so on) in order to try to escape this haunting existential reality. Human beings were made for God, but something has gone deeply wrong. Due to sin and the fall, human beings are cut off and out of sync with life and with themselves.[41]

Because of their sinful condition, people often think they want or need various things to fulfill their desperate longings. Yet, the apprehending of genuine and lasting meaning and purpose in life remains elusive and fleeting.

However, when individuals rise above their existentially alienated state, they discover that what they really want and need is God himself. Cornelius Plantinga Jr. explains: "Our sense of God runs in us like a stream, even though we divert it toward other objects. We human beings want God even when we think that what we really want is a green valley, or a good time from our past, or a loved one."[42]

Part of the sinful condition in man is confusion over what will even satisfy his longings. Reflective human beings know that something is wrong or missing but cannot identify it. This fallen and out-of-sync condition has led to the creation of whole fields of study such as psychology and psychiatry. Yet, in the Christian worldview, the answer to man's estranged and desperate condition is not far off. Jesus Christ—the way, the truth, and the life—graciously responds: "I have come that they may have life, and have it to the full" (John 10:10).

Human beings were originally made in the image of God for the very purpose of serving and glorifying their Creator. Placing faith in the life, death, and resurrection of the God-man, Jesus Christ, is the way to fulfill man's yearning for meaning, purpose, and significance.

In his famous work *Pensées*, the French great thinker and writer Blaise Pascal (1623–1662) discusses the God-shaped hole human beings have inside of them:

> What else does this craving, and this helplessness, proclaim but that there was once in man a true happiness, of which all that now remains is the empty print and trace? This he tries in vain to fill with everything around him, seeking in things that are not there the help he cannot find in those that are, though none can help, since this infinite abyss can be filled only with an infinite and immutable object; in other words by God himself.[43]

The message of historic Christianity is that this God-shaped hole or vacuum inside of human beings can only be filled with the God-shaped person of Jesus Christ. Christianity, if authentically embraced, holds the cure to the desperate predicament of searching for purpose, meaning, and significance. Pascal explains the Christian worldview further:

> Not only do we only know God through Jesus Christ, but we only know ourselves through Jesus Christ; we only know life and death through Jesus Christ. Apart from Jesus Christ we cannot know the meaning of our life or our death, of God or of ourselves.[44]

Pascal and Augustine believed that individuals find both themselves and God through their redemptive encounters with Jesus Christ. They demonstrated how Christianity not only explains the puzzle of man's nature but also provides the solution for his existential estrangement from God and from himself. A redemptive relationship with Christ fills the previously empty person.

Augustine elaborates with questions that have but one answer: "Who will grant me to rest content in you? To whom shall I turn for the gift of your coming into my heart and filling it to the brim . . . ?"[45]

The Uniqueness and Enigma of Man

If the biblical vision of human beings is indeed true, certain traits will uniquely characterize their existence. But how would people be different if they naturally evolved from other creatures? What difference would being created in God's image make compared to being one with the universe? How well does the Christian worldview's basic anthropology correspond with what is known experientially about human nature? Is there an actual way to put anthropological theories to the test?

In assessing the viability of the historic Christian view of man, the relationship between human beings and animals must be explored. How are people like and unlike the animals? Is there a mere difference of degree or a profound difference of kind? Secular evolutionary theory and historic Christianity are clearly at odds on this important issue. But which viewpoint has the most explanatory power?

Is Man Different in Degree or in Kind from the Animals?

Human beings are similar to animals in some very important ways. But if the Bible is true, this likeness can be expected. For example, Scripture indicates that the body of man was created from the same dust of the ground that God used to create the animals:

> The LORD God formed the man from the dust of the ground and breathed into his nostrils the breath of life, and the man became a living being.
>
> Genesis 2:7

> Now the LORD God had formed out of the ground all the beasts of the field and all the birds of the air.
>
> Genesis 2:19

The Hebrew verbs used in Genesis for "make" ('āsāh, 1:26), "created" (bār'ā, 1:27), and "formed" (yāṣār, 2:7; 19) imply a divinely created physiological affinity between man and animals.[46] Genesis makes this affinity evident in other ways as well. For example, human beings eat much the same food as the land animals,[47] and the first human is called a "living being" (*nefeš ḥayāh*), a term also applied to animals.[48] Therefore, from a biblical perspective certain physical similarities (anatomical, physiological, biochemical, genetic) between man and other primates, for instance, should not be surprising.

The actual genetics of humans and chimpanzees are amazingly alike. In terms of raw genetics, chimpanzees are estimated to be over 90 percent similar to man.[49] While this affinity is often presented as strong support for naturalistic evolution, in reality the Genesis creation account anticipates this finding and others like it. There may well be a number of important ways that man and animals differ only in degree.

However, according to Genesis the *imago Dei* specifically makes man *different in kind* from the animals. If the biblical view of humanity is correct, then man should share certain physiological characteristics with the animals, but there should also be profound differences between them.

How Do Human Beings Differ from the Animals?

Specific qualities and traits set people apart from all other creatures. According to the Christian worldview, and specifically in light of the *imago Dei*, these profound differences are expected. Philosophers in particular have noted at least seven ways in which humans differ dramatically and significantly from animals:[50]

1. Human beings have an inherent spiritual and religious nature. The vast majority of people pursue some form of spiritual truth. They generally have deep-seated religious beliefs and engage in intricate rituals. Common practices such as prayer and worship demonstrate their pursuit of God or the transcendental. This defining characteristic of humankind is so apparent that some have designated humans as *Homo religiosus*—"religious man."

Formal atheism appears largely inconsistent with the overall history of human nature and practice. Even professed nonbelievers (atheists, skeptics) pursue questions concerning life's meaning and purpose and are drawn to whatever they consider of paramount importance and value. American philosopher of religion Paul Tillich suggested that there are no true atheists because all people have an "ultimate concern." And philosopher Harold H. Titus has said that even agnostics and atheists "tend to replace a personal god with an impersonal one—the state, race, some process in nature, or devotion to the search for truth or some other ideal."[51]

The ancient Greek philosopher Socrates (ca. 470–399 B.C.) once said, "The unexamined life is not worth living." Humans alone contemplate what philosophers call "the big questions of life." Though animals can be very intelligent they show no sign of spirituality or of concern with ultimate issues.

Only people are cognizant of their imminent death. This awareness generates personal angst, contemplation of God, and the possibility of immortality.

2. Human beings possess unique intellectual, cultural, and communicative abilities. They are thinkers capable of abstract reasoning and able to recognize, apply, and communicate the foundational principles of logic. Only human minds develop propositions, formulate arguments, draw inferences, recognize universal principles, and value logical validity, coherence, and truth. Only people recognize, appreciate, and wonder about such things as why the physical universe corresponds to abstract mathematical theorems.

Human beings communicate their conceptual apprehension of truth utilizing complex symbols (language). Propositional language is intricate, complex, and flexible (verbal, written). Language networks humanity and is a necessary vehicle in establishing human culture and societal institutions. People have a deep need to communicate with each other and accomplish that interaction through a sophisticated intellectual process.

In contrast, animals can do some pretty amazing things; they can be taught (by humans) to count, use a vocabulary of human words, and so forth. However, animals apparently lack any ability to work with abstractions and they cannot ask philosophical questions.

3. Human beings are conscious of time, reality, and truth. People alone recollect the past, recognize the present, and anticipate and worry about the future. They live their entire lives within and aware of the constraints of time. Yet human beings also have a desire to transcend time; they think about living forever.

Reflective people wonder whether their perception of reality matches reality. Only human beings pursue truth including the founding and development of philosophy, science, mathematics, logic, the arts, and a religious worldview. What is real (metaphysics), what is true (epistemology), and what is rational (logic) are paramount questions, but again, just for man.

Although animals can have a keen intuitive sense of concrete time, even surpassing that of a human's (for example, some birds are more attuned to the changes of seasons), animals utterly lack any capacity for abstractions concerning time. Likewise, they may seem aware of reality in its concrete particulars but do not inquire into metaphysical, epistemological, and logical questions.

4. Human beings possess a conscience, identify a value system, and legislate moral laws for society. People have an inner sense of moral right and wrong or good and bad (conscience). They deliberate about moral choices, feel the pull of prescriptive moral obligation and duty, and attempt to conform their lives according to a system of ethical conduct.

Individuals also know the reality of violating their own moral standards. Most people believe that universal, objective, and unchanging moral principles exist; and even those who reject absolute standards find it difficult to live that way.[52] Human society, by necessity, legislates morality and punishes the violators.

Christian philosopher Alvin Plantinga poignantly stated: "It is extremely difficult to be a normal human being and not think that some actions are wrong and some are right."[53] Questions of what is good (ethics) and what is of genuine worth (values) are solely in humanity's domain.

Animals are certainly capable of doing good, even heroic acts (for example, a dog saving its master from a burning house or guiding soldiers through dangerous obstacles during combat), but they are not capable of making morally reflective judgments (a dog cannot debate the merits of risking its life to save another).

5. Human beings are uniquely inventive and technological. Philosopher J. P. Moreland has noted that, in terms of technology, people living at the time of the American Civil War had more in common with the Old Testament patriarch Abraham (ca. 2000 B.C.) than with people living today.[54] Technological advancement in the twentieth century alone was breathtaking. Tracing the advance of military technology (airplanes, submarines, tanks, missiles) from World War I to the present day is astonishingly sobering. In less than a century, military technology advanced from the trench warfare of World War I to the "blitzkrieg" and atomic bomb of World War II to the intercontinental ballistic missiles of the Cold War, and finally to the stealth aircraft and smart bombs of today.

Human beings create and utilize complex tools, and they design and manufacture advanced machines. People confront natural obstacles and take dominion over nature. Philosopher Harold H. Titus marveled at the ability of humans: "They have learned to fly, to journey under the sea, to travel to interstellar space . . . and to project their images and voices around the world."[55]

Though human technology is constantly progressive, it is also a double-edged sword. Human innovation has not only lengthened the human life span but also brought the world to the brink of nuclear destruction. In this sobering and humbling fact, people once again prove themselves unique among all living creatures.

Animals have a very limited capacity for utilizing objects in nature as tools, lacking entirely the creativity of human beings. While often powerful and instinctive creatures, animals have never had the ability to take dominion over nature with inventive ideas.

6. Human beings possess an intense curiosity to explore and understand the entire created realm. Human beings are driven to explore and understand the world they live in. They seek out the most desolate and dangerous places on and in Earth and even beyond. Though animals often explore and try to understand their immediate habitats, their investigations appear to pertain to furthering their survival or enhancing their fun.

Whereas animals may play with a pretty stone or twig, human beings want to understand the smallest fundamental entities that make up the stone or twig and how these entities arise and interact. Birds may look to the star patterns in the sky to guide them in their migrations, but humans seek to comprehend the source of starlight and what lies beyond it.

The desire of animals to explore and understand their immediate environment appears to be constrained by their body size. Humans, on the other hand, want to explore and understand the full range of existing entities, even down to the very smallest (for example, strings that measure less than a trillionth of a trillionth of a trillionth of a meter across). Likewise, they are not content to just explore and understand their immediate environment. Their curiosity ranges from the core of the Earth to that which lies beyond the most distant galaxy.

Stephen Hawking summarizes humanity's insatiable curiosity about the created realm in his bestselling science book, *A Brief History of Time*. According to this great scientist, no human being is content until he or she has complete answers to the following questions: "What is the nature of the universe? What is our place in it and where did it and we come from? Why is it the way it is?"[56] Hawking indicates that he will remain dissatisfied until he "would know the mind of God."[57]

7. *Human beings possess aesthetic taste and appreciation for more than just practical purposes.* People distinctly create, recognize, and appreciate beauty. This aesthetic taste and value extend to art, music, film, literature, and the natural world itself. Humans often create because they are moved by a deep and mysterious sense of the beautiful. Many people place aesthetic concerns at the level of basic needs for survival. Anthropological finds have clearly shown that humankind's aesthetic need and expression date virtually from the very beginning of its existence.

Animals' creative capacities are of a lower order and are apparently motivated exclusively by practical necessity (for example, birds make nests and beavers build dams). They do not seem to create for sheer pleasure.

Distinguishing dynamics. These seven characteristics clearly place human beings in a different category than the rest of Earth's creatures. In many respects man is different in kind, not just in degree, from the animals. And the distinct attributes of humankind comport well with what Scripture reveals concerning the *imago Dei*.

Can a Theory of Human Nature Be Put to the Test?

If the Christian vision of reality is true, profound differences between humans and animals would be expected. Any acceptable worldview must possess real explanatory power, and so far the Christian position corresponds well to the real world. But to be worthy of belief, a religion or philosophy must also account for the meaningful realities a person encounters in life. And the enigma of humanity itself poses one of the most complex challenges.

Can Christianity account for the mysterious and enigmatic nature of man? How does this worldview explain what one famous observer called humankind's "greatness and wretchedness"?

The Greatest Enigma—Man

Blaise Pascal described human beings in his classic work *Pensées* as a strange and freakish mixture of "greatness and wretchedness,"[58] as simultaneously both the "glory and refuse of the universe."[59] Part of man's nobility is demonstrated in his unique ability as a reflective thinker to recognize his own wretchedness. Pascal thought only the Christian faith could account for this schizophrenic condition. Christian philosopher Thomas V. Morris explains further:

> One of the greatest mysteries is in us. How is the naked ape capable of grasping the mathematical structure of matter? How can one species produce both unspeakable wickedness and nearly inexplicable goodness? How can we be responsible both for the most disgusting squalor and for the most breathtaking beauty? How can grand aspirations and self-destructive impulses, kindness and cruelty, be interwoven in one life? The human enigma cries out for explanation. Pascal believed that only the tenets of the Christian faith can adequately account for both the greatness and wretchedness of humanity. And he was convinced that this in itself is an important piece of evidence that Christianity embraces truth.[60]

Just how does Christianity explain humanity's paradoxical nature? The Christian worldview asserts that human greatness is a direct result of the *imago Dei*. As creatures made in the image and likeness of God, human beings reflect the glory of their Maker.

Wretchedness, on the other hand, can be traced to Adam. The first man succeeded in plunging all humanity into sin and corruption (Genesis 3). From a biblical worldview, any understanding of human behavior must include recognition of the sin nature.[61]

While important differences exist among the various theological segments within Christianity concerning this doctrine of original sin,[62] the following explanation may correspond best to the biblical perspective.

Adam, in his relationship to God, was not merely the first man—a distinct, isolated individual. He was also the "representative man."[63] In terms of God's covenant with Adam (often referred to as the Covenant of Works), he represented humanity as a whole.[64] By this covenant, God's treatment of all humankind would be based upon Adam's actions (either by his obedience or disobedience to specific commands).

Therefore, when Adam was placed in the garden, all humanity was on probation before God. Because Adam rebelled against God's command, not only did he suffer divine disapproval, but so did all his descendants. Adam's fall transmitted sin and guilt from him to all human beings.[65] So through Adam, all people sinned and are morally accountable to God. Thus, original sin, as defined by theologian John Jefferson Davis, refers to "the sinfulness, guilt, and susceptibility to death inherited by all human beings (except Christ) from Adam."[66]

The doctrine of original sin also means that all of Adam's progeny are conceived in sin and consequently inherit a sin nature. This severely incapacitating force permeates the heart of every individual.[67] Consequently, human beings are not sinners simply because they happen to sin; rather, they sin because they are sinners by nature. This underlying bent produces all manner of sin.

Humanity's problem therefore, should be thought of more as a condition than a struggle with specific acts. As a universal phenomenon, sin affects each and every person[68] with Jesus Christ being the only exception.[69] Inherited from Adam this nature resides at the very core (inner being) of each human being,[70] and affects the entire person—including the mind, will, affections, and body.[71] Human beings are thus "totally depraved."[72]

This doctrine of total depravity doesn't mean that people are utterly or completely evil, but it does mean they are pervasively sinful (sin has affected their total being). This state makes it impossible for human beings to merit the favor of God.[73] While fallen people are still capable of doing certain morally good acts, their sin nature makes them incapable of living in a way completely acceptable to almighty God.[74]

Given God's holy and righteous moral character,[75] man in his sinful state must rightly face God's just wrath or anger.[76] By necessity God must punish the responsible sinner. Yet in the midst of humanity's despairing circumstance, God graciously intervened and provided people with a way of escaping divine judgment through divinely imparted forgiveness. That forgiveness comes in and through the life, death, and resurrection of the divine Messiah, Jesus Christ.[77]

The result of being simultaneously great and wretched is that man can paint the Sistine Chapel and write the plays of Shakespeare but also be capable of creating Auschwitz and the Gulag. The astonishing moral dissonance evident in the life of the high-ranking Nazi leader Reinhard Heydrich demonstrates the depths of the problem. Considered the mastermind behind the Nazi plan to exterminate European Jewry (the final solution),[78] Heydrich was considered a highly educated and cultured individual who greatly appreciated the classical music of Schubert, Wagner, and Beethoven. In the same life he displayed both brilliance and sheer unadulterated evil.

The Reality of Man

According to astronomer and Christian apologist Hugh Ross, man is far too evil for naturalistic evolution to be true.[79] Unlike animals, humans often use their intellectual endowments to commit acts of wickedness. Human malevolence is enhanced by human intelligence and creativity. Experientially speaking, people appear just as expected—that is, if Christianity is indeed true. Could it be that Christianity actually explains the ultimate enigma—man? If so, that kind of explanatory power goes a long way in substantiating the truth-claims of historic Christianity.

The historic Christian worldview contains deep understanding and insight into the human condition. As Scripture predicts, man is different in both degree and in kind from the animals. And human beings are both great and wretched, just as could be expected from a creature that is Godlike in many respects but also deeply fallen.

As complicated creatures, humans often struggle with questions of morality and ethics. The next chapter explores how the Bible offers specific insights into these concerns that dramatically impact the Christian worldview.

Discussion Questions

1. What does it mean to be made in the image of God? What are the natural and moral components of the *imago Dei*? Theologically speaking, just how are human beings like and unlike God?
2. How has the fall affected the *imago Dei*? What does the phrase "effaced but not erased" actually mean?
3. What are the humanitarian implications of the *imago Dei*?
4. What does it mean that humans differ from the animals in both degree and kind? How does the Bible present these differences? Just how do humans differ from the animals?
5. What did Pascal mean when he said humans are both "great" and "wretched"?

For Further Study

Augustine. *Confessions*. Translated by R. S. Pine-Coffin. New York: Penguin, 1961.

Hoekema, Anthony A. *Created in God's Image*. Grand Rapids: Eerdmans, 1986.

Lewis, C. S. *The Abolition of Man, or Reflections on Education with Special Reference to the Teaching of English in the Upper Forms of School*. New York: Macmillan, 1947.

Machen, J. Gresham. *The Christian View of Man*. New York: Macmillan, 1937.

Pascal, Blaise. *Pensées*. Rev. ed. Translated by A. J. Krailsheimer. New York: Penguin, 1995.

Rana, Fazale, with Hugh Ross. *Who Was Adam? A Creation Model Approach to the Origin of Man*. Colorado Springs: NavPress, 2005.

11

THE HISTORIC CHRISTIAN VIEW OF MORAL VALUES

If God exists, objective moral values exist. To say that there are objective moral values is to say that something is right or wrong independently of whether anybody believes it to be so. It is to say, for example, that Nazi anti-Semitism was morally wrong, even though the Nazis who carried out the Holocaust thought that it was good; and it would still be wrong even if the Nazis had won World War II.

William Lane Craig, "The Indispensability of Theological Meta-Ethical Foundations for Morality," *Foundations*

Many people express the view that so-called matters of truth and morality are private, personal, and individual matters of choice. Some of them think the greatest wrong is being intolerant of the beliefs and moral choices made by others. I've often heard students say, "Whatever a person thinks is right is right for them."

One evening in my ethics class, we explored whether certain actions are always morally wrong. In the midst of this protracted and emotionally laden discussion I brought up Samantha Runnion's kidnapping. She was the five-year-old girl snatched from in front of her home in Stanton, California, during the summer of 2002. Her abductor sexually assaulted and murdered her. He then left her nude body alongside the road.

I considered that act shockingly evil—monstrous—and told my students so. Surely a crime like this was proof that some actions are evil and always wrong—for all people, at all times, everywhere. To my amazement, approximately one-fourth of that class of more than thirty students disagreed.

A number of them said that while they didn't agree with what the murderer had done, and while they would never engage in such behavior themselves, they nevertheless could not say that such actions were always morally wrong for everybody, at all times, everywhere. These students were willing to concede that murder and rape were wrong for them, but they could not assert that these atrocities were necessarily wrong for others. Intelligent young adults insisted on holding onto the relativistic view that there are no universal moral absolutes.

I wonder if they had thought through the moral implications of their position. Maybe these young people had professors who presented a relativistic view of truth and morality but offered no instruction about the monumental problems associated with this perspective. But then again, many of those professors are probably unaware of the insurmountable difficulties inherent in relativism.

The Foundation of Christian Ethics

Moral values are as real and consequential as the law of gravity. All people experience the pull of conscience, consider various ethical options, make choices, then face the inevitable consequences or rewards of their actions. Students frequently decide whether to run the risk of cheating on an exam in order to get a better grade. Young women often face the dilemma of whether to have an abortion. Executives are confronted with daily decisions about being honest in their business dealings. Values are a critical component of human life.

Central to any world-and-life view is its description, explanation, and justification of the moral sphere. The historic Christian position teaches that moral responsibility is a necessary and positive feature of being human. To be made in God's image is to bear ethical rights, responsibilities, and obligations. An overview of the ethical foundations of the Christian worldview begins to distinguish the position of theistic-based moral objectivism from the destructive relativism so common in today's world.[1]

Absolute Ethical Values

An objective approach to ethics contrasts sharply with a relativistic viewpoint. Five points express the historic Christian foundation for absolute norms.

1. Morality originates in God's perfect character and immutable nature.

Objective moral principles are not only compatible with the Christian worldview, but are also exactly what would be expected in a world made by an infinite, eternal, personal, holy, just, and loving Creator. The source and foundation for the ethical absolutes reflected in Christianity are found in the God of the Bible. Moral ideals stem from his perfect character and unchanging nature.

Skeptics sometimes attempt to apply what is known as the "Euthyphro Problem" (taken from Plato's Socratic dialogue *Euthyphro*) to the relationship between the biblical God and ethics: Is something right or wrong because God wills it (implying that morality is arbitrarily determined by divine choice)? Or, does God will things to be right or wrong because morality resides on a higher sphere (implying that morality transcends God)? The Euthyphro conflict implies that God is either arbitrary in nature or limited in nature; neither position is acceptable in the Christian theistic worldview.

This dilemma fails because of the biblical God's unique relationship to moral value. God doesn't arbitrarily or capriciously invent right and wrong. He doesn't invent moral values at all—they stem from his eternal, unchanging being. Nor are moral values somehow above God's being as transcendent realities to which he must defer. This view would be inconsistent with his status as the sovereign and ultimate King and Ruler. Rather, ethics extend to humankind as expressions of God's own transcendent nature.[2]

God possesses a perfect ethical character. His moral standards have been revealed through the created order (for example, in the human conscience) and through explicit historical and revelatory statements in Scripture (as in the Ten Commandments, the Golden Rule, and the Sermon on the Mount). As the infinite and necessary "Good," God is the objective and fixed ground upon which ethical values rest.

Without God such characteristics as inherent human dignity, moral worth, objective human rights, and personal moral responsibility and obligation would have no basis. Christian philosopher Paul Copan noted that a "natural context for moral values and human dignity is the theistic one—in which we've been made by a personal, self-aware, purposeful, good God to resemble him in certain important ways."[3]

2. Moral values are objective, universal, unchanging, and discoverable.

The ethical principles so central to the historic Christian worldview are distinct from and independent of the human mind and will. Therefore, they are objective instead of subjective. These universal values are an "abiding and fixed reality common to all."[4]

Because ethical laws flow from an immutable God, these standards have an unchanging nature. And because God built these invisible principles into the structure of the universe, morals are discovered by man—not invented. Thus, although moral ideals are absolute, human understanding of them is not.

Human beings often disagree about these issues. Even apart from such dissidence, people do not always completely understand or properly apply the values they do recognize. Unlike God, human beings have to grow in their moral insights over time. Yet while people strive to uphold their beliefs, evolve in their thinking, and discover new insights over the course of time, core ethical values always remain the same.

Ethical objectivism is commonly embraced by the theistic religions (among other worldview orientations, including even some secularists), and it especially reflects the historic Christian worldview. However, in today's world, ethical subjectivism—an individualistic form of moral relativism (as opposed to cultural relativism)—is also very popular. Table 11.1 sets forth these two basic views.

Table 11.1
Two Views of Ethical Foundations

Ethical Subjectivism	Ethical Objectivism
Whatever a person thinks or feels is morally right is right for him.	*A binding moral order exists independent of human opinion and/or approval.*
The rightness or wrongness of actions depends upon a person's thoughts, opinions, intentions, and desires (moral truth is relative to the individual).	Universal and valid ethical principles exist outside of and distinct from the minds and wills of human beings (moral truth stands apart from human convention).
Moral values are:	**Moral values are:**
Subjective	Objective
Invented	Discovered
Conventional	Nonconventional
Relative	Absolute
Descriptive	Prescriptive
Consequential	Nonconsequential
Particular	Universal

3. Moral values are prescriptive in nature.

Prescriptive moral values involve the distinctly ethical "ought" or "should." To have objective morality, requires a "right" that should be followed and a "wrong" that ought to be avoided. The prescriptive nature of ethics (an immediate and direct moral awareness in humans) compels right or correct conduct. Secular varieties of ethics, inevitably stemming from self-interest, lack this necessary "ought-" or "should-oriented" element. With genuinely prescribed morality, specific behavior is objectively right or wrong.

Acting in an expedient, convenient, or pragmatic way (based on self-interest) does not equate with prescriptive morality. The two approaches may overlap, but philosophically they are not the same thing. Grounding ethics in the existence of a perfectly moral divine being grants Christian ethics a specific prescriptive nature the secular position lacks by definition. Objective prescriptive morality presupposes an ontological or metaphysical foundation. What is good (ethics) cannot be separated from what is real and true (metaphysics). Goodness cannot exist in an ontological and/or metaphysical vacuum.

4. Subjective ethics are inadequate, incoherent, and pragmatically unlivable.

An ethical approach to life based solely upon an individual's likes, tastes, or preferences cannot function as a viable moral philosophy. A morality relative to either a person or culture is ultimately incoherent (in effect, such a morality denies itself). Moral relativism, which pervades much of Western culture, leads to the logical quagmire of thinking that no human is better than another, no code of values exceeds any other, and all moral choices are equal.[5]

Conventional or invented ethics can neither account for moral obligations nor compel and justify real moral action. Life is inconceivable without such ideals and unlivable without their objective grounding in nature or reality. The God of the Bible is that fixed ontological ground upon which objective ethics rest.

All types of moral relativism[6] are antithetical to the historic Christian worldview. Table 11.2 briefly defines the two most popular types, ethical subjectivism and ethical conventionalism, and sets forth some major objections that make these two relativistic theories logically and morally untenable.

Thought Box: Problem of the Good

As a Christian and serious student of World War II, the thought of why a good God would allow such a horrific event as the Holocaust (the Nazi extermination of six million Jews and several million other ethnic minorities and political dissidents) and other such evils has greatly perplexed and intrigued me. My reflections on this problem indicate, however, that a benevolent God (a transcendental ground of goodness) must exist in order for the Holocaust to be deemed evil in the first place.[7] Evil is by definition the violation of an objective moral standard.

Could a person appropriately reason that the cataclysmic evil of the Holocaust demands an objective moral standard of goodness that is best accounted for by the existence of the biblical God? And if this reasoning is sound, would not the existence of evil be support for God rather than evidence of his nonexistence? Instead of the "problem of evil," maybe there is a "problem of the good."

Table 11.2
Insurmountable Problems with Moral Relativism

Ethical Subjectivism (individual relativism)	Ethical Conventionalism (cultural relativism)
Whatever I think is morally right is right.	*Whatever my culture says is morally right is right.*
Moral truth is relative to the individual person.	Moral truth is relative to a person's culture or society.
Four Problems:	**Four Problems:**
1. If right is what each person thinks is right, then nothing can be wrong (but it seems intuitively obvious that the moral thinking of some [for example, mass murderers Adolf Eichmann and Saddam Hussein] is clearly wrong).	1. If what a person's culture says is right is in fact right, then one culture cannot validly criticize the moral actions of another culture (Americans cannot legitimately condemn the treatment of Afghani women by the Taliban).
2. If right is what each person thinks is right, then there is no difference between a person's opinions about morality and actual morality (the crucial feature of moral deliberation is thus eliminated).	2. Ethical conventionalism leaves no possibility for the reform of a culture because such reform is unnecessary. (The efforts of Wilberforce, Lincoln, Gandhi, and King were thus of no value and morally misguided.)
3. If morality is reduced to personal taste or preference, then logical arguments have no proper application in the moral sphere (a person's taste can't be invalid or wrong).	3. Cultural relativism suffers from a serious practical dilemma: "culture" is a difficult concept to define and in this pluralistic age a person may belong to multiple cultures.
4. Individualistic relativism fails to distinguish between virtue and vice (Adolf Hitler was just as moral as Mother Teresa so long as both did what they thought right).	4. From the historic Christian perspective, ethical conventionalism ignores the transcultural Law of God ("Thou shalt not murder" is a transcultural moral imperative).

5. The God of the Bible endowed the universe and especially humankind with value, meaning, and significance.

Imagining how a universe without God (and in particular the sovereign Lord revealed explicitly in Scripture) could have value, meaning, and purpose, especially with regard to individual human beings, is problematic. If the universe and humanity are merely products of blind, accidental, and purely natural processes—then a genuine enduring value for life is extremely difficult to identify and justify. Accidental creatures with no ultimate purpose or end are hard-pressed to impart any permanent significance to their own lives.

According to the Christian worldview, the created order's value comes from its relationship to God. Being made in the image of God gives human beings immeasurable worth. Philosopher Thomas V. Morris makes the point that

> something has meaning if and only if it is endowed with meaning or significance by a purposive personal agent or group of such agents. . . . Meaning is never intrinsic; it is always derivative. . . . We can endow with meaning only those things over which we have the requisite control.[8]

If Morris is right, then the limitations of the human condition cause some real inner existential consternation. For when people begin to reflect upon the profound circumstances over which they have little or no influence, it awakens the realization that life is largely beyond human control. Much of reality lies outside the possibility of endowing it with meaning. A few specific situations beyond human ability to change are:

- being conceived into existence
- the DNA that defines a person
- the timing, place, and circumstances of a person's own birth
- the family into which one is born
- the ideas, education, philosophy, religion, and worldview to which an individual is exposed
- social and environmental factors
- much of a person's own suffering and death

Even the everyday choices individuals make, over which they have some measure of control, are shaped and influenced by the profound things that happen beyond their consent. Recognizing that so much of what is critically important to life lies outside a person's direct authority should motivate that individual to analyze critically his adopted worldview. The question of control and meaning should also lead to reflection about the question of God.

Sovereign Control

According to the Christian worldview, the God of the Bible is the transcendent Creator and immanent Sustainer of his creation. Therefore God is in complete control of all things. Scripture states that God "works out *everything* in conformity with the purpose of his will" (Eph. 1:11, emphasis added). While God sovereignly directs all things, he provides a special providential promise to the believer concerning his ultimate goodness: "We know that in all things God works for the good of those who love him, who have been called according to his purpose" (Rom. 8:28).

An infinite, eternal, and morally perfect being, God possesses intrinsic value, meaning, and purpose. By creating and sustaining the universe (Gen. 1:1) and making human beings in his expressed image (Gen. 1:26–27), God endowed his world (and especially those made in his image) with significance. People can thus discover genuine and enduring value, meaning, and purpose in their own lives.

Not only did God grant dignity and value to human beings through creation, he also extended those traits all the more through the immeasurable gift of redemption. Repentant sinners have been purchased and forgiven by the life, death, and resurrection of God the Son.[9]

The Christian worldview considers humanity in general, and the individual person in particular, to possess a derived value from the Creator, Lord, and Redeemer. In contrast, how could limited human beings possess meaning if no such God exists? If Morris is right in his claim that meaning is always endowed and derivative and never intrinsic, then the naturalistic, atheistic worldview would by necessity be nihilistic (entailing that human life is meaningless and purposeless).

The Christian worldview grounds its ethical values in the existence of an infinite, eternal, and morally perfect God. These enduring values are extended to human beings through God's works in creation and in redemption. As a result Christian ethics are objective, prescriptive, and universal in nature. This divinely grounded system of values grants to humanity a meaning, purpose, and significance that a secular-based moral relativism is incapable of providing.

Part 3 puts four competing worldviews to the test. Naturalism, postmodernism, pantheistic monism, and Islam each have their own distinctive features. The next chapter checks out how one view—naturalism—fares in the marketplace of ideas.

Discussion Questions

1. What is God's relationship to ethics? How would you respond to the Euthyphro challenge?
2. How does the historic Christian understanding of ethics differ from secular ethics based upon self-interest? What does it mean for ethical principles to be "prescriptive" in nature?
3. What are the strongest criticisms of moral relativism (both individualistic and cultural)?
4. Explain Thomas Morris's argument about endowed meaning. Do you agree with him? Why or why not?

5. How would you argue from morality to the biblical God? How does God serve as a foundation for objective morality?

For Further Study

Beckwith, Francis J., and Gregory Koukl. *Relativism: Feet Firmly Planted in Mid-Air*. Grand Rapids: Baker, 1998.

Davis, John Jefferson. *Evangelical Ethics: Issues Facing the Church Today*. Phillipsburg, NJ: P & R Publishing, 1993.

Harris, Robert A. *The Integration of Faith and Learning: A Worldview Approach*. Eugene, OR: Cascade, 2004.

Pojman, Louis P. *Ethics: Discovering Right and Wrong*. Belmont, CA: Wadsworth, 1990.

Purtill, Richard L. *Thinking about Ethics*. Englewood Cliffs, NJ: Prentice-Hall, 1976.

Rae, Scott B. *Moral Choices: An Introduction to Ethics*. Grand Rapids: Zondervan, 1995.

EVALUATING
WORLDVIEW
COMPETITORS

12

NATURALISM

A SECULAR WORLDVIEW CHALLENGE

With me the horrid doubt always arises whether the convictions of man's mind, which has been developed from the mind of lower animals, are of any value or at all trustworthy. Would any one trust in the convictions of a monkey's mind, if there are any convictions in such a mind?

Charles Darwin, *The Life and Letters of Charles Darwin*

As a philosopher, I had frequently spent time reflecting upon death, recognizing both the brevity of life and the inevitability of my death. I even taught a philosophy course titled Perspectives on Death and Dying. Yet the frank medical assessment of my fragile health condition described earlier forced me to consider as never before that my death might indeed be quite imminent. As the comedian and movie maker Woody Allen is said to have quipped, "I know that I am going to die, I just don't want to be there when it happens."

More than the fear and angst, I experienced great sorrow at the thought of leaving my family. My job as a father was not yet sufficiently completed. I was especially concerned for my son, Michael, who was only a child. My two daughters were in their teens and I'd spent more time with them, but still not enough. And my heart ached at the thought of my wife, Joan, becoming a widow.

Thinking about my death no longer in theoretical terms, but as an actual real-ity, led me to consider what I truly believed about immortality. Though the brain lesions made clear and careful thinking difficult, I candidly reevaluated what I believed about God, death, and the afterlife. I also reflected upon how different my Christian convictions were from the other religions and philosophies that I'd studied and taught about. I wondered what it would be like to hold a naturalist worldview and face the prospect that death resulted in permanent extinction with the loss of personal consciousness forever.

An Incredible Congruence

Physicists study the physical universe through the prism of mathematics. Recognizing the important role mathematical constructs play in attempting to understand the cosmos raises a critical philosophical question: How can the conceptual principles present in the human mind actually correspond to the structure of the physical universe itself?

This astonishing affinity—between the mathematical thoughts of man's mind, in the form of equations, with the objective cosmos—corresponds well with the Christian worldview. For according to Scripture, God created both the physical universe and the minds of human beings. And because people were created in the image of God, they have the necessary cognitive facul-ties and sensory organs to recognize the intelligible order of the universe. The conceptual enterprises of logic, mathematics, and science are expected features of a universe made by a perfectly rational Creator.

On the other hand, how can this stunning correspondence be explained if there is no God and the physical cosmos is all that exists? The probability seems as though it would be utterly staggering for human beings to not only evolve through blind, unguided, purely impersonal natural processes but also for those same undirected processes to develop a human brain and mind capable of grasping the very conceptual nature of the universe.

Yet, according to the worldview of naturalism, that's what happened. Does this dilemma raise an intractable problem for the evolutionary position?

Any worldview that argues for a rational basis of the scientific enterprise must account for the remarkable congruence between the universe and a human mind.

If the cosmos evolved by chance with no anticipation of man, and if there was no created correspondence between the human mind and the physical cosmos, is there any good reason to trust the mind's conceptual apprehension of the cosmos? Can naturalism provide a connection between the human mind and the universe, other than what must be considered an incredible coincidence?

As a non-Christian worldview, naturalism vies for the attention of many people in today's global and largely pluralistic world. Because this prominent secular worldview strongly competes with Christianity in the twenty-first century's marketplace of ideas, it deserves serious consideration. How does it fare when evaluated by the same criteria used for testing Christian truth-claims?

A Naturalistic Perspective

The number of people worldwide who embrace a godless worldview remains a relatively small percentage compared to the large majority of people who embrace some type of religious perspective.[1] However, secularism appears to be growing in popularity and is well-entrenched in many parts of the Western world, especially in the centers of academia. Naturalism may be the most familiar secular philosophy of life, capturing the attention and devotion of many intellectuals.

A brief exploration of the naturalistic worldview begins by describing its distinctive features or beliefs. Identifying some of this position's most prominent representatives leads to some of the positive elements it contributes toward understanding the world and the human condition. Then, application of some appropriate worldview tests (discussed in chapter 2) evaluates naturalism's negative implications.

Nature Is the Whole Show

Naturalism,[2] as traditionally defined, is the worldview system that regards the natural, material, and physical universe as the only reality.[3] The world of nature is viewed as the sum total of reality, the whole show, all that actually exists.

The *Britannica Concise Encyclopedia* defines naturalism as "the theory that affirms that all beings and events in the universe are natural and therefore can be fully known by the methods of scientific investigation."[4] Naturalists typically view the universe as a closed and uniform system of material causes and effects with nothing existing outside the realm of nature. All reality is located within the exclusive domain of the spatiotemporal world of physical objects, events, processes, and forces.

The universe stands ontologically on its own—complete, self-contained, self-sufficient, and self-explanatory. Naturalists reject both a supernatural realm of existence and immaterial agencies or realities such as God, angels, and immaterial human souls. Secular scientist Carl Sagan expressed the position of strong naturalism in a famous statement from his television series, *Cosmos*: "The cosmos is all that is, or ever was, or ever will be."

Yet while the earlier definition holds consistent among naturalists, a great deal of diversity nevertheless exists in their specific philosophical worldview.[5]

Naturalists readily disagree amongst themselves. Michael Rea, a philosopher who has written extensively about naturalism, notes these differences, especially with regard to the fundamental question of being: "The house of naturalism is a house divided. There is little agreement about what naturalism is, or about what sort of ontology it requires."[6]

Naturalism's Distinctive Features

An affirmation of the naturalistic worldview frequently involves eight important beliefs that can be identified as varieties of or subcategories within the broad worldview known as metaphysical or ontological naturalism. These points might be considered its so-called family traits.

1. Monism

From the Greek *monos*, meaning "one," monism is the metaphysical view that all reality is one thing or stuff.[7] By rejecting the supernatural, naturalists affirm that "everything is composed of natural entities."[8] While lacking unanimity as to the exact nature of the one (some assert "matter" while others do not), naturalism asserts that all things in the universe can be explained by natural, physical, and material objects and forces.

Everything is reducible to or explainable in terms of nature itself as studied and interpreted by science. Reductive naturalists believe all things are physical and material in nature. Nonreductive naturalists consider all things to be physical in nature, but allow for irreducible or emergent properties resulting in intangibles such as consciousness, intentionality, and values. Naturalists agree that the physical universe—with its constituents of matter, energy, time, and space—is the one fundamental reality from which all things are derived.

2. Materialism

"Materialism" (matter is the one ultimate reality) is a particular type of monism. But while materialism is common among metaphysical naturalists, naturalism does not necessarily entail materialism[9] (though naturalism offers few other ontological options).

This metaphysical view considers everything in the universe to be matter (that is, composed of material objects).[10] Everything can be reduced to or explained in terms of matter or is ultimately dependent upon it. Nonmaterial entities or substances—souls, spirits, and angels—simply do not exist. And, because the God of the Bible is an immaterial nonphysical being, materialists dismiss God as nonexistent and illusory.

Materialists view matter either as eternal (in some form) or as somehow having emerged spontaneously into existence from nothing by nothing. Some nonreductive materialists, who believe in such things as consciousness, intentionality, and values, assert that these phenomena represent a yet-to-be understood "matter in motion."

Reductive materialists assert that the material physical brain with its related electrical-chemical processes produces or causes the mind (but not the reverse; the mind has no effect upon the brain). That the brain causes the mind is thought to be analogous to how an engine causes exhaust or fire causes smoke. This particular mind-body theory (epiphenomenalism)—with a one-way causal relationship moving from matter to mind—is commonly held by naturalists. The application of materialism to the nature of the mind is often referred to as "physicalism."

3. Physicalism

The ontological theory of physicalism[11] is an extension of materialism, particularly in attempts to explain the mind-body problem (the difficulty of relating the seemingly immaterial, nonphysical, and unobservable "mind" to the demonstrably material and observable "brain" or "body").

Physicalism asserts that what actually exists is ultimately constituted of physical realities. This theory entails the idea that all realities can be described and explained using only the vocabulary of chemistry and physics. Sometimes physicalism implies a reductionism or eliminativism that denies the very existence of distinctively mental entities. The naturalists who affirm this type of physicalism simply assert that mental states are identical to brain states, so that sensations and the like are nothing more than neurological conditions taking place in the human brain.

Physicalism outright rejects all forms of mind-body dualism (the view that the mind and body are distinct substances but nevertheless influence each other in a two-way causal connection). Mind-body dualism (also known as substance dualism) has typically been attractive to Christian theistic philosophers and theologians in their attempts to come to grips with the mind-body enigma. On the other hand, physicalism usually asserts that the brain is the definitive cause of so-called mental events. Apparent mental events are considered a property or function of the brain and thus a mere function of matter.

4. Scientism

Broadly speaking, "science" refers to the empirical method for observing, analyzing, and interpreting the data of the natural world. This term also defines the knowledge gained by using such a method. While naturalists and nonnaturalists agree on its value, naturalists tend to consider science as having privileged status with regard to knowledge. Some naturalists even readily embrace the exalted principle that sums up the optimistic attitude reflected in what is called "scientism":[12] "Science is the measure of all things."

Definitely more than science, scientism asserts that science is either the only reliable method (strong scientism) or the best, most dependable method (weak scientism) for obtaining genuine knowledge. Naturalists who embrace scientism are convinced that the natural sciences are the only path that lead to knowledge and truth.

Scientism maintains a very narrow focus in the types of things it permits as candidates for authentic knowledge and truth. One article explains this position:

> Naturalism as a world view is based on the premise that knowledge about what exists and about how things work is best achieved through the sciences, not personal revelation or religious tradition. . . . Scientific empiricism has the necessary consequence of unifying our knowledge of the world, of placing all objects of understanding within a single, overarching causal context.[13]

Restricting the possibility of knowledge to the realm of the natural sciences means that religious, philosophical, aesthetic, and moral statements have little or no contribution to make in terms of knowledge and truth. The naturalist's faith clearly resides in science (whether embracing a strong or weak scientism). Those who embrace scientism also must readily embrace Darwinian or some other form of naturalistic evolution because it is the only origin-of-life theory that plays by the rules. As a result any explanatory theory for life,[14] and especially for humankind, must come purely from the natural universe, for any supernatural explanation has already been ruled out, *a priori*.

5. Darwinian Evolution

Following the theory set forth by the English scientist Charles Darwin (1809–1882), naturalists assert that all life is the result of purely natural processes. Evolution[15] as a biological theory asserts that complex life-forms developed from more primitive life through a variety of mechanisms that include natural selection, sexual selection, and genetic drift. Typically unfit life-forms (species poorly adapted to their environments) are eliminated through the struggle for survival, whereas life-forms better adapted to their environments survive.

Evolutionary theory claims that new and more adaptive life-forms are generated through the process of random genetic mutation in conjunction with natural selection. This process is thought to produce genetic variations within species that eventually result in the emergence of new species. Evolutionary theory postulates that human beings evolved from lower primates and thus are solely a part of nature.

Naturalists staunchly defend some form of evolutionary theory because biological evolution is the only naturalistic explanation for life and the appearance of *Homo sapiens*.[16] The theory of evolution is a necessary explanatory component in the overall worldview of naturalism.

6. Antisupernaturalism

By insisting on natural causes, naturalism by its very definition dismisses the existence of the supernatural realm. Philosopher Peter A. Angeles explains this single-minded focus on the physical world: "No reality exists other than processes (events, objects, happenings, occurrences) in space and time."[17]

Naturalists assert that because nature is the exclusive reality, all phenomena can and must be adequately explained within the matrix of this cosmos without recourse to supernatural explanations. Appeals to the supernatural to explain events transpiring in the world of time and space are considered unscientific and illegitimate. Though complex in structure and organization, all events, objects, and phenomena in the world must have purely natural explanations. As one naturalist put it, "Naturalism, in essence, is simply the idea that human beings are completely included in the natural world: there's nothing supernatural about us."[18]

7. Atheism/Agnosticism

Naturalists are typically atheistic in outlook, believing that no God or gods exist.[19] Because no supernatural realm exists, there can't be a supernatural deity to affect the natural universe from the outside. Atheism asserts that no God or gods are real entities, thus rejecting the biblical God who (by definition) is an infinite, eternal, spiritual being.

Atheists believe rather that the human mind invented God and, therefore, he is illusory. While atheism seems a more ontologically consistent fit for anyone who embraces the naturalistic worldview, some naturalists instead embrace agnosticism.[20] Agnostics assert either that they personally do not know if God exists (soft agnosticism) or that no one can know if God exists (hard agnosticism).

Hard agnosticism alleges that the evidence is insufficient to prove or disprove God's existence and calls for an intellectual suspension of judgment concerning whether God actually exists. Whether it manifests as hard or soft agnosticism, the naturalistic worldview is highly skeptical about both God and religious worldview explanations such as those found in theism.

8. Secular Humanism

The philosophical viewpoint of secular humanism[21] strongly embraces all seven previous points that reflect the subcategories or family traits of the naturalist worldview. This position emphatically opposes belief in God, religion, and anything supernatural. Rather, it firmly endorses some form of scientism, biological evolution, and usually a materialist/physicalist ontology (state of ultimate being).

Because humans are different only in degree from the rest of nature and have reached the highest step on the evolutionary ladder, they hold a privileged position and value in the purely naturalistic scheme of things. Some would therefore say that secular humanism can be summed up in the statement: "Man is the measure of all things."

From the humanist perspective morals, values, and societal norms find their source, foundation, and justification in the conventional agreement of humankind. Humanism's value system typically reflects such principles as libertarianism (maximizing individual liberty), utilitarianism (promoting the greatest good for the greatest number), relativism (subjective and changing standards), and pragmatism (truth is found in workability that results in positive human consequences).

Great confidence is placed in science and technology's capacity to solve human problems. Human beings are considered highly complicated yet solely physical organisms—merely the product of genetic, chemical, and physical processes and forces. Exactly how purely material causes produced human beings has yet to be understood by science.

Humanists typically reject mind-body dualism, and they either reject or are quite skeptical about the prospects of any kind of immortality. Thus, most advocates of secular humanism view death as the extinction of human consciousness and the loss of individual and personal identity forever. The secular humanist philosophy has been set forth in such historical documents as Humanist Manifesto I (1933), Humanist Manifesto II (1973), Secular Humanist Declaration (1981), and Humanist Manifesto III (2003).

Prominent Representatives of Naturalism

Over the years, distinguished scientists and social scientists in a variety of fields have been advocates for the naturalist worldview,[22] especially since the seventeenth- and eighteenth-century Enlightenment period. Such scientists included Charles Darwin and Thomas H. Huxley. Outspoken scientists such as Carl Sagan, Stephen Jay Gould, and Richard Dawkins have carried the naturalist perspective to the present day. The founders and influencers in the fields of the social sciences include other prominent naturalists such as Sigmund Freud, Auguste Comte, and Karl Marx.

Many recognizable philosophers, both past and present, have also promoted a purely naturalistic worldview. These include the ancient pre-Socratic philosophers Democritus and Lucretius. Philosophers associated with the logical positivist movement of the early twentieth century, such as A. J. Ayer and Bertrand Russell, embraced naturalism, as did the atheistic existential philosophers Friedrich Nietzsche and Jean Paul Sartre.

Pragmatist philosopher and educator John Dewey was also an influential naturalist, as were the prominent mathematical logician Willard V. O. Quine and the Oxford philosopher J. L. Mackie. Current philosophers of mind such as Paul and Patricia Churchland and John Searle also reside in the confines of this camp.

Putting Naturalism to the Test

Such distinguished adherents make a person wonder about some of naturalism's features as a worldview. All prominent worldviews that compete for attention in the marketplace of ideas include both positive and negative elements. The positive features of naturalism attract many people to this particular comprehensive explanation of reality.

But questions remain. No worldview perspective is perfect (including the historic Christian position)—all worldviews have challenges, tensions, and difficulties to face and attempt to resolve. (For example, consider how much attention Christian philosophers and theologians have given to answering the so-called problem of evil.) However, some challenges can be fatal. Is the problem of the congruence between the universe and the human mind one of them? Are there other insurmountable obstacles? How does naturalism fare using the worldview tests discussed in chapter 2?

At least three positive features can be identified and examined before identifying the negative elements.

Positive Elements

First, naturalism is, at least in one sense, a simple explanatory theory about the nature of reality. Even some Christian philosophers view naturalism as "a simpler hypothesis than theism."[23] William Wainwright, an academic philosopher and a Christian by conviction, explains that "naturalism is simpler in the sense that it denies the existence of transcendent reality and thus postulates fewer entities."[24]

Naturalists believe in one realm of existence, whereas Christianity postulates two. Ockham's Razor (see chapter 2) makes this principle of simplicity an important consideration when evaluating worldview systems.

However, in weighing naturalism's supposed simplicity, it should be noted that naturalism is not science itself (though this worldview greatly stresses and endorses the continued practice and development of science). Rather naturalism is a metaphysical theory that attempts to explain reality (as does Christianity). And when it comes to worldview tests, simplicity itself simply cannot carry the day. A worldview must also have genuine explanatory power and scope. This condition becomes an important component in testing the worldview a little later in this chapter.

Second, naturalism affirms the genuine existence of the physical universe and the need to investigate the cosmos through the practice of science. This positive aspect of naturalism is shared with Christianity but not with the Eastern mystical worldview. Both the naturalistic and Christian worldviews concur that the physical cosmos is authentically real, meaningful, and therefore valuable. Both belief systems recognize the importance of the scientific enterprise. Naturalism does possess some important explanatory power when it comes to the empirical facts of nature, but the scope of this power is clearly limited.

Third, naturalists emphasize the importance of relevant, practical, and workable consequences for human beings—especially when it comes to matters relating to science and technology. This practical, science-oriented feature appeals to many people who appreciate a so-called realistic approach to the world and life. Naturalism's "this-world" and humanistic focus scores high marks on the pragmatic test.

In terms of a short worldview scorecard, naturalism's positive worldview features lie in its basic simplicity (balance test), its insistence that science can interpret and explain the natural, empirical aspects of the cosmos (correspondence test), and in its practical focus upon this world (pragmatic test).

Negative Elements

Other worldview tests also reveal rather intriguing insights. However, these characteristics may not be quite so positive.

1. Coherence Test: Does naturalism have a reason to trust reason? Testing a particular position for coherence demonstrates its level of logical consistency. Any sound worldview must contain legitimate grounds for reason and argumentation, making this question appropriate. Three arguments illustrate some extremely serious concerns:[25]

Coherence problem A: An irrational source. According to the naturalist worldview, the source or foundation of man's reasoning was not itself rational (endowed with reason), nor was it personal (self-aware, intelligent), and it was not teleological (purposive) in nature. Rather it was a nonrational and impersonal process without purpose consisting of a combination of genetic mutation, variation, and environmental factors (natural selection). Naturalism postulates that a combination of random chance and blind impersonal natural process (physical and chemical in nature) produced humanity's rational faculties.

However, presuming that this kind of nonrational, chance origin lies behind human intelligence raises legitimate questions about whether human reason can then be trusted. As a matter of epistemological protocol, if not sound logical intuition, the nonrational should not be thought to produce the rational; nor the impersonal, the personal; nor the a-teleological, the teleological.

For the nonrational to cause the rational does not comport with normal everyday experience. According to the presumptions of science, an effect requires an adequate and sufficient cause, and indeed that effect cannot be greater than the cause. But in the case of evolution, the effect of human intelligence is magnitudes or exponentially greater than its supposed cause.

Even if these nonrational factors did succeed in producing the rational faculties of human beings, how can it be known that the product of this basically nonintelligent process (the human brain and mind) can and should be trusted to deliver rational content? Therefore, when one discovers that the source of human reason is not itself rational, then a valid reason has been raised to doubt and distrust the outcome of that reason. Philosopher Paul Copan describes this epistemological crisis and self-defeating dilemma: "I am relying on the very cognitive faculties whose unreliability is the conclusion of my skeptical argument. I am assuming a trustworthy reasoning process to arrive at the conclusion that I can't trust my reasoning."[26]

This dilemma places the worldview of naturalism in an extremely difficult position. Naturalists are fond of asserting that they have embraced their worldview based upon purely rational factors, appealing to such things as logic and sound scientific understanding. They also often claim to have rejected theism because the problem of evil makes belief in God logically untenable.

But if the source of human cognitive faculties were not rational, then the naturalist doesn't necessarily have good reason to trust that he has embraced this worldview on the basis of sound rational factors. Nor is he in a position to justifiably dismiss theism based upon rational grounds. In other words, if that which produced human reasoning was not itself rational in nature, why then have any confidence in one's present ability to reason? This consideration shows naturalism to be logically self-defeating.

Coherence problem B: A necessary physical determinism. Many, if not most, naturalists embrace some form of materialism or physicalism. With limited ontological options, their purely natural worldview mandates that the physical universe (a matrix of matter, energy, time, and space) is the sole or fundamental level of reality.

However, if naturalism involves some form of materialism or physicalism as its basic ontology (basis for being), then it follows that all actions, events, and processes are the result of purely material and/or physical forces. And if humans and their thoughts, ideas, and convictions are the result of these forces, then how can naturalism avoid some form of physical determinism that undermines such things as intention, rational deliberation, logical inference, and authentic choice? How can naturalists legitimately claim that they have embraced their worldview and rejected theism based solely upon rational considerations if fundamental physical forces have determined all things including their cognitive faculties?

Rational considerations do not fit the blind, accidental operation of the physical laws of nature. They connect with intelligence, personhood, and purposefulness.

A further difficulty can be found in the amoral implications of determinism. If physical determinism is true with respect to humanity, then human actions are neither blameworthy nor praiseworthy. A person might claim: "My molecules made me do it."

Coherence problem C: Survivability doesn't guarantee objective truth. If an individual embraces naturalistic evolutionary theory, then she has to accept the idea that complex human cognitive faculties and sensory organs arose through purely accidental, blind, mindless, and purposeless processes in nature. The evolutionary process (natural selection) that is said to have taken billions of years to produce intellectual and sensory capacities in people functioned solely in light of survival value and reproductive advantage (involving such things as genetic variation and random genetic mutation).

The mechanism of evolution functioned only to enhance a particular organism's survival chances. But evolution's function and focus raise a serious challenge to the naturalist worldview. If evolution's sole activity is to promote a species' survivability, then how can people who have embraced evolutionary naturalism have confidence that their cognitive faculties provided reliable, true beliefs? In other words, if naturalism is correct, then it seems highly questionable that humans would have belief-forming faculties (mind, brain, sensory organs) that produce reliably true beliefs. Evolution's intention doesn't promote true beliefs, it promotes survival. And, yet, a sound basis for truth is necessary if a person is to embrace naturalistic evolution over other explanations.

Some naturalists have even suggested that human belief in such things as God, immortality, and objective moral values was produced in man as a means of promoting human survivability.[27] So even though these ideas (e.g., God) are actually false, they somehow supported man's ability to survive and even thrive. But this theory would mean that false beliefs may at times do more to promote human flourishing than true beliefs.

A blind source that functions on the mechanistic track of survivability alone cannot guarantee that the human cognitive system provides truth; it may even promote what is false. Survivability and truth are two very different outcomes.

Humankind's intellectual endowments also seem to range profoundly above what could be expected from mere survivability (see chapter 10). Humans are capable not only of arriving at truth seemingly useful in survival (for instance a *true* knowledge of how to grow food and make weapons to kill animals), but also of contemplating abstractions with no apparent survival benefit (for example, thinking about beauty). If this evolutionary argument against naturalism (survivability over truth) holds logical merit, then naturalists have no sound reason (or guarantee) to trust their reason in their worldview.

The coherence test asserts that to avoid being self-defeating, a worldview must provide a sufficient and meaningful basis for rationality itself. Any position that cannot justify this process cannot possibly be true but would instead be incoherent. Essential incoherence shows that a worldview must be false. Based upon the arguments just presented (among others), some philosophers (including this author) consider naturalism to be self-defeating and thus incoherent and untrue as a comprehensive system of belief.[28] Naturalism fails to pass the critical test for coherence.

2. Explanatory Power and Scope Test: How does naturalism compare with Christian theism in terms of explaining reality? If naturalism is to be accepted as an adequate worldview, then it needs to possess genuine explanatory power and scope. Table 12.1[29] provides a way of comparing the explanatory power and scope of naturalism with Christian theism. These two respective worldviews explain how twelve of the most meaningful realities observed and/or experienced in life are differentiated. The emphasis is upon how these realities are accounted for (their foundation) or how they came to be (their origin).

Naturalism has some explanatory power, especially when attempting to account for the regular processes and forces of nature. For example, methodological naturalism (the approach to science in which only natural causes and explanations are permitted) is generally viewed by the scientific community as successful in investigating the physical world. However, both metaphysical and methodological naturalism are extremely limited in the scope of their explanations.

The mistake of scientism is in thinking that science can explain everything. In reality, science alone cannot explain some of the most meaningful human realities of life (for example, values, aesthetics, and meaning).

As a world-and-life view naturalism can only offer extremely weak explanations for the meaningful and diverse realities encountered in life. This criticism may be considered unfair because from the naturalist perspective no final or ultimate explanations exist, except for the physical universe as an alleged collective and self-explanatory whole. But that point illustrates one of the gaping holes in this belief system. If the particular and contingent human

Table 12.1
Explanatory Power and Scope

Naturalist Worldview	Christian Worldview
Origin of the Universe	**Origin of the Universe**
The physical universe emerged from nothing, by no one, and without a specific plan or purpose.	The universe was created *ex nihilo* by an infinite, eternal, and tripersonal God for his own glory.
Design in the Universe	**Design in the Universe**
Order, regularity, and fine-tuning in the universe emerged coincidentally (possibly with other worlds).	Order, regularity, and fine-tuning in the universe came from God's creative plan and purpose.
First Life	**First Life**
Life somehow emerged accidentally from nonliving matter through purely natural processes.	God, who possesses life in himself (as an eternal and everlasting being), created the various life-forms.
Personhood	**Personhood**
Persons emerged from impersonal and unintelligent natural processes and forces.	As a superpersonal (Triune) being, God made human beings personal and intelligent creatures.
Minds	**Minds**
Mindless and/or nonconscious natural processes produced beings with minds that are self-conscious.	God's infinite, eternal, and self-conscious mind is the cause of the finite self-conscious minds of his creatures.
Rationality	**Rationality**
Human rational faculties and sensory organs came from a blind, nonrational survival mechanism.	Human rational faculties and sensory organs were created in the image of the all-wise God.
Morality	**Morality**
Blind, impersonal, and nonmoral natural forces stand behind purely human moral conventions.	God is a perfect moral being, and his holy character is the source and foundation of all moral goodness.
Epistemological Content	**Epistemological Content**
Information, knowledge, and truth came from a blind, impersonal, and unintelligent natural source.	Information, knowledge, and truth came from an infinitely wise and rational God who is Truth.
Aesthetics	**Aesthetics**
Beauty and elegant theories came from blind, purposeless, and valueless natural processes.	Beauty and elegant theories came directly from God's creative power and infinitely wise mind.
Human Value	**Human Value**
Humans are the product of valueless, purposeless, and accidental natural processes and forces.	Humans have inherent dignity, moral worth, and absolute rights because they bear God's image.
Human Volition	**Human Volition**
People emerged from mechanistic natural forces beyond their personal volitional control.	People were created with free agency by a God who has supreme freedom of choice and action.
Human Meaning	**Human Meaning**
While there is no ultimate meaning to human life, there may be subjective meaning in life by choice.	Human beings find their ultimate meaning, purpose, and significance in their Creator and Redeemer.

realities of life (reason, morality, values) are to have significance, then they need an ultimate source and foundation upon which their objective validity can be established. Without such a foundation, naturalism is metaphysically and ontologically challenged as a worldview.

The branches of philosophy known as epistemology (knowledge), axiology (values), and logic (rationality) all depend upon an adequate view of metaphysics (reality) and ontology (being). For this reason the best ancient Greek and Christian philosophers insisted upon "first philosophy," the study of essences (or the "whatness" of things). A necessary reality is required to make sense of reason, values, and purpose and to ground their objective basis.

Yet when the naturalist worldview must be defended in the realm of first philosophy, metaphysics, and ontology, inadequate nominalist theories are typically offered to account for such realities as abstract entities and universals. Explanations about how reason, consciousness, mind, and personhood came from an evolutionary mechanism that lacked each of these profound qualities are incoherent. Consequently, there is no reason to trust that human rational faculties are indeed presenting true beliefs about evolutionary theory.

When naturalists are confronted with the deterministic and reductionistic fallacies inherent in the ontological theories of materialism and physicalism, the common rejoinder is that naturalism doesn't necessarily entail these particular approaches. But since naturalism insists that at the fundamental level all things are physical in nature, how can naturalists escape some form of bottom-line physicalism or materialism?

When faced with the enormously probative cosmological data that the physical universe (including all matter, energy, time, and space) had a sudden and singular beginning a finite period of time ago—thus clearly implying that this present universe is not self-contained, self-explanatory, and closed—many naturalists immediately began to look to speculative theories within physics to try to retain their commitment to a purely naturalistic viewpoint. Some exotic theories arose as a result.

About a decade ago, some naturalists entertained the idea that at a very early stage leading to the big bang, a quantum fluctuation allowed something to pop into existence from absolute nothing. This speculative theory meant that something could come from nothing, without a cause, and that being could come from nonbeing (violating both scientific and philosophical maxims). This exotic physics concept, since it appeals to unobserved physical laws, however, is no longer popular among today's astrophysicists.

Probably the most appealing cosmological approach that currently attempts to salvage a purely naturalistic view of reality is known as the *multiverse* theory. This idea postulates that a near infinite number of universes may have burst into existence by a mechanism that stands behind and beyond the physics of the known universe. According to its advocates, human beings have won the cosmic lottery by emerging from purely natural processes in what may be the only particular universe that has all the narrowly drawn physical characteristics necessary to permit complex life.

This exotic theory, while having some basis in speculative (yet to be verified) mathematics, nevertheless has serious explanatory problems. First, as yet no direct empirical data supports the existence of these multiple universes or of the mechanism that supposedly brings them forth. Therefore, the multiverse principle currently can neither be verified nor falsified—a defining factor in science. Second, naturalists, usually fond of the Ockham's Razor principle, may appropriately want to consider whether this exotic theory, in effect, multiplies entities beyond necessity or is at least ad hoc in nature.

Third, presuming that this multiverse actually exists may amount to a type of infinite regression fallacy. In other words, how did the multiverse begin and what is its source? (Some conceive of the multiverse as an infinite or eternal mechanism, which invites the question of whether the multiverse theory actually defies the traditional definition of naturalism.) Fourth, are naturalists willing to bet their destiny on an unseen and unverified speculative theory when they chastise Christians for considering such things as Pascal's Wager?[30] Fifth, multiverse sounds like it is virtually metaphysical (beyond the physical) in nature. So can this theory be purely naturalistic when it utilizes a mechanism that exists outside the physical realm?

Historic Christian philosophers and theologians think that the explanatory power and scope of naturalism is woefully inadequate. Many Christians highly trained in the natural sciences think that naturalism, physicalism, and scientism have failed to provide an adequate explanation for the meaningful realities evident in the universe. They argue on scientific, mathematical, logical, and philosophical grounds that a metaphysical explanation that includes the supernatural proves to be a more adequate explanatory theory, both in power and scope.

3. Existential Test: Does naturalism adequately address the internal needs of humanity? Human beings have an intrinsic need to make moral sense of the universe. To do so requires an objective basis for moral values because a relativistic approach to ethics is incoherent, unworkable, and subjective. Therefore naturalism cannot serve as a prescriptive basis for individual or social morality. Furthermore, people need to know that as human beings they have special value, they possess genuine moral obligations, and they will be held accountable for their moral actions.[31]

Yet naturalism, a worldview that considers ethics to be merely invented by human beings with no ultimate standard of goodness, is not able to justify the basis for objective moral values. Because of the belief that humans merely evolved as animals that came from impersonal, unguided, valueless processes, naturalism has no basis for affirming that people have authentic inherent dignity and moral worth. Neither can this theory meet the human need to live with a certain moral accountability because there is no ultimate judgment. At death humans simply drift into extinction.

Plato explains that without an afterlife there can be no ultimate justice. Thus Adolf Hitler, who committed suicide, can never be held accountable for the incredible suffering he inflicted upon millions of people. A purely naturalistic worldview leaves humankind's moral needs unfulfilled.

Human beings also need to discover authentic meaning, purpose, and significance in their lives. Without a sound and enduring reason to live, people often succumb to a sense of despair. Humans need purpose and hope as much as they need food, shelter, and clothing—maybe even more. And that significance must include genuine meaning to life, not just a subjective and arbitrary purpose.

Yet again, naturalism as a worldview seems unable to offer the kind of meaning, purpose, and hope that humans require and yearn to experience. Instead, the ultimate fate of the individual, humanity, and even the universe will inevitably be the same regardless of what any person may do.[32] Nothing that anyone thinks, says, or does will change the fact that each individual person, all of humankind collectively, and the universe itself (due to entropy) will someday be utterly extinct, lifeless, and cold. The outcome of naturalism is an inevitable hopelessness.

Test Scores

As a secular worldview, naturalism scores well on three of the comprehensive tests. It receives high marks in: (1) its basic simplicity (one half of the balance test), its ability to explain many of the empirical aspects of the cosmos (part of the correspondence test), and (3) its practical, this-world focus (the pragmatic test).

However, naturalism scores exceedingly poor on two critically important tests and outright flunks the third, which is the foundational worldview examination. (1) Naturalism is very limited in its ability to explain or account for reality, especially in its range of explanation (the explanatory power and scope test). (2) It miserably fails to provide people with an enduring meaning and purpose in life (the existential test). (3) Naturalism appears to be self-defeating because it cannot provide a sufficient and meaningful basis for rationality and thus fails to justify the rational enterprise (the coherence test). Because coherence is a necessary condition for truth, naturalism as a worldview must be false as it proves itself incoherent.

But how might yet another skeptical worldview fare when put to the test? Postmodernism, quite popular on many college and university campuses, is evaluated in the next chapter.

Discussion Questions

1. How would you define the worldview of naturalism? What necessary components distinctly reflect the naturalist viewpoint?
2. Why does naturalism have great difficulty in providing a basis for human rationality? Explain the argument against naturalism from reason and rationality.
3. How does naturalism compare with Christian theism in terms of explaining reality?
4. What is the multiverse theory? What are its weaknesses as an ultimate cosmological theory?
5. In what specific ways does naturalism fail to account for and address the internal needs of humanity?

For Further Study

Beckwith, Francis J., William Lane Craig, and J. P. Moreland, eds. *To Everyone an Answer: A Case for the Christian Worldview: Essays in Honor of Norman L. Geisler*. Downers Grove, IL: InterVarsity, 2004.

Craig, William Lane, and J. P. Moreland, eds. *Naturalism: A Critical Analysis*. London: Routledge, 2002.

Harris, Robert A. *The Integration of Faith and Learning: A Worldview Approach*. Eugene, OR: Cascade, 2004.

Moreland, J. P., and William Lane Craig. *Philosophical Foundations for a Christian Worldview*. Downers Grove, IL: InterVarsity, 2003.

Rea, Michael C. *World without Design: The Ontological Consequences of Naturalism*. New York: Oxford University Press, 2002.

Reppert, Victor. *C. S. Lewis's Dangerous Idea: A Philosophical Defense of Lewis's Argument from Reason*. Downers Grove, IL: InterVarsity, 2003.

13

POSTMODERNISM

A SKEPTICAL WORLDVIEW PERSPECTIVE

Enlightenment thinkers believe we can know everything, and radical postmodernists believe we can know nothing.

Edward O. Wilson, *Consilience*

*M*y nickname as a youth was "professor." Both my father and my baseball coach insisted that I asked far too many philosophical questions. Strangely enough, as a kid, funerals fascinated me far more than weddings. I actually enjoyed going with my father to Forest Lawn cemetery to observe the graves of family and friends. The topic of death has always gotten my attention.

But actually experiencing a catastrophic health crisis is a different story. The "big questions" of philosophy really strike home. While hospitalized I thought a lot about dying. Was death actually a wall or a door? Is it the end or the beginning? Because something transpires at death (either oblivion, reincarnation, divine judgment, or life eternal), people are forced to form beliefs about what lies ahead. Recognizing the inevitability of death has a profound way of impacting how people live their lives.

However, some people avoid thinking about death by focusing all their attention upon the things of this life. And there are certainly plenty of things in this world to divert one from concentrating on serious philosophical reflection.

219

Some people insist upon reserving judgment about the big questions. A basic skepticism pervades their thinking concerning ultimate issues. According to them, no one can truly know about such things as God, death, and immortality. My experience with encountering the prospect of death, however, underscores for me that skepticism is existentially unlivable.

An Ancient Clash over Truth

The most well-known quote in the history of Western philosophy may come from Socrates (ca. 470–399 B.C.), who said, "The unexamined life is not worth living." This philosophical dictum makes perfect sense because he believed that fixed and abiding truth was knowable by the mind of man.[1] For Socrates, objective truth could be discovered through human reason and dialogue.

Thus, to fail to pursue truth about the meaning of life and morality was to live an inauthentic and shallow human existence. Socrates considered life itself a quest for knowledge and truth about the unchanging reality and the nature of justice.

Socrates's views about truth clashed, however, with those held by a group of early Greek teachers called the Sophists.[2] These itinerant rhetoricians taught that it was impossible to know the nature of truth and thus embraced a form of skepticism. Reality was therefore only what each person perceived it to be—a type of relativism. Rather than being objective and discoverable, truth was subjective and invented according to human cultural conventions.

The Sophists emphasized that to succeed in life people should believe that which is useful and practical. For the Sophists, rhetoric—the persuasive power of language—replaced philosophical reflection and logical argumentation. Some of them even viewed life as nothing more than the pursuit of power, influence, and pleasure.

The classical debate over truth in ancient Athens isn't merely a distant controversy. It actually illuminates the clash of worldviews happening today in the twenty-first century. Philosophically speaking, as much as things change, they inevitably remain the same. The issue of truth is at the heart of the differences between the worldviews of Christian theism and secular postmodernism.

Questioning the Foundations of Truth

The term *postmodernism* refers not only to a historical era but also to a loosely connected system of beliefs much like that of the Sophists. This pattern of thought roughly constitutes a worldview, though (as demonstrated later) postmodernism by and large rejects the concept of any comprehensive belief system.[3]

An important distinction exists between embracing postmodernism as a basic philosophical (essentially worldview) system and affirming certain postmodern perspectives or beliefs.[4] This study focuses primarily on setting forth the secular worldview of postmodernism (sometimes referred to as "radical postmodernism").[5] Other works examine the question of whether the postmodern mindset from the vantage point of historic Christianity is either a plague, a welcome opportunity, or something in between.[6]

Rather than offering an exact and detailed description of postmodernism, this work presents more of a paradigm (or model) for the secular worldview. Understanding the model's distinctive features then permits testing of the postmodern position.

In an important sense, postmodernism is a reaction to modernism; and modernism in turn is a reaction to premodernism. Brief summaries of these three complex and evolving historical eras reveal critical insights into their basic worldview orientations.[7] Then, short descriptions present what historians and philosophers know as the Zeitgeist (or the "spirit of the age") for each particular time period.

Premodernism

Marking the time in history prior to the seventeenth century, premodernism includes the ancient, Medieval, Renaissance, and Reformation periods. In Western civilization, this intellectual era was roughly characterized by the belief that some type of supernatural agency (a supreme being or God) existed and transcended the physical universe. Different interpretations were given to that supernatural agency (monotheism, polytheism, etc.), though the universe was typically viewed as being independent of the human observer and thus an authentic reality (realism). This realm possessed an intelligible order and design (teleology).

The classical philosophers (especially Plato and Aristotle) generally held this overall perspective as did other pagan philosophies or religions of the time. Christendom, possibly the "grand example"[8] of the premodern era, sustained the deep conviction that an infinite, eternal, and personal God existed and had created the cosmos and human beings.

Created in God's image, human beings were thus considered distinct from nature. Building upon the ancient Hebrew Scriptures and the basic theological views of Judaism, Christendom further asserted that this Creator had revealed himself as the Redeemer of sinful humankind in and through the life, death, and resurrection of the God-man (divine Messiah) Jesus Christ.

Christian theism affirmed that objective truth existed and that when a person's beliefs corresponded with reality, he knew truth (a basic correspondence theory of truth).[9] The historic Christian conviction was that God had revealed himself both in the created order and in special supernatural redemptive events, actions, and words. This later revelation was embodied through the inspired writings of Scripture, thus presupposing that human language was a reliable means of conveying meaning, reality, and truth (a referential view of language).[10]

Furthermore, Christianity viewed history as moving in a linear direction: beginning in creation, finding its fulfillment in redemption, and moving toward an apocalyptic end. Christians discovered truth, meaning, purpose, and value uniquely in their God and through what he revealed.[11] This worldview was drawn from Scripture and theologically formulated and articulated through the writings of such influential thinkers as Athanasius, Augustine, Thomas Aquinas, Martin Luther, John Calvin, and John Wesley, to name a select few.

Modernism

The period from the Enlightenment (seventeenth and eighteenth centuries) through the end of the Cold War (late twentieth century) is known as modernism. With the coming of the Enlightenment—sometimes referred to as the "Age of Reason"—modernity began to take shape. The Enlightenment age was extremely skeptical of religious or church authority and doctrine (considered mere dogma). The movers and shakers of this largely but not exclusively secular movement (Descartes, Hume, Kant, Voltaire, Rousseau) emphasized the rationality, goodness, and potential of man.

To those with a so-called "enlightened rational mind" the church, the Bible, and institutionalized religion largely represented superstition. Thus, the Enlightenment (often viewed as the "beachhead of modernism"[12]) sought to build a philosophy of life and a civilization upon rational reflection and empirical investigation. The deliverances of the emerging modern scientific enterprise (fueled by men like Bacon and Newton) gradually eclipsed ecclesiastical authority. The Enlightenment emphasized that human beings could grasp the objective truth about reality through reason alone, and that concept laid the epistemological foundation for the modern era.

With the emergence and large-scale acceptance of Darwin's theory of evolution in the mid-nineteenth and early twentieth centuries, modernism saw increasing acceptance of the naturalist worldview with its emphasis upon scientism and secular humanism. Modernity has been characterized as the era claiming "certainty of knowledge" and "grand explanatory theories."

Over roughly four centuries modernism's large-scale systems and dogmatic philosophies have included Enlightenment rationalism, Romanticism, logical positivism, totalitarianism (including Marxist-Leninism and National Socialism), and atheistic existentialism. All of these systems, however, increasingly sought to discover truth, meaning, purpose, and value for human beings without any reference to God.[13]

Modernism by and large retained the premodern ideas that the universe is real and intelligible, that language is a basically reliable tool for communicating truth and reality, and the epistemological principle that truth is found when one's ideas, beliefs, and statements correspond to reality.[14] However, as it evolved, modernism clearly jettisoned such concepts as God, the transcendental realm, revelation, and the miraculous.

The major positions reflective of premodernism and modernism are still well represented in the world today. This current age (which may be defined as pluralistic) includes premodern, modern, and postmodern viewpoints. In fact, in some quarters of Western society, modernism still holds significant sway.

Postmodernism

Premodernism and modernism set the stage for understanding postmodernism. Beginning near the end of the Cold War, the postmodern era can be understood as both a reaction to and a logical extension of modernism.[15] Some have even suggested that this period might best be called "ultramodernism"[16] because it reflects the next stage or disintegration of modernism.

The transitions made by the three eras of thought in their views of such critical realities as truth, meaning, purpose, and values have been of crucial significance. While premodernism (particularly Christendom) grounded the universal nature of these ideals in their Creator and Redeemer God, modernism ultimately sought to evict God from them. This viewpoint insisted that all universal realities could be grounded elsewhere—in man, nature, or science.

However, secular postmodernism, while agreeing with modernism's rejection of God, nevertheless rejected its bold and optimistic claims to certainty and to human potential and advancement. In effect, postmodernism (in light of two catastrophic world wars and the prolonged tensions of the Cold War) proclaims that an objective foundation for truth, meaning, purpose, and values simply does not exist. Its proponents assert that there is no way of knowing ultimate reality and therefore no way of judging which view best corresponds to reality.

Postmodernism, then, is characterized by (1) a deep suspicion and ultimate rejection of large-scale explanatory systems, and (2) a profound sense of relativism, subjectivism, and pluralism. These features extend to such areas as truth, knowledge, morality, and language.[17]

Three Eras' Perspectives

A brief summary statement for each era's position[18] makes them easy to remember.

Premodernism: The objective foundation for truth, meaning, purpose, and value *is found in God*.

Modernism: The objective foundation for truth, meaning, purpose, and value *is found in man, nature, or science*.

Postmodernism: The objective foundation for truth, meaning, purpose, and value *does not exist*.

Postmodernism's Distinctive Features

Four important characteristics help define the secular postmodern worldview:[19]

1. Suspicion and Rejection of Metanarratives

Postmodernism tends to reject all grand narratives (stories) or explanatory systems (ideologies) as failed experiments of the modern age. Leading postmodernist thinker Jean-François Lyotard even sees the emergence of postmodernism as a direct reaction to the concept of a metanarrative.[20] Christian author Stanley J. Grenz explains this reaction:

> The postmodern outlook entails the end of the appeal to any central legitimizing myth whatsoever. Not only have all the reigning master narratives lost their credibility, but the idea of a grand narrative is itself no longer credible. We have not only become aware of a plurality of conflicting legitimating stories but have moved into the age of the demise of the metanarrative. . . . The demise of the grand narrative means that we no longer search for the one system of myths that can unite human beings into one people or the globe into one "world." Although they have divested themselves of any metanarrative, postmoderns are still left with local narratives.[21]

Postmodernist philosophers consider comprehensive systems that attempt to account for all reality (like a worldview) as masks for social and political power structures that tend to oppress and exploit the marginalized of society. In the eyes of postmodernists, large-scale appeals to ultimate truth and reality are never really based upon reason per se (that is, pure, neutral, or unbiased reason), but rather tend to serve someone's agenda. Postmodernists would undoubtedly be suspicious of this book because it attempts to explain and advocate the historic Christian world-and-life view as the most objective, rational, and explanatory system available.

2. No Absolute or Objective ("God's-Eye" View of) Truth

To the postmodern way of thinking, the reason metanarratives must be rejected is simply because absolute, objective, and universal truth does not exist. There is categorically no independent divine (transcendent) perspective available. Truth is solely a matter of context or perspective that is invented or socially constructed (known as perspectivalism).

The best that people and communities can do is to construct and tell stories (micro- or local narratives) about their views of truth, reality, and values. But no single idea can actually be correct or true. Grenz summarizes this position:

The postmodern understanding of knowledge, therefore, is built on two foundational assumptions: (1) postmoderns view all explanations of reality as constructions that are useful but not objectively true, and (2) postmoderns deny that we have the ability to step outside our constructions of reality.[22]

Postmodernists therefore reject the correspondence view of truth essentially affirmed by both premodernism and modernism. In its place they affirm a type of neopragmatism asserting that what a person or group finds helpful, useful, or beneficial to believe is therefore true for them. It is therefore easy to see why relativism, multiculturalism, and pluralism have flourished during the age of postmodernism's popularity.

3. Language Considered Arbitrary and Incapable of Communicating Clear, Objective, and Ultimate Meaning

Postmodernists consider language as being capricious and whimsical (obeying no overarching linguistic laws or rules). It therefore makes an unstable vehicle for conveying meaning and knowledge. There can be no one-to-one correspondence between words and the meanings they intend to convey.

Language cannot and does not reliably convey truth, but rather uniquely shapes human thought and actually creates truth. Postmodernists believe that people and cultures engage in "language games," meaning that they subjectively define their own perspectives of truth that may, and in fact do, conflict with the views of other people and communities. This belief system is the inevitable result of a naturalist metaphysical perspective. Subjectivism and relativism abound without an objective foundation. By rejecting both the unified nature of truth and knowledge and the basic *referential* nature of language (its function of referring to actual realities), postmodernism departs from the two preceding eras.

4. Textual Deconstruction

Postmodernism's approach to literary criticism aptly illustrates its highly skeptical view concerning the nature and function of language. A number of this position's leading thinkers are known more for their work in literary criticism than for their general philosophical achievements. According to the theory of deconstructionism ("taking it apart"), no text (whether historical, religious, or literary) can unambiguously communicate truth, meaning, and reality.

Meaning cannot be found intrinsically in the text itself but materializes as the reader interacts and dialogues with the text. Christian textual scholars D. A. Carson and Douglas J. Moo elaborate:

Deconstructionists are no less text-centered, but they add to the brew a radical skepticism. Convinced that no text is stable or coherent, deconstructionists argue that all texts are indeterminate in meaning and inevitably contain inherent contradictions. That leaves the thoughtful reader with only two alternatives: abandon any search for meaning in texts, which is tantamount to abandoning reading itself, or find meaning in the interplay between the reader and contradictory (though frequently evocative) ideas sparked by the text. . . . Deconstruction locates more and more of the "meaning," not in the text itself, but in the readers, or in the readers' interaction with the text, and thus in some gray space between text and reader.[23]

According to deconstructionism, texts possess no inherent authority or objectivity in communicating the author's original intent, thus leaving no possibility for a single correct reading of a particular text. In fact, as many valid interpretations may exist as there are readers. An author's intentions certainly do not control the meaning of a given text, and some would even assert that the intentions of the author are irrelevant considerations in interpreting (or deconstructing) a text. As Chris Rohmann notes, "To the deconstructionist, language, truth, and meaning are elusive, equivocal, and relative."[24]

Postmodernism is characterized by an utter skepticism about the nature of reality and truth. So-called "truth" can only be subjective, relativistic, pluralistic, and socially constructed. Language is incapable of conveying objective meaning, and grand (worldview) theories are considered pure power plays. Postmodernism rejects objective meaning and the correspondence theory of truth in place of pure subjectivism and pragmatism.

There appears to be an amazing parallel between contemporary postmodernism and the Sophists of ancient Athens. Table 14.1 presents two distinct and competing views of the all-important question of truth. This debate over the nature of truth began in the ancient world and continues today.

Table 14.1
Two Competing Views of Truth

For Socrates (and Christian Theists)	For Sophists (and Postmodernists)
Truth is:	*Truth is:*
Objective	Subjective
Absolute	Relative
Knowable	Unknowable
Discovered	Invented
Correspondent to reality	What is useful and workable
The proper object of life's pursuit	Less important than power

Postmodernism's Prominent Representatives

German thinkers Friedrich Nietzsche (1844–1900) and Martin Heidegger (1889–1976) are influential philosophers who may be identified as forerunners of postmodernism. While both had close ties to the atheistic existentialism movement, Nietzsche's broadly relativistic ideas and his concept of the "will to power" are clearly detected in postmodernism. Heidegger's ideas influenced the hermeneutics of deconstructionism.

French philosopher Jacques Derrida (1930–2004) helped develop postmodernism through his strong denials of ultimate metaphysical certainty and his development of the critical literary theory of deconstructionism. Other influential secular postmodern thinkers include Michel Foucault (1926–1984), Jean Baudrillard (1929–2007), and Jean-François Lyotard (1924–1998). American philosopher Richard Rorty's ideas concerning the nature of truth (pragmatism over correspondence) have significantly influenced postmodern considerations relating to epistemology.[25]

Putting Postmodernism to the Test

As with any worldview, postmodernism's distinctive characteristics can be defined and tested. Exploring some of this position's strong points leads into a detailed examination of some of its more troubling aspects.

Positive Elements

Postmodernism's strengths lie in its insightful criticisms of the excesses of modernity.[26] At least three important worldview-oriented features are worth considering:

First, in addressing the state and needs of human beings in society, postmodernism appropriately recognizes that the ideologies characteristic of modernism have often oppressed and marginalized those outside its ranks. This truth was horrifically underscored by the totalitarian ideologies of the twentieth century that oppressed, terrorized, and engaged in systematic mass murder of those people groups deemed inferior, unwanted, or politically dissident.

In this way postmodernism agrees with the values of the historic Christian worldview. The care for and assistance of people who are disenfranchised by the political kingdoms of this earth (the poor, weak, and disadvantaged) should be encouraged. And Christians should take note that they are not immune to treating non-Christians less than civilly when Christian ranks are in the political or social ascendancy.

Second, postmodernists are right to point out that in spite of modernism's optimistic view of human beings and their advancement—people individually and humanity corporately suffer from corruptions, imperfections, limitations, biases, prejudices, and power trips. The Christian worldview asserts that the most experientially verified truth-claim of the Bible is that human beings are sinners. The Age of Enlightenment was dead wrong about granting man an essential goodness. A realistic anthropology should remain skeptical of man's inherent virtue.

Third, postmodernism is justified in being skeptical of the exalted knowledge-claims made by advocates of modernism. Human beings often face limitations when it comes to knowledge. They are seldom in a position of possessing certainty.

However, the Christian worldview is also critical of postmodernism's excessive skepticism. Knowing something on the basis of probability or plausibility does not rule out real knowledge. Human knowledge can be limited yet also objective in nature. Modernism's knowledge-claims were too exalted, but postmodernism's knowledge-claims are far too dismissive.[27]

While postmodernism has some attractive features, the problems with this worldview perspective need to be identified and carefully scrutinized.

Negative Elements

Severe weaknesses also present themselves in the postmodern system of thought. The all-important question of coherence makes a good place to start this examination.

1. Coherence Test: Does postmodernism pass the test of reason? Many of this position's central claims involve inherent contradictions. The following examples should be considered:

Coherence problem A: Rejection of all metanarratives (grand stories, systematic explanations of reality, worldviews). This bold rejection of all metanarratives actually becomes a metanarrative itself. It's as if postmodernism claims to be the grand story that dismisses all grand stories, or the particular worldview that rejects the very concept of worldviews.[28]

When postmodernism attempts to eliminate ultimate claims to reality, it actually asserts an ultimate declaration. Applied back to itself, that assertion violates its own claim and thus renders this position self-referentially absurd.

Coherence problem B: Denial of reality backfires. Another of postmodernism's bold declarations is that no one has access to the ultimate nature of reality, yet this claim too is peculiar for it conceals for itself the very thing it attempts to deny for all others. In other words, to assert that no one has access to the ultimate nature of reality requires that very access. Only knowing about ultimate reality can reveal the position that access to it is denied. This postmodern claim logically backfires. It cannot meet its own standard.

Coherence problem C: Perspectivalism is self-defeating. A third postmodernist position is essentially that all truth-claims are merely a matter of perspective (they reflect a particular biased view of either an individual person or group). However, to assert that everything is a matter of perspective is to claim a universal perspective that categorizes all other perspectives.

Postmodernism's claim of perspectivalism is self-defeating. First, if the declaration "all is a matter of perspective" is just one more biased perspective, then it has no objective authority and can't serve as a proper classification. On the other hand, if this assertion that "all is a matter of perspective" reflects a universal perspective that stands above all other perspectives, then this postmodern perspectival claim is false.[29] Either way this view so central to postmodernism is logically contradictory.

These three examples not only illustrate that postmodernism's central claims are self-refuting, but they also reveal a problem about the nature of denying critical realities such as truth, reality, and objectivity. Their denial must start with their affirmation. As Christian philosopher Paul Copan properly notes: "In the end, we cannot deny truth or knowledge or objectivity without affirming them by our denials."[30] Skepticism, of which postmodernism is yet another version, is self-defeating.

2. Pragmatic Test: Does postmodernism promote workable consequences? Certain elements of postmodernism seem practically unworkable, if not self-contradictory in nature. The approach to literary criticism known as deconstructionism shows this impracticality. If deconstructionism is correct in its basic claims, then the meaning of a text depends not upon the original intent of the author but rather upon the various and subjective interactions on the part of the readers. Yet when Jacques Derrida (the father of deconstructionism) set forth this intended theory in his writings, couldn't his text have been deconstructed? In fact, couldn't a text be deconstructed virtually *ad infinitum*? And if this process went on and on, where would meaning be found?

Surely Derrida wanted his personal intention to be derived by his readers. But the linguistic relativism of postmodernism makes written communication totally arbitrary and ineffectual. Therefore postmodernists themselves have difficulty living and functioning within their self-defined relativistic system. For surely these advocates want their specific intents to be derived from their words by their readers. This exaggerated approach to language is a strong indicator of postmodernism's basic incoherence and practical unworkability as a worldview.

3. Existential Test: Does the postmodern worldview address the internal needs of humanity? Postmodernism insists that no one can have access to an ultimate foundation for such critical realities as moral values. The best individuals and communities can do is tell mininarratives (small-scale stories) that express their subjective opinions about ethics. But if relativistic morality is the only option humankind has open, as postmodernists insist, then what justification do they have in rejecting metanarratives? Furthermore, if ultimate right or wrong in a moral sense cannot be determined, then on what basis do postmodernists criticize the totalitarian regimes that oppressed and enslaved millions of people in the twentieth century? This relativistic approach to ethics suffers from logical inconsistency.

To genuinely make sense of man's moral obligation and actually have prescriptive morality, there must be an objective basis for morality. Humankind needs a fixed moral foundation in order to ground the moral sphere of life. However, postmodernism as just another skeptical variety of naturalism has no place to ground morality. By questioning and eliminating any access to an ultimate foundation for such things as truth, values, and meaning, postmodernism has, in effect, left human beings adrift in a sea of subjectivity.

4. Competition Test: Can postmodernism compete in the marketplace of ideas? If all things are a matter of mere perspective and every viewpoint involves bias and prejudice, then how can the postmodernist position rise above the others and provide a superior answer? The reality is that this worldview cannot. It has no viable and enduring answers to the great questions of life.

Postmodernism is the most recent stage in an overall bankrupt naturalistic worldview. Maybe the real reason for dismissing metanarratives is that this position has no big-picture perspective to offer humankind; instead, it offers a retreat back to skepticism, which becomes a self-perpetuating, subjective, and ultimately meaningless cycle. Can such a view last among people who cannot live without ultimate truth, meaning, purpose, and values? Postmodernism does not appear to have the proper weaponry to compete for long in the coliseum of today's worldview battleground. Only time will tell.

Test Scores

Though not logically and rationally sound, the postmodern "spirit of the age" permeates current culture in certain respects. And, it poses a greater potential threat to the veracity of the historic Christian worldview than naturalism. How can the truth-claims of Christianity be correct if truth, morality, and language are ultimately relative? If the worldview of postmodernism is correct, then Christianity is not only hopelessly deluded but is an oppressive agent on Earth.

The strengths of postmodernism lie in its valid criticisms of the exaggerated claims of modernism (of which historic Christianity, the product of the premodern era, would for the most part concur). However, the weaknesses of this skeptical perspective are truly devastating. Some of postmodernism's central features reflect convoluted reasoning and end up being self-defeating (coherence test) and practically unworkable (pragmatic test). This viewpoint also scores very poorly in terms of meeting the internal needs of human beings (existential test) and it has great difficulty in competing against alternative worldview perspectives.

Postmodernism's essential claims do not score well on the critical battery of worldview tests. Therefore, it is very difficult to consider this position a viable and logically legitimate worldview. It may be better to think of postmodernism not as a worldview but as an attempt to sidestep the wide-ranging categories that worldview thinking brings to the forefront. And yet those goals cannot be achieved.

The next chapter ventures East, exploring and evaluating the worldview of pantheistic monism.

Discussion Questions

1. How would you characterize premodernism, modernism, and postmodernism when it comes to the questions of truth, meaning, purpose, and values?
2. List and describe some of the essential claims of the system of postmodernism.
3. In what ways are the essential claims of postmodernism incoherent?
4. In what ways is postmodernism practically unlivable?
5. Why might postmodernism be considered a greater threat to Christian theism than naturalism?

For Further Study

Copan, Paul. "That's Just Your Interpretation": Responding to Skeptics Who Challenge Your Faith. Grand Rapids: Baker, 2001. Chapters 1–4.

Erickson, Millard. Truth or Consequences: The Promise and Perils of Postmodernism. Downers Grove, IL: InterVarsity, 2001.

Groothuis, Douglas. Truth Decay: Defending Christianity against the Challenges of Postmodernism. Downers Grove, IL: InterVarsity, 2000.

Honeysett, Marcus. Meltdown: Making Sense of a Culture in Crisis. Grand Rapids: Kregel, 2005.

Oden, Thomas C. After Modernity . . . What? Agenda for Theology. Grand Rapids: Zondervan, 1990.

Veith, Gene Edward, Jr. Postmodern Times: A Christian Guide to Contemporary Thought and Culture. Wheaton, IL: Crossway, 1994.

14

PANTHEISTIC MONISM

AN EASTERN MYSTICAL VIEWPOINT

If the human self is really divine—if there is no difference between God and humans—then doesn't it seem strange that so many human beings have forgotten this? How do we account for this cosmic amnesia?

Paul Copan, *"That's Just Your Interpretation"*

My studies in philosophy and religion have made me well aware that there are arguments against the historic Christian faith being true. The world's religions, for example, have very different ways of conceiving of God, human beings, and immortality.

Frankly, at times, during the more insecure moments of my illness, especially those filled with pain and exhaustion, I wondered if my deeply held religious convictions could be wrong. The reality of being a reflective person means that, at least on occasion, I must deal with intellectual doubt. Yet from a biblical perspective, doubt is not the same as unbelief. My faith is uniquely compatible with reason, and the Scriptures encourage believers to thoroughly put ideas to the test. For Christians, thinking, reasoning, and believing go together.

Nevertheless, I wondered what people with an Eastern mystical worldview thought as they faced death—anticipating successive lifetimes through reincarnation, inevitably facing a total loss of personal identity through being absorbed into an impersonal deity. How would I feel if my hope for life after death involved multiple rebirths into a world full of suffering and pain?

Religious Worldview Rivals

Many religious perspectives compete for influence and adherents in the twenty-first-century marketplace of ideas.[1] Religious pluralism certainly characterizes the age.

One philosophical and religious orientation that permeates the East and has become increasingly popular in the West during the last half century is pantheistic monism. This deeply influential belief system represents one of Christianity's greatest religious worldview rivals today. An exploration of this basic system of thought begins with a journey to the East.

The Undifferentiated One

The worldview of pantheistic monism[2] proclaims that all reality is an undifferentiated one, and that unity is God or Ultimate Reality. This Eastern ontological and metaphysical theory may be summed up in the statement: "All is God and God is All."

Everything that is real—including the universe and the souls of human beings—is one in essence with this single all-encompassing Ultimate Divine Reality. All reality is one and there are no distinctions. Everything that is not one and divine is illusory and/or deceptive in nature. This worldview represents a type of philosophical idealism that says all reality is composed of mind, idea, soul, or spirit. Sometimes this worldview is called "transcendentalism."

This brief presentation of pantheistic monism represents a generic and simplified approach to a broad philosophical perspective. The position described here represents some of the foundational ideas upon which diverse and complex Eastern religious systems ground their beliefs and practices.

A number of Eastern-based religious traditions, as well as Western cults and sects, embrace this basic viewpoint but each has its own individual orientation and special points of emphasis. Therefore this discussion supplies more of a general paradigm (model or pattern) rather than referencing any specific religious system. However, overall this study reflects in general the position of philosophical Hinduism—a religion among the oldest and most influential traditions of the Eastern philosophies.

Within the history of religion and philosophy, at least five distinct types of pantheism are represented. The model presented here most nearly represents absolute pantheism.[3]

Pantheism's Distinctive Features

To unwrap this unusual and mystical Eastern perspective, eight distinctive features of the pantheistic monistic worldview need to be examined. Understanding these philosophical and religious characteristics helps in coming to grips with this world-and-life view.

1. Monism

From the Greek word *monos* meaning "one," this metaphysical and ontological viewpoint asserts that all reality is an undifferentiated one (or unity). Rejecting all types of dualism (two distinct realities) and pluralism (many distinct realities), reality is avowed to be a seamless garment without distinctions of any kind and therefore signifies a complete and total oneness. True reality has no parts, dualities, or particulars.

Ultimate Reality is viewed as neither material nor physical (like naturalistic monism) but rather purely spiritual in nature. This solely spiritual reality is also considered totally impersonal (or transpersonal—beyond personal and impersonal) and therefore nonrational and amoral. The Ultimate One is said to have no boundaries or divisions. It is the all-pervasive being.

This singular entity reflects and encompasses all of reality and is considered wholly interrelated and interpenetrating. All divisions and distinctions are viewed as being only apparent, not real, and therefore ultimately illusory.

2. Pantheism

From the Greek *pan* ("all" or "every") and *theos* ("God"), *pantheism* is the belief that "all is God." Building on the concept of monism, pantheism asserts that the unified Ultimate Reality is God.

Nothing exists that is not God, and all real things collectively (the world or universe) constitute God. All true reality is in some way identified with the divine essence; thus God is said to be in, with, and through all things. Pantheism is correctly understood to reflect the idea that "God is all and all is God." This Ultimate Reality (identified as "Brahman" in the philosophical form of Hinduism) is often considered infinite, absolute, immutable, and indivisible. Also classified as impersonal, nonrational, and amoral, this "world soul" (as described in Hinduism) is an "It" rather than a "He."

Some forms of pantheism proclaim that the physical universe only appears to be real but is in actuality an illusion. Other forms of pantheism declare that the universe somehow emanates from God or is created out of God (*ex Deo*, as opposed to the biblical doctrine of *ex nihilo*; see chapter 9). Eastern religions consider this pantheistic conception of the divine to be beyond the description of human thought and speech.

3. Man's Divine Soul

If all is one (monism) and the one is God (pantheism), then it follows that man is God. The true human "self" (identified in Hinduism as the *atman*) is identical in essence to Ultimate Reality or God. This atman is not merely related to, or part of, Brahman; rather atman *is* Brahman (the true self is God). Because human beings are part of the universe and that universe is collectively considered divine, man's essence is divine.

The soul of each human being is the cosmic or world soul. Yet while man is God, man mistakenly perceives himself as being separate and distinct from God. This grand case of mistaken identity on the part of human beings is humanity's basic predicament, and the unenlightened state is described as one of ignorance and illusion.

4. The Problem of Illusion

Eastern religion asserts that human beings suffer from a type of metaphysical amnesia—an ignorance of their divine nature. While one in essence with God or Ultimate Reality, human beings erroneously perceive themselves as separate, distinct, and particular entities. This striking error in identity results in *maya* (the Hindu term for illusion). Understood as a type of false knowledge or dream state, this condition deceives man in terms of his ultimate self-perception.

When humans make wrong or immoral choices in life and when they attach themselves to that which is ultimately unreal or insubstantial, this deception supposedly increases. The illusion about one's true identity must be overcome to, in a sense, "reunite" with Ultimate Reality. Religion scholar Winfried Corduan explains man's mission in life according to this philosophy: "The key to Vedantic thought, then, is to transcend the world of experience, which is only maya, and to uncover one's identity as the atman-Brahman."[4] But to do this, man must be awakened or enlightened from his state of meta-physical forgetfulness.

5. The Law of Karma

The word *karma* literally means doing, deeds, action, or work. The law of karma refers to a cosmic principle of justice. Eastern philosophies affirm a universal moral law of cause and effect that is operative in the universe. Human actions have direct consequences, and a person thus reaps what she sows. The effects of a person's actions, both good and bad, follow a person from one lifetime to the next. In fact, past-life decisions and actions impact present-life circumstances. World religions scholar John B. Noss explains:

> One's future existence is determined by the Law of Karma . . . the law that one's thoughts, words, and deeds have an ethical consequence fixing one's lot in future existences. Looked at retrospectively, Karma is the cause of what is happening in one's life now.[5]

This principle may be thought of as a cosmic form of the expression "what goes around comes around."

Being ignorant of their divine nature due to maya, human beings inevitably attach themselves to illusory things and artificial distinctions—thus building up a negative karmic debt that will affect them in future lifetimes. That albatross compounds their metaphysical amnesia. This principle should not be understood as constituting a sin committed against a deity and requiring divine retribution. Rather karma is the inevitable consequences of one's actions and operates somewhat like a natural law.[6]

6. Reincarnation

The word *reincarnation*, from the Latin *re* ("again") and *in carne* ("in flesh") literally means to be put back in the flesh again. This Eastern doctrine teaches that people undergo successive lives because following death, the soul of a person passes or wanders into another (and new) body. He is then reborn in the world again.

Thus human beings are born, they build up karmic debt through unjust and inauthentic behavior, then they subsequently die. Because of the debt they've incurred, people must be reborn over and over again until that karmic debt is eliminated through mystical enlightenment. This process includes an awakening to a person's inherent unity with the cosmic One and ultimately liberation from karma's oppressive hold. Actions from previous lives dictate a person's state and condition in each lifetime; thus individuals receive payment or reap what they have sown.

The more philosophical branches of Hinduism call this cycle of rebirths due to karma, *samsara* (the wheel of reincarnation). Individuals may return for an untold number of human lives and in some versions of Eastern thought, even animal lives including insects or worms. Another term frequently used for reincarnation is "transmigration."

Reincarnation is often viewed by Western advocates in a very positive light, as an opportunity for a second chance to advance and improve one's state in life. In the East, on the other hand, reincarnation is viewed in a very negative light because it involves a return to an unenlightened state of ignorance and illusion and suffering cosmic forgetfulness as to one's true and ultimate identity.

7. Mystical Enlightenment

Because man suffers in a state of amnesia with an unawakened conscious-ness (humanity's greatest predicament), he desperately needs spiritual en-lightenment or, more specifically, self-realization. Thus, human beings must transcend their attachment to the illusory world if they hope to discover their true selves—their oneness with the One Ultimate Reality. This ignorance of a person's true identity can only be overcome through the transformation or alteration of consciousness. This process involves following a mystical path (devotion, works, contemplation) that makes it "possible or necessary to achieve communion with, knowledge of, or identity with God through direct contemplation unmediated by human reason, logic, or observation."[7]

Mystical and/or occult practices and experiences are considered the door-way to spiritual awakening and enlightenment among the spiritual teachers of the East. Religious syncretism (combining elements of different religions) and pluralism (the idea of many religious paths to enlightenment) are considered viable options in an Eastern mystical context. Eastern gurus exhort people to renounce the world of attachment and to pursue discipline and mystical contemplation in order to find self-realization.

8. Liberation

In Eastern pantheism, because all is one and the one is God, man is in reality at one with the Cosmic All. Yet man's spiritual amnesia must be over-come for him to reunite with God, and mystical enlightenment makes that possible. When someone experiences release from the illusion of individual attachments and distinctions, then the wheel of reincarnation is broken and he experiences ultimate freedom and true spiritual liberation.

On the more philosophical side of Hinduism, this emancipation (*moksha*) represents the end of man's journey to be reunited with Brahman. In the pan-theistic monism worldview man's mind, consciousness, and soul are completely absorbed into the impersonal, cosmic World Soul. This loss of individual iden-tity and consciousness involved in man's final destiny stands in stark contrast to the eternal, conscious, and personal relationship with a superpersonal and perfectly moral God offered in the redemption found in Jesus Christ.

Pantheism's Prominent Representatives

The Eastern philosophy that most nearly corresponds to the pantheistic mo-nism worldview is the more philosophical branch of Hinduism, known as Ad-vaita Vedanta.[8] This type of Hinduism reflects the absolute pantheism taught in the sacred writings known as the Upanishads (considered commentaries on the Vedas). The Eastern philosopher most closely associated with this type of Hinduism is Shankara, who lived around A.D. 800.

To a large extent the belief system of pantheistic monism is reflected in the world religions of Jainism, Buddhism, and Sikhism, all considered offshoots of Hinduism. However, Buddhism has a different understanding of the nature of ultimate reality and the nature of the human self. In large measure, this overall worldview is reflected in the popular beliefs of the New Age movement.

Other Eastern cults and sects embrace a basic pantheistic monism, including Transcendental Meditation, Self-Realization Fellowship, the International Society for Krishna Consciousness (ISKCON, popularly known as Hare Krishnas), and such mind-science groups as Christian Science and Religious Science. ISKCON, however, has adopted a view of God that in some respects is more theistic in orientation (a personal human relationship with a personal God).

Putting Pantheistic Monism to the Test

Just as with the analysis of skeptical worldviews, some positive elements of the pantheistic monism worldview can be noted before moving to specific criticisms. It is worth keeping in mind that historic Christianity affirms that all people were created in God's image (Gen. 1:26–27) and that the universe bears witness to the Creator (Rom. 1:18–21). Therefore, Christians can expect that people in other religious systems will have some awareness of divine truth, though, because of sin, it will inevitably be mixed with much error.

Positive Elements

Three positive points about the pantheistic monism worldview stand out.[9] These aspects are generally consistent with how most people through the centuries have viewed the world and life, and in very broad strokes they agree with the Christian worldview.

First, pantheistic monism concurs with the intuition shared by most human beings that an Ultimate Reality exists and is spiritual in nature. Certainly the God of pantheistic monism is fundamentally different from the God of the Bible (who is superpersonal as well as perfectly rational and moral). But the conviction that an essential spiritual reality is involved in life matches the strong spiritual impulse felt by most people. The religious history of humanity reflects this awareness and deep desire.

Second, pantheistic monism affirms a holistic unity to existence. Again, the stark philosophical unity expressed in this Eastern belief system is quite contrary to the dominant religious views of the West. However, its emphasis upon a basic unified existence shows an appreciation for consistency and coherence. Nevertheless, as shall be seen, pantheistic monism founders on the issue of rational consistency.

Third, the basic principle of karma affirms a sense of justice governing the lives and actions of human beings. The principle of cosmic justice strongly resonates with all people who desire to live a reflective and good life.

While these three elements (spirituality, unity, and justice) reflect the positive aspects of the pantheist worldview, the negative aspects show that this position has no coherent or moral basis to ground, justify, and guarantee these crucial and meaningful realities about life and the world. A more detailed critical examination reveals why.[10]

Negative Elements

Though pantheistic monism offers a few positives, testing this position raises legitimate philosophical concerns.

1. Coherence Test: Are the basic beliefs of pantheistic monism logically consistent? Pantheistic monism fails the coherence test in at least two ways. First, its monistic view of atman and Brahman is incoherent. Second, its view of reincarnation is also incoherent.

Problem A: The monism/atman/Brahman incoherence. According to this form of Eastern monism, all reality is an undifferentiated one without any particular distinctions. Yet this philosophy identifies the distinct human self (atman) as being essentially one in essence with Ultimate Reality. This "distinct true self" idea logically conflicts with monism's basic assertion that there are no distinctions. In other words, the critical concepts of monism and atman in the worldview of pantheistic monism contradict each other. The concept of atman affirms what monism denies. However, the logical contradictions do not end there.

Another question is how the human self or soul can be identical to God in nature or essence yet also—at the same exact time and in the same exact way—be separated from God. How is it logically possible for the self to be simultaneously one (united) with God and also not be one (separated) with God? Moreover, how will the self or soul be reunited with God or Ultimate Reality (at liberation or moksha) when the self or soul is already (and has always been) one with God? This clearly asserts that "A" can equal "A" and also equal "non-A" (a violation of the law of noncontradiction).

An advocate of this worldview may simply insist that the self is merely deceived about its perceived separation from God, but in reality the self is always united with God. However, that response also creates logical problems because the illusion that deceives the self is a distinction that conflicts with the principle of monism, which doesn't allow for such distinctions.

The states of illusion and reality constitute two things or two concepts. In other words, separating reality from illusion violates monism's fundamental assertion that no such distinctions are possible. These problems almost make a person wonder if pantheistic monism ends up asserting that maya (illusion) is not itself maya.

Another objection offered by Eastern philosophers to these logical criticisms is to assert that logic does not apply to Ultimate Reality. However, this assertion is self-defeating, for logic is involved in the very claim that logic does not apply to reality. Furthermore, this assertion creates a distinction (logic involves necessary distinctions) that again runs contrary to monism. Without logic, the monist could not vocalize his objection (for logic makes meaningful thought, speech, and action possible), nor could he offer any reason for his position being true in the first place.

Problem B: The reincarnation/monism incoherence. The doctrine of reincarnation implies and involves many critical distinctions. It distinguishes between different selves or souls (such as Mother Teresa and Adolf Hitler), as well as separates those who have been enlightened from those who haven't. It even distinguishes between the individual self and Ultimate Reality.

However, all of these critical defining characteristics fly in the face of monism's fundamental claim. Christian philosopher Paul Copan notes: "It seems that the distinctions presupposed by the doctrine of reincarnation undermine the notion of undifferentiated oneness of Reality—and vice versa."[11] Reincarnation involves the need for many distinctions, whereas monism insists there are no distinctions at all. Therefore, reincarnation and monism, two necessary features of the pantheistic monism worldview, are logically incoherent.

Because these two principles are contradictory, they cannot both be true. But to embrace pantheistic monism, both concepts must be accepted. To do so requires adopting that which must be false.

Pantheistic monism is fraught with incoherence and absurdity.[12] Its distinctive features and doctrines (monism, atman, pantheism, reincarnation) logically conflict with each other. As a worldview, it clearly fails the necessary coherence test.

2. Explanatory Power and Scope Test: Can pantheistic monism explain personal reality? According to this worldview, Ultimate Reality is completely impersonal. God is beyond all rational and moral categories and is thus less or other than personal. In fact, at the end of the karma-samsara cycle, the soul loses its personal identity and is absorbed into the completely impersonal world soul. The analogy of this Eastern concept of moksha is one of a single drop of water being placed into the ocean where the drop of water loses all trace of its individual characteristics and becomes indistinguishable from the whole. Therefore at the end of reincarnation's journey is the loss of personal identity forever. The goal in Eastern religion, then, is to lose or extinguish personal consciousness.

Yet the supposedly impersonal nature of Ultimate Reality raises serious explanatory problems for this worldview.[13] How, for example, did personal agents such as human beings come forth from a completely impersonal source? And isn't personhood a greater state than the impersonal?

Personal agents are capable of thought, volition, and emotion, whereas an impersonal entity is not. Does this not mean that the personal state transcends the impersonal state and that human beings possess qualities or faculties that the Eastern Ultimate Reality does not? How then is the personal dimension of life explained? It appears that in pantheistic monism even personhood is chalked up to illusion and deception. But if personhood is part of the experience of maya, then *who* is actually being deceived?

The issue of an impersonal God also raises the question of how this entity can be known. For those who embrace a theistic perspective concerning God, this concern is critical. Christian philosopher Richard Purtill explains: "But the issue is a profoundly important one for our attitude to the Supreme Being, for if God is not a person, we cannot have a personal relationship with God."[14] Pantheistic monism has no rational explanation for the fundamental human condition of personal conscious experience. This position therefore lacks any significant explanatory power when it comes to one of the most meaningful realities of human life. This worldview at its fundamental level fails the explanatory power and scope test.

3. Correspondence Test: Does pantheistic monism correspond with empirical facts and match with human experiences of the world? One of the most blatant difficulties with pantheistic monism is that its description of reality is so counterintuitive to a person's everyday normal experiences. Two examples demonstrate the problems.

First, the assertion that human beings are divine and suffer from a severe case of metaphysical amnesia is completely foreign to virtually every person's normal experience and awareness. Human beings are normally painfully aware of both their finitude and their imperfections. How could such a suppressive state come about, and why would it come to dominate the conscious awareness of entities supposedly one with Ultimate Reality? Rather than classifying this condition as forgetfulness, it might more reasonably be assessed as a broad explanatory theory that borders upon a fundamental distortion of and/or departure from reality itself.

Second, the assertion that the material, physical universe is an illusion completely undercuts the correspondence test. The universe and an individual's conscious and empirical awareness of it strikes human beings as self-evidently real and true. Why would a person choose to embrace the illusionistic philosophy of monism when his reason, senses, and intuition tell him that the opposite is true?[15]

Pantheistic monism is completely out of touch with what seems to the vast majority of human beings to be the undeniably real experience of the world and the personal experiences within it. Perhaps a more rational affirmation is that pantheism is an illusionary philosophy that declares that all is an illusion.

4. Pragmatic/Existential Tests: Is reincarnation a practical, viable, livable, and hopeful belief? Westerners favorable toward reincarnation tend to view it in an optimistic light as a second chance to improve a person's lot in life. However, India's attachment to reincarnation reveals a very different story. The lower castes in that religious/cultural/ societal structure have recognized that a reincarnation-based religious philosophy is practically unworkable, oppressive, and fatalistic in nature.[16] Members of India's lower echelon are consistently marginalized in society, suffer stigma and discrimination, and feel trapped in a religious determinism beyond their ability to change. The practical fruit of reincarnation has proven quite sour in those parts of the world that take this philosophical system seriously.

Reincarnation also proves to be a convoluted moral system. It claims that people suffer because of injustices performed in their past lives. However, this claim leads to monumental intellectual and moral problems. First, it means impoverished children living in India are suffering because of their past-life injustices. But if these children are reaping justice for their previous evil actions, then why would anyone want to help them? Why give them food, shelter, and clothing if such acts interfere with the just punishment they so rightly deserve?[17]

Just as people wouldn't help a criminal escape justice, they shouldn't help guilty children who obviously committed evil in their past lives and need to work out their karma. Yet, does this reasoning seem rational and consistent with a sound moral philosophy? Drawn to its logical conclusion, the law of karma would hinder rather than encourage people's attempts to extend compassion to the less fortunate in society.

Second, suppose Reinhard Heydrich, the Nazi mastermind behind the Holocaust, were reincarnated following his death in 1942. Though Heydrich was responsible for great evil in his previous life, in his new life he'd have no knowledge or memory of what he did before and his old evil dispositions would be gone.[18] Having a fresh start, so to speak, wouldn't Heydrich be a brand new person? If so, why punish the new person for what the old one did?

Further, because Heydrich would have no memory of his past deeds of genocide against the Jews, how would he know he was being justly punished and that he needed to change his ways in order to avoid building up negative karmic debt? How could reincarnation change a person who's oblivious to his past actions?

The popular music artist and entertainer George Harrison, an advocate of Eastern mysticism, once said that he was destined to become a member of the Beatles (the world-famous music group) because of something he did in a previous life. But Harrison became the victim of a crazed fan who broke into his home in England and stabbed the ex-Beatle numerous times with a knife. Would Harrison have also said that this violent crime committed against him happened because of something evil he did in a past lifetime? In light of the law of karma, could not one reason that victims of violent crimes had obviously done something horrific in a previous life? Does this type of moral reasoning seem sound?

Third, if a person's fate in this life is sealed by her actions in a previous life, how did this process start and how does she escape a type of fatalism? Once the cards have been dealt, what is a person to do? Reincarnation does not seem like a viable and livable worldview that gives people genuine hope and purpose.

A worldview should offer individuals a viable reason to live and to die. A life filled with illusion and deception, where man's ultimate purpose is to lose his complete personal identity by becoming one with an impersonal Ultimate Reality, does not offer any sense of hope for the present or for the future. Pantheistic monism offers only an impersonal absorption. A sense of hopelessness permeates this belief system.

Test Scores

Pantheistic monism miserably flunks five of the most important worldview tests. The tests for coherence, explanatory power and scope, correspondence, pragmatism, and existentialism show that this system of belief is neither rational nor empirically based. And it is practically and existentially unlivable.

The next chapter explores and tests yet another popular and controversial religion—Islam.

Discussion Questions

1. If you were asked to give a clear and concise definition of the worldview of pantheistic monism, what would you say? What points would you emphasize?
2. How would you describe God or Ultimate Reality as presented in pantheistic monism? What specific characteristics does this God possess?
3. What is the true nature of man (or of the self) according to pantheistic monism? What is man's basic problem? What solution is offered to resolve man's predicament?
4. What specific types of contradictions are evident within the worldview of pantheistic monism? How might advocates of this worldview respond to these logical criticisms?
5. How does pantheistic monism compare to Christian theism in terms of livability and extending hope and purpose to human beings?

For Further Study

Clark, David K., and Norman L. Geisler. *Apologetics in the New Age: A Christian Critique of Pantheism*. Grand Rapids: Baker, 1990.

Copan, Paul. *"That's Just Your Interpretation": Responding to Skeptics Who Challenge Your Faith*. Grand Rapids: Baker, 2001. Chapters 5–6.

Corduan, Winfried. *Neighboring Faiths: A Christian Introduction to World Religions*. Downers Grove, IL: InterVarsity, 1998. Chapters 7–9.

Sire, James W. *The Universe Next Door: A Basic Worldview Catalog*. 3rd ed. Downers Grove, IL: InterVarsity, 1997. Chapters 7–8.

Smith, Huston. *The World's Religions: Our Great Wisdom Traditions*. Rev. ed. San Francisco: HarperSanFrancisco, 1991. Chapters 2–3.

15

ISLAM

A RADICAL MONOTHEISTIC CHALLENGE

Despite all the names of God in the Qur'an, in orthodox Islam we confront a
God who is basically unknowable. These names do not tell us anything about
what God is like but only how God has willed to act. God's actions do not
reflect God's character.

Norman Geisler and Abdul Saleeb, *Answering Islam*

*My personal relationship with God made a tremendous difference while
I was deathly sick. That intimacy was possible because God the Father
sent his only Son into the world. Jesus Christ came as God in human flesh—the
Lord, Messiah, and Savior who decisively revealed God in an up close and personal way. At Christ's incarnation, people encountered God in a tangible way in
history. The New Testament declares that to see, encounter, and know Jesus is to
see, encounter, and know God himself (John 14:7–11).*

*The words from the Gospel of John reminded me that to place my trust in Jesus
Christ was to cast my confidence in God himself (John 14:1). When I recalled
these words was about the time I learned that my health crisis stemmed from a
rare bacteria known as nocardia, which even though it wasn't cancer might still
kill me. During weeks of uncertainty, my personal Lord and Savior cared for my
every need, encouraging me through his Word, his people, and his presence.*

I wondered what it would be like for a Muslim who cannot know his God in a personal way.

Islam: The Straight Path

The fastest growing religion in the world, Islam considers itself the only straight path to God. What is Islam's relationship to Christianity? Is Islam by nature a violent religion that promotes terrorism? Understanding Islam's tenets and practices can lead to understanding the millions of people who hold this position's views.

At the center of the Islamic religion is the belief that there is one and only one God (absolute monotheism). This single, sovereign, and personal God—"Allah"—uniquely revealed his will for humankind through his prophet Muhammad (A.D. 570–632). The specific content of this divine revelation was set forth in the holy book known as the Qur'an. It calls all people, everywhere, to worship the one true God—the creator and judge of humanity considered supreme over all. People, therefore, need to submit their lives to his expressed will.

The Arabic term *Islam* incorporates the meanings of "peace" and "surrender." Ironically, these two terms are not often associated with Muslims, especially by Westerners. However, the religion of Islam teaches that human beings will only find true peace, both in this life and in the hereafter, by surrendering their wills to the will of Allah. The word *Muslim* means one who submits his life and seeks to follow the proclaimed straight path of God. Islam, like modern Judaism, is a religion that stresses what an individual practices more than what he believes (placing emphasis upon devotion over doctrine and law over theology).

Now considered the second-largest religion in the world after Christianity, Islam has approximately 1.3 billion adherents worldwide or about 20 percent of the world's population.[1] In 1900, the world's inhabitants numbered roughly 1.5 billion, of which about 33 percent (roughly 500 million) were Christians and about 12 percent (roughly 200 million) were Muslims. In 2000, world population was approximately 6 billion, about 33 percent (2 billion) Christian and about 20 percent (1.2 billion) Muslim.

In other words, Islam's "market share" grew substantially, while Christianity's has apparently not risen at all. Although large numbers of Muslims live in the Middle East, the largest populations are found on the continent of Asia. For example, the largest concentration of Muslims in any country is currently found in Indonesia.[2] The next three in order are Pakistan, Bangladesh, and India; no other countries even come close.

Muslims are also increasingly moving to the West, with their numbers rising steadily in Europe and to a lesser but consistent extent in North America.[3]

Islam is a significant and influential belief system whose collective world-and-life view continues to impact the world economically, politically, culturally, and religiously. Islamic scholar Seyyed Hossein Nasr notes: "Islam is both a religion and a civilization, a historical reality that spans over fourteen centuries of human history."[4]

The growth and influence of Islam make it historical Christianity's primary competitor in the marketplace of worldview ideas. While Islam and Christianity are both monotheistic religions, ultimately their views of God, man, and salvation differ considerably. A brief exploration of the core beliefs and practices of Islam[5] helps with evaluating its positive and negative worldview-related elements.[6]

Islam's Core Beliefs

Though Islam's religious practices are its central focus, several theological tenets must also be noted. These doctrines reflect the deepest beliefs of orthodox Muslims.

God/Allah

The heart of Islamic theology is its rigorous and uncompromising commitment to monotheism. The personal name of this singular and undivided deity is Allah, a common Arabic noun meaning "the divinity." Allah's name appears more than 2,500 times in the Qur'an.[7]

Islam affirms a strict unitarian form of monotheism that stresses the absolute indivisible unity of God (*tawhid*). Allah has no partners, equals, rivals, companions, or associates. Unlike the Triune God of Christianity, Allah is not begotten nor does he beget (therefore Allah has no son). This vigilant commitment to an absolute form of monotheism is the reason that any attempt to identify God with another being or finite creature is viewed as blasphemy or idolatry (*shirk*). To do so is regarded as one of the worst sins in Islam.

The Qur'an speaks of God in theistic terms as having sovereign control over all things. Georgetown University scholar of Islam John L. Esposito summarizes: "Muhammad declared the sole existence of Allah, the transcendent, all-powerful, and all-knowing Creator, Sustainer, Ordainer, and Judge of the universe."[8]

Some 99 different names for Allah in the Qur'an attempt to convey certain qualities—for example, he is just, compassionate, beneficent, merciful, and loving.[9] However, the God of Islam differs from the God of the Bible in three important ways. First, the revelation given Muhammad does not identify Allah's essence, character, and personhood, but rather only his divine will and commands. In fact, because Allah's revelation was mediated entirely through the angel Gabriel, even Muhammad never encountered God. As Esposito explains, "In Islam, God does not reveal Himself, for God is transcendent, but rather His will or guidance."[10]

Second, there is no allowance for any plurality within Allah's one divine nature. Third, in Islamic theology, either Allah is viewed as wholly transcendent or there is less emphasis upon God's immanence.[11] While some consider this perception a matter of theological emphasis,[12] a strong case can be made for concluding that orthodox Islam's concept of God stresses his transcendence at the expense of his immanence.

These points are discussed in more detail when Islamic theology is put to the test.

Angels and Spirits

Allah's role and action in creation are prominent features in Islamic theology. Muslims view their God as the creator of heaven and Earth (the physical universe) and of the spiritual realm as well. They claim he created an untold number of angelic beings, as well as other spiritual creatures called *jinn*.[13]

Angels play an important role in Islam because Muslims believe it was through the angel Gabriel (the same angel that spoke to the virgin Mary) that Allah revealed his will to the prophet Muhammad. Gabriel is identified as an archangel, as are other figures such as the biblical angel Michael. Angels are also involved in the judgment of human beings.

Jinn are more mysterious in nature, thought to be intelligent and powerful creatures (somewhere between angels and humans[14]). Some are benevolent and others malevolent. Islamic theologians debate whether Satan might be a jinn, as some Muslims believe Allah would not allow one of his angels to fall into such great evil.[15]

Prophets

According to Islamic theology, throughout the centuries Allah sent some 124,000 prophets[16] (*Nabi*) into the world to remind humanity of the truth of monotheism (Allah as the one true God). They also warned people to submit to God's laws in light of the impending divine judgment.

Many of the prophets mentioned specifically in the Qur'an are biblical figures including (but not limited to) Abraham, Noah, Moses, David, Solomon, Job, Joseph, and Jesus.[17] Islam views Jesus as merely a human prophet, not as the Son of God or Savior, and he is given less prominence than Muhammad. Prophets in Islam are considered holy, perhaps even faultless or sinless, individuals.

While meditating in a mountain cave on the outskirts of Mecca (Mount Hira), Muhammad is said to have received divine revelation, making him the conduit of Allah for revealing the content of the Qur'an. As a result, Muhammad became the prophet for all times and places—the final and supreme prophet (seal of the prophets).[18] He stands as the culmination of the long prophetic line, and no legitimate successor will come after him.

Muhammad's importance in Islam is not limited to his prophetic or revelatory role. For Muslims, he's also the principal moral example. Esposito says, "Muhammad serves both as God's human instrument in bearing his revelation and as the model or ideal whom all believers should emulate."[19] In a practical sense, Muslims may ask when confronted with a dilemma, "What would Muhammad do?"

Nasr explains: "The Prophet is seen by Muslims as the most perfect of all God's creatures, the perfect man par excellence . . . whom the Quran calls an excellent model."[20] Of course, it should be underscored that Islam views Muhammad as being solely a human being. But some Muslims revere Muhammad's moral example to the degree of calling him the "living Qur'an."[21] The Hadith, a commentary on the Qur'an and a practical guide to living, is said to record many actual details of Muhammad's life.

Holy Book / Qur'an

As has been mentioned, Muslims believe that Allah sent many prophets to humankind in order to convey his will. This revelation included the critical truth of monotheism, the human need to submit to God's laws, and the warning of future divine judgment. According to Islamic belief, some of those prophets were also apostles (rasul) who produced scriptural or revelational writings for their communities. These early revelatory prophets and apostles are said to have included Zoroaster (Avesta), Moses (Torah), David (Psalms), and Jesus (Gospels).[22]

Islam teaches that all these scriptural books convey the same basic message of monotheism and the need to perform good works in obedience to God. These religious communities are referred to as "People of the Book," and the Qur'an even encourages people to believe in the truth of the previous scriptural writings (Surah 4:136).

However, with the coming of the Qur'an, it became apparent that these earlier writings did indeed conflict with the revelation that came through Muhammad. Islamic theology explains these differences by saying that following the revelatory prophets' deaths, extraneous and false beliefs infiltrated the biblical texts, corrupting them. This distortion allowed heretical and false doctrines to arise within both the Jewish and Christian communities.

Esposito notes the Muslim view of the Hebrew and Christian Scriptures: "The current texts of the Torah and the New Testament are regarded as a composite of human fabrications mixed with divine revelation."[23] Muslims believe that the Bible as originally given completely agreed with Islamic theology, but Jewish and Christian corruption caused these writings to conflict with the Qur'an.

From the Islamic viewpoint, the Jewish and Christian Scriptures are incomplete and corrupted (*tahrif*). However, the Qur'an stands as the complete, final, and perfect revelation from God par excellence.[24] It has been said that "the Qur'an is the foundation of Islam."[25]

Nasr explains this holy book's prominent position: "The Quran is that central sacred presence that determines all aspects of Muslim life and the source and fountainhead of all that can be authentically called Islamic."[26]

According to Islamic theology the content that makes up the Qur'an was revealed through the angel Gabriel to Muhammad over a 23-year period. Muhammad then relayed these revelations orally ("Qur'an" means "reciting"). Later they were written down and became a single volume of sacred scripture. Tradition holds that those who served as Muhammad's scribes (*Zayd*) wrote the content on "pieces of paper, stones, palm-leaves, shoulderblades, ribs, and bits of leather."[27] Paper was undoubtedly scarce in the Arabian desert in the seventh century.

The Qur'an is approximately four-fifths the size of the New Testament. It includes 114 chapters (called *surahs*) with a total of about 6,000 verses (called *ayat*). The chapters are arranged according to length (long to short) rather than chronologically or topically. The longer ones are said to contain the later Medinan revelations, whereas the shorter chapters contain the earlier Meccan revelations, both allegedly given to Muhammad.[28]

For all Muslims, the Qur'an is the literal word of God (dictated in Arabic to Gabriel, then by Gabriel to Muhammad) and therefore eternal, absolute, and irrevocable. Allah spoke in the first person, a feature unique to this holy book. The literary form of the Qur'an reflects a type of Arabic poetry and prose. Characteristically theological and ethical in nature, each chapter except one starts with what is called the *bismillah*, which reads as follows: "In the Name of God, the Compassionate, the Merciful."[29]

Judgment

The basis of divine judgment[30] in Islam comes from the view that human beings are fully responsible for their actions, and God is all-knowing and completely just. This belief system rejects the idea of original or inherited sin and instead teaches that human beings are born good. Self-discipline and divine guidance make them capable of living lives morally acceptable to God.

Muslims do not believe, as Christians do, that sin is a state of being; rather, they insist that sin is merely the result of willful disobedience. In Islam, humans are limited, weak, and generally forgetful of spiritual realities, but they are not fallen sinners trapped in sin. Allah, though spoken of as merciful in the Qur'an, does not offer redemption to humankind, but rather fair and impartial justice.

Though claiming to be heirs of the biblical tradition, Islam is clearly not a religion of grace and redemption. Paradise is considered a just reward and hell a rightful punishment.

For Muslims, judgment day or the "day of reckoning" is a future cataclysmic event whose time is known only to Allah. According to Islam, this day will begin with the sound of a trumpet followed by a general resurrection of the dead. All people will appear before God with their actions perfectly recorded in the Book of Deeds.

It is a common belief that two angels follow each Muslim throughout life. The angel on the person's right records his good deeds, while the angel on the person's left records his bad deeds. In effect, a person's destiny rests upon the preponderance of his actions as measured upon a scale. Generally speaking, Muslims have no assurance that they will earn paradise, but this dilemma often is understood as an incentive to strive for greater submission to God's laws.

Paradise involves both spiritual and physical pleasures (often described in sensual terms for men), whereas hell consists of eternal banishment from God's presence accompanied by despair and physical punishment. While this judgment seems based solely upon a human being's actions, Muslims also believe that Allah consigns people to paradise or hell based upon his sovereign or arbitrary will.

The Five Pillars of Islam

Some Muslim scholars assert that the Qur'an stresses deeds over ideas. This emphasis upon obedience and devotion to the law of God over doctrine makes the basic religious practices engaged in by Muslims crucial in terms of this worldview's answers to the "big" questions. These essential and obligatory practices in Islam are known as The Five Pillars (*arkan*).[31] Upon these pillars "rests the whole ritual structure of the [Islamic] religion."[32]

1. Profession of Faith (Shahadah)

"There is no god but the God (Allah), and Muhammad is the messenger of God." This brief creedal statement is probably the best-known creed among all the world's religions. It is said that in the Muslim world the shahadah is usually the first words a person hears at birth and the last words heard at death. World religions scholar Huston Smith says, "The shahadah is the ultimate answer to all questions."[33] Reciting this proclamation is the way a person professes faith and becomes a Muslim.

Religious creeds usually express in a few words the very essence of a religion. The shahadah succeeds in that task for it stresses two foundational theological beliefs—"the alpha and omega of the Islamic message."[34] First, the creed affirms Islam's uncompromising commitment to absolute monotheism. Allah is considered the one and only God. Muslims understand this affirmation to exclude not only polytheistic religions, but also Christianity (Muslims misunderstand the doctrine of the Trinity as a compromise of monotheism). Second, the creed underscores the important conviction that Muhammad stands as the last and greatest of Allah's prophets or messengers to humankind.

Huston Smith explains the importance of reciting the creed: "At least once during his or her lifetime a Muslim must say that shahadah correctly, slowly, thoughtfully, aloud, with full understanding, and with heartfelt conviction."[35]

2. Prayer (Salat)

Muslims are expected to pray five times per day (canonical prayers). Prior to prayer a Muslim engages in a ceremonial cleansing whereby he washes his face, mouth, hands, and feet. While praying, he faces east toward the holy Islamic city of Mecca, where Muhammad is said to have first received the revelation from Allah.

Prayers involve bowing, prostrating, and kneeling before God. They can be done alone or in a group, at home or in a mosque (known as "the place of prostration"[36]). Recited in Arabic at dawn, midday, midafternoon, sunset, and nightfall, these prayers express gratitude to God. Considered "the most central rite of Islam," prayer gives a proper perspective on life.[37] Muslims usually gather for congregational prayer at the mosque on Friday, though that day is not considered a Sabbath.

3. Almsgiving (Zakat)

Muslims have an obligation both to assist the poor and to help in the spread of Islam's message. Adherents are expected to give one-fortieth (approximately 2.5 percent) of their net worth in assisting the less fortunate. This money is often collected at the mosque and held in a public treasury. Earlier in Islam's history, almsgiving provided a type of social welfare for poorer Muslim communities.

4. Fast of Ramadan (Sawm)

During the ninth month of the Islamic calendar—"Ramadan"—all healthy adult Muslims are expected to fast during the daylight hours. From sunrise to sunset, an individual abstains from food, drink, and sex. This fasting commemorates the "Night of Power" when the prophet Muhammad supposedly first received the revelation from Allah that eventually became the Qur'an.

Muslims view Ramadan as a time of spiritual reflection and physical discipline. Many read enough of the Qur'an each evening to finish the book by Ramadan's end. This culmination takes place with a grand celebration and feast that lasts several days and is comparable to Christmas for Christians.

5. Pilgrimage to Mecca (Hajj)

The end of Ramadan marks the beginning of the season of pilgrimage. All Muslims physically and financially capable are expected to take a trip to Mecca at least once during their lives. This seasonal pilgrimage is intended to heighten spiritual awareness and commitment to God and to reinforce the importance of human equality. The rituals involved in visiting Mecca (located in Saudi Arabia) center around the historical events of Muhammad's life that led to the founding of the Islamic community in the seventh century. Nasr remarks: "The *hajj* signifies a return both to the spatial center of the Islamic universe and to the temporal origin of the human state itself."[38]

Jihad

Some Muslims add the concept of *jihad*[39] or "holy war" to the obligatory practices found in The Five Pillars. An obviously controversial topic considering the present war against terrorism, the concept of jihad can refer to either an internal spiritual striving or exertion (against one's own evil inclinations) or to military warfare when an Islamic state is under siege or its practices and propagation are being repressed.

After the catastrophic events of September 11, 2001, many people in the Western world have seriously wondered if Islam is not largely a religion that promotes hatred and violence. However, present-day Islam is not as rigidly monolithic as it may appear at first glance. As a worldwide religion, it encompasses some diversity of thought and practice as demonstrated by three broad perspectives: (1) traditional or orthodox, (2) modernist or secularist, and (3) extremist or fundamentalist.[40]

Most Muslims embrace traditional Islam (described above). The activism and terrorism within Islam appear to be more closely associated with a variety of fundamentalist groups, the Wahhabi movement being a notable example.[41] These factions have their own religious and political agendas and use violence and terror to achieve their ends.

People who desire freedom and justice in the world certainly hope that the radical elements of Islam responsible for horrific acts of terror only represent a small minority within this large religion. Nevertheless, it would be encouraging and reassuring to see more mainstream Islamic leaders publicly condemn the acts of Osama bin Laden and al-Qaeda. If Islam hopes to be considered a genuine religion of peace and justice, then it must police its own ranks and clamp down on the Islamo-fascist types who thrive on murdering people in the name of Allah. Some experts in the history of religion think Islam may indeed need to experience a type of reformation to demonstrate just how traditional Islam differs from the radical terrorist elements.

Putting the Islamic Worldview to the Test

The basic beliefs and central practices of Islam can now be put to the test by identifying its positive and negative elements. Application of some tests from chapter 2 shows how those characteristics fare in terms of viable worldviews.

Positive Elements

In spite of the fact that some Muslims either engage in or are supportive of acts of terror, Islam contains some commendable features. Four constructive points demonstrate these positive elements.

First, Islam as a broad historical religion values human reason, argumentation, and legitimate tests for rationality (coherence). Islamic civilization experienced a powerful intellectual and cultural renaissance in the ninth and tenth centuries that for a time threatened to outpace the Christian civilization of the West. Muslim thinkers through the centuries have made significant contributions in the areas of mathematics, philosophy, and medicine.[42]

Second, Islam scores high marks in terms of the correspondence test because it affirms the real and independent existence of the physical universe (scientific realism[43]). Additionally, Muslims view Allah as the divine craftsman who stands behind the world's complexity and design. Appreciation for a theistic (even Islamic) approach to science[44] has characterized Islam for much of its history.

Third, Islam's historical background makes it possible to test (verify or falsify) at least some of its truth-claims. For example, Islam's tenets are much more open to rational evaluation than the claims of the pantheistic monism worldview.

Fourth, Islam shares some important beliefs with the historic Christian faith. Both religions believe in a single God who is the transcendent Creator of the universe. And though Islam denies the deity of Christ and his role as Savior (certainly critical truths of Christianity), Muslims do affirm that Jesus was a historical figure born of a virgin. They consider him to be a human prophet who lived a sinless life and performed miracles.

Negative Elements

Evaluating the Islamic perspective further reveals some aspects not quite so positive. Answers to the following questions reveal some troubling insights.

1. Coherence Test: Are Islam's revelatory claims concerning the Judeo-Christian Scriptures and the Qur'an logically consistent? The religion of Islam claims to be part of the biblical tradition. Muslims assert that like Jews and Christians, they are also "People of the Book." They attempt to trace their religious lineage back to the Old Testament prophet Abraham (through Ishmael instead of Isaac), thus claiming to also be "Children of Abraham" and affirming Abrahamic monotheism.

The Qur'an itself even encourages people to accept and believe the Scriptures—the Bible's Old and New Testaments—that preceded the so-called revelation given to Muhammad. Islamic truth appears tied to biblical truth, for Islam teaches that the revelation in the Qur'an via Muhammad completes the revelation that began with such prophets as Moses (Torah) and Jesus (Gospels). According to Muslim scholars, the writings of the Jewish Torah and the New Testament Gospels confirm Muhammad's unique prophetic role (Surah 7:157).

However, Islam also claims that both the Old and New Testament Scriptures are incomplete and corrupted (*tahrif*). Yet this assertion raises a very serious question about the logical consistency of the overall Islamic position concerning revelation. On one hand, Islamic theology teaches that Islam is part of and dependent upon the truth of the biblical revelation (finding justification within it and building upon it). But on the other hand, Islamic theology considers biblical revelation largely inadequate and untrustworthy. This claim is at best inconsistent and at worst logically incoherent. To further understand this vital issue requires an appreciation for how Islamic theology responds to such criticism.

Muslim apologists try to sidestep the revelatory criticisms of inconsistency and logical incoherence by arguing that what the biblical prophets originally wrote was indeed consistent with later Islamic teaching found in the Qur'an. Jews and Christians who came after the prophets' deaths corrupted the text and invented false doctrines that now conflict with what Allah's prophets always taught.

In effect, Islamic theology considers Islam as coming before Judaism and Christianity and yet also fulfilling and correcting these two religions. Esposito explains:

> Thus, Islam is not a new religion with a new Scripture. Instead of being the youngest of the major monotheistic world religions, from a Muslim viewpoint it is the oldest. Islam represents the "original" as well as the final revelation of the God of Abraham, Moses, Jesus, and Muhammad.[45]

However, the historical facts concerning the biblical texts do not support Islam's grand claim to be the first and last revelation. Judaism and Christianity both have extensive collections of biblical manuscripts that span centuries. Textual critical studies have demonstrably shown that the biblical texts, even with the problem of transmissional errors, have not been substantially corrupted through the centuries.[46] Looking backward, the biblical texts from the time of Muhammad (seventh century A.D.) are no different from the texts that appeared earlier, during the years of Christianity's greatest expansion in the first three centuries after Christ. Moreover, the manuscripts are the same at the time of Christ and even before.

Table 15.1 describes a variety of biblical manuscripts written throughout the centuries. After careful textual analysis, these documents amply illustrate that, even when accounting for copying errors, the biblical text has not been substantially corrupted as Muslim scholars claim.

Table 15.1
Key Biblical Manuscripts Copied throughout the Centuries

Title	Description
Bodmer Papyri Manuscripts ($\mathfrak{P}^{66}$, $\mathfrak{P}^{72}$, $\mathfrak{P}^{75}$)	Include parts of the New Testament (including most of the Gospels of Luke and John) and date to approximately A.D. 200.
Chester Beatty Papyri Manuscripts ($\mathfrak{P}^{45}$, $\mathfrak{P}^{46}$, $\mathfrak{P}^{47}$)	Contain almost all of the New Testament (including large portions of the four Gospels) and date to about A.D. 250.
Codex Vaticanus (B)	Comprises almost the entire Bible. It resides in the Vatican Library and dates from A.D. 325–350.
Codex Sinaiticus (א)	Includes the entire New Testament and parts of the Old Testament. Located in the British Museum, this manuscript dates from about A.D. 340.
Codex Ephraemi (C)	Contains part of the Old Testament and most of the New Testament. This manuscript resides in the French National Library and dates from about A.D. 400.
Codex Alexandrinus (A)	Comprises most of the Bible. It is located in the British Museum and dates from about A.D. 450.
Codex Bezae (D)	Written in Greek and Latin, this manuscript includes parts of the New Testament (including most of the four Gospels). It can be found in the Cambridge University Library and dates between A.D. 450–550.

This table is drawn from material in Norman L. Geisler and William E. Nix, *A General Introduction to the Bible*, rev. ed. (Chicago: Moody, 1986); Bruce M. Metzger, *The Text of the New Testament: Its Transmission, Corruption, and Restoration*, 3rd ed. (New York: Oxford University Press, 1992).

Therefore, no evidence exists to support Islam's claim that the biblical texts have been substantially corrupted. At the same time, it can be shown through the writings of the Christian church fathers that such doctrines as the Trinity and the deity of Christ (considered perversions by Muslims) actually had a very early origin in the history of Christianity and were drawn from the canonical writings produced by Jesus's apostles.[47]

Some Muslim apologists, however, argue (usually borrowing from liberal and/or radical New Testament scholarship) the untenable textual position that Jesus's apostles themselves corrupted Christ's teaching. Often the apostle Paul is accused of inventing a divine Christ and, in effect, being the second founder of Christianity.

Ironically, Islam's claim of textual corruption appears to backfire. While an examination of the biblical texts disproves the Muslim allegation of corruption over time, the same cannot be said for the Qur'an. The third orthodox caliph—Uthman (A.D. 644–656), following in the authoritative line of Muhammad—selected one version of the Qur'an and burned all the others. Common sense seems to indicate that Uthman would only burn the other texts because clear textual variations were involved. Therefore, to restore the Qur'an to the state it was in before Uthman is historically and textually impossible.

The destruction of all versions but one raises the question, "How do Muslim scholars objectively know whether Uthman picked the Qur'anic text in its purest and most authentic form?" Shi'ite Muslims protest that he eradicated the parts of the Qur'an that taught Muhammad's true successor was his relative Ali. In light of Uthman's action, the Muslim claim to have one original version[48] of the Qur'an's text can neither be historically nor textually supported. The Bible stands in a much stronger position than the Qur'an when it comes to textual authenticity.

Islam is a religion intended to restore the biblical faiths, but textual and doctrinal history with regard to the Bible shows no sign that they ever needed such restoration. The truth-claims of Islam appear to rest, at least to some degree, on the scriptural writings of Judaism and Christianity. Yet Islam simultaneously dismisses the essential truth of those two religions (sometimes declaring that the Qur'an abrogates the Bible). While Islam builds upon the borrowed theological capital of Judaism and Christianity, it nevertheless rejects the historical theological essence of the biblical religions, namely their clear redemptive focus.

But one may wonder if Christianity doesn't do to Judaism what Islam attempts to do to these biblical religions in terms of restoration. However, Christianity's relationship to Judaism is quite different. Historic Christianity accepts and embraces the complete reliability and truth of the Hebrew Scriptures. Christianity also embraces, for the most part, the central theological system of Jewish theology but insists there has been progressive revelation. In addition, the Christian faith affirms that Jesus of Nazareth was Israel's Messiah who came to fulfill the laws of Judaism, not to abolish them. In effect, Christians affirm much of the truth of Judaism, even to believe that the Hebrew Scriptures have been fulfilled by the Jewish Messiah.

Because Islam cannot prove its grand revelatory claims of corruption in the Jewish and Christian Scriptures, it seems proper to embrace the initial revelation—one with objective, historical support for its reliability: the Bible.

2. Existential Test: Do Muslims have a personal relationship with Allah?
While the Qur'an mentions many names that apparently intend to describe Allah, in reality the Qur'an does not reveal Allah's person, character, or essence. Rather the Qur'an only unfolds Allah's will and law, attempting to give human beings guidance in living a submissive life. Esposito notes: "Thus, people cannot know God directly. The Quran does not reveal God, but God's will or law for all creation."[49]

The Muslim has an unknowable God. A Muslim can know the will of Allah but cannot have a personal relationship with him. Additionally, a Muslim may know God's will but cannot know his character or essence.

So how can Muslims relate to their God if they know nothing about his person, character, and essence? The claim of Muslim scholars to see the fullness of God's face[50] in the Qur'an seems rather ironic because in reality they only experience a theological agnosticism.

The religion of Islam cannot offer a personal relationship with God. Adherents are expected to follow divine rules and devote themselves to religious practices, but an interpersonal relationship with the transcendent Allah is beyond reach. This religious scenario is quite different from the biblical concept of God—a loving, caring Father who watches over orphans and widows and desires to have an intimate, redemptive relationship with all his children.

With relationships as one of life's most meaningful experiences, the importance of a personal relationship with God cannot be overstated. In Islam, how can an individual Muslim's deepest needs be met when the creature cannot know the Creator? In a worldview context, it is difficult to see how the religion of Islam meaningfully and sufficiently addresses the internal needs of humanity.

A further point needs to be raised about the radical oneness of Allah's nature. This extreme unitarian approach to theology has inherent philosophical problems. The greatest of the Christian church fathers, Augustine[51] (A.D. 354–430), explained in his monumental work *De Trinitate* (*On the Trinity*) that only a God who has plurality within unity can adequately account for God being love and for the use of his divine mind. If God is a single solitary being, as Islamic theology describes Allah, then before creation God had no one to love and could not distinguish between the knower and the known (a requisite of self-knowledge). The Trinity doctrine, which Muslims mistakenly reject as tritheism, resolves the philosophical problems inherent in Islam's uncompromising and rigid monotheism.

3. Explanatory Power: Is Islam's optimistic view of man realistic or even in accord with Islamic history? An adequate worldview should be able to account for and explain the meaningful realities of life. One of the most important realities to make sense of is man himself. However, Islam's view of man seems unrealistic and even naïve. According to Islam, human beings are born innocent with an unequivocally good and positive nature. The worst that can be said about people is that as finite creatures they are weak, limited, susceptible to temptation, and generally forgetful of God.

In contrast to Christianity, Islam describes no catastrophic fall that resulted in original sin, which is then passed on from one generation of people to the next. Islam rejects the concept of original sin and instead views sin not as an inner destructive moral state of being, but rather as individual acts of disobedience. Because Muslims don't believe they are fallen, they don't acknowledge a need for a Savior. Individual people, Islam insists, are capable of living in obedience to God with his guidance.

Yet, does this anthropological viewpoint comport with the reality of human experience? Can one really pull oneself up to live in a way morally and ethically pleasing to God? And even if external moral behavior can be controlled, the human heart upon honest inspection often seems dominated by a radical selfishness—powerfully influenced by such dispositions as envy, greed, lust, and pride. The history of humanity—while having many intellectual, moral, and spiritual bright spots—is also filled with brutality, war, racism, and genocide. And the history of Islam, in particular, has had more than its own share of hostility and bloodshed. Humankind's profound predicament of confronting its own sin and evil is not explained by Islam's naïve optimism concerning man's allegedly basic benevolent nature.

In denying original sin, Islam embraces an unrealistic anthropology that is simply unable to explain the depths of human sin and evil, especially the evil committed by so-called devoted Muslims (for example, the al-Qaeda operatives on 9/11 who murdered almost 3,000 innocent people). The wars of the twentieth century alone illustrate that human beings are capable of incredible evil (Nazi death camps, Soviet Gulags, religion-based genocide). The problem of moral sickness runs far deeper than Islam's superficial prognosis indicates. Blaise Pascal's paradoxical diagnosis of human nature seems much more accurate. According to Pascal, man is simultaneously the "glory and refuse of the universe" (see chapter 10).[52]

Islam's high view of man also seems to run counter to its teachings about ultimate submission to God. If man's nature is good and humans are merely limited and weak, then why can't devout Muslims achieve moral perfection? And why are they so uncertain about their standing in the judgment? Given Islam's positive assessment of the human condition, one would expect Muslims to have more assurance in approaching Allah on the day of reckoning.

Explanatory power and scope are crucial to a worldview, and on this point Islam cannot seem to explain the enigma of man or why humans are the way they are.

Test Scores

The Islamic worldview is to be commended for its appreciation of reason, argumentation, scientific realism, and the testability of its historic truth-claims (scoring high on parts of the coherence, correspondence, and verification tests). However, Islam's grand revelatory claims concerning Muhammad and the Qur'an are convoluted and historically and textually unsupportable. Furthermore, Islamic theology fails to meet humankind's greatest need because the God Muslims are to submit to is unknowable (existential test). Additionally, the anthropology of Islam is unrealistic and at odds with Islamic history (explanatory power and scope test). Islam's greatest theological deficiency, however, lies in its rejection of Jesus Christ as the Incarnate Lord God and Savior.

Traditional Islam's Relationship to Historic Christianity

While Christianity and Islam are both broadly theistic religions, the two religions nevertheless clash doctrinally. Such doctrines lie at the heart of Christianity, particularly the Trinity (one God in three persons), the Incarnation (Jesus Christ as God in human flesh), the fall of humanity (original sin passed from Adam to all humankind), and the Atonement (Jesus Christ appeased God's wrath against human sin by suffering and dying on the cross). However, Islam categorically denies all four of these essential Christian doctrines.

Islamic theology rejects the Trinity doctrine as idolatrous polytheism (Surah 5:73) and denounces the teaching of the Incarnation as blasphemy (Surah 5:116) in light of Allah's absolute oneness. Muslims reject the doctrine of original sin and assert that man is merely disobedient instead of a depraved and lost sinner. In effect, the Islamic religion denies that human beings need a Savior, and Muslims do not believe that Jesus Christ even died upon the cross of Calvary (Surah 4:157–59).

The logic is clear in evaluating the possible truth of these two religions. If Islam is true, then historic Christianity is false. If Christianity is true, then orthodox Islam is false. The two religions cannot affirm one another without denying what is essential to their own faiths. The two largest monotheistic religions in the world, while sharing some common secondary beliefs, are in direct doctrinal conflict with each other when it comes to the theological essentials.

So how does the Christian theistic worldview fare overall when all nine tests are applied? The next chapter further evaluates how the Christian position stands up in the marketplace of ideas.

Discussion Questions

1. What are the core beliefs of Islam? Which of these beliefs stands as the most important?
2. Can you list and explain The Five Pillars of Islam? What does it mean when people say that Islam exalts practices over doctrines?
3. How would you respond to Islam's claim that the Bible is an incomplete and corrupt revelation?
4. Which anthropology has greater explanatory power, historic Christianity or Islam? Explain your answer.
5. How do Muslims and Christians differ in their views of Jesus Christ?

For Further Study

Corduan, Winfried. *Neighboring Faiths: A Christian Introduction to World Religions*. Downers Grove, IL: InterVarsity, 1998. Chapter 3.

Esposito, John L. *Islam: The Straight Path*. 3rd ed. New York: Oxford University Press, 1998.

Geisler, Norman L., and Abdul Saleeb. *Answering Islam: The Crescent in Light of the Cross*. 2nd ed. Grand Rapids: Baker, 2002.

Halverson, Dean, ed. *The Illustrated Guide to World Religions*. Bloomington, MN: Bethany, 2003.

Nasr, Seyyed Hossein. *Islam: Religion, History, and Civilization*. San Francisco: Harper, 2003. This volume is written by a Muslim scholar who explains and defends traditional Islam.

Pickthall, Muhammad M., trans. *The Glorious Qur'an: Text and Explanatory Translation*. 2nd ed. Elmhurst, NY: Tahrike Tarsile Qur'an, 1999.

Samples, Kenneth Richard. *Without a Doubt: Answering the 20 Toughest Faith Questions*. Grand Rapids: Baker, 2004. Chapters 5, 7, 9, 12–13.

16

TESTING THE CHRISTIAN THEISTIC WORLDVIEW

This [worldview] vision derives from Scripture, centers on the person and work of Jesus Christ, and grows rich from the contributions of ecumenical creeds, church confessions, and the thinking of such heavyweight theologians as Augustine, Aquinas, Luther, Calvin, and Barth.

Cornelius Plantinga Jr., *Engaging God's World*

*A*lone in my hospital room I thought a lot about the person of Jesus Christ—his suffering and death on the cross, his atonement for all my sins. The factual truth of his victorious bodily resurrection from the dead deeply comforted me. Even death itself could not defeat the divine Messiah—my Lord, Savior, and High Priest. The truth that Jesus Christ was even then in heaven interceding for me at the time of my greatest struggle greatly encouraged me. To know that Christ had suffered and died and that he, though God, could empathize with my suffering because he was also a man uplifted my spirit.

I also contemplated the first question and answer of the Heidelberg Catechism:

Q: *What is your only comfort in life and in death?*
A: *That I am not my own, but belong—body and soul, in life and in death—to my faithful Savior Jesus Christ.*

He has fully paid for all my sins with his precious blood, and has set me free from the tyranny of the devil. He also watches over me in such a way that not a hair can fall from my head without the will of my Father in heaven: in fact, all things must work together for my salvation.

Because I belong to him, Christ, by his Holy Spirit, assures me of eternal life and
makes me wholeheartedly willing and ready from now on to live for him.[1]

This catechism captures the ultimate existential question of life. In the end, in
what or in whom can I confidently place my trust?

By God's grace (which included the common grace of good medicine as well
as the grace extended via intercessory prayer offered on my behalf by family
and friends[2]*), and to my doctor's surprise, I fully recovered from the illness that*
threatened to take my life. It took many months of treatment, but whether I lived
or died my Christian beliefs indeed made a world of difference.

Arguably the most influential philosopher ever to live was Aurelius Augustinus. As a young adult, Augustine turned his back on his Christian roots and pursued hedonism, paganism, raw political power, and career advancement in the Roman Empire. He initially thought the religion of his youth contained logical contradictions and was anti-intellectual. To this brilliant and proud man, Christianity seemed unworthy of his deepest intellectual and spiritual commitment.

However, through a series of events, Augustine was challenged to reconsider Christianity's truth-claims. Through a lengthy process of rigorous testing, he became convinced that the historic Christian faith is true, rational, and viable. He recorded this extraordinary intellectual and spiritual journey in what may be the first autobiography in Western civilization—*Confessions.*

Upon Augustine's conversion, he subsequently became a church bishop, theologian, and philosopher—a versatile and intuitive apologist for the Christian faith. These accomplishments earned him high regard as many scholars considered Augustine the most influential Christian thinker outside the New Testament. His numerous writings further developed and defined the theological distinctives of the Christian worldview.

The same process of testing Christianity's truth-claims that persuaded Augustine persuades many people today. And, with the passage of time, the case for the Christian worldview becomes increasingly more compelling.

Historic Christianity's Worldview Test Scores

While even a brief exploration of naturalism, postmodernism, pantheistic monism, and Islam reveals some deeply troubling logical aspects, an even tougher evaluation of Christianity conveys quite a different message. Part 2 of this book explains the main features of the historic Christian worldview and discloses some aspects of their cogency and viability. But summarizing how Christian theism fares on all nine tests shows the features that distinguish this perspective from every worldview rival.

1. Coherence Test: Is a particular worldview logically consistent?

Christian theism scores well on this crucial logic test for two basic reasons. First, it provides a sufficient and meaningful basis for rationality. The historic Christian world-and-life view offers a foundation upon which reason may be properly anchored. It also supplies an adequate explanation for why reason and rationality exist in the universe at all. Christian theology teaches that a perfectly rational being, God, is the ontological ground and source of reason (see chapter 5). Therefore such conceptual realities as logic, mathematics, knowledge, and truth flow from a supremely intelligent divine mind.

These vital abstract entities uniquely characterize the universe God created *ex nihilo*. And because God made human beings in his image with rational faculties and sensory organs that generally function properly, humans are able to discover the world's basic intelligible and empirical order. God's objective existence is the fixed ontological reference point that makes authentic knowledge of the world possible.

The omniscient and wise Creator networked the intelligibility of the world with the mind of man. Evangelical theologian John Jefferson Davis explains reason's divinely intended role in the Christian world-and-life view: "Human reason, a good gift of the creator God, is to be a servant to the church in its mission of subduing the earth (Gen. 1:28) and discipling the nations (Matt. 28:19–20) to the glory of God."[3]

Second, while the great revealed truths of historic Christianity (such as the doctrines of the Trinity, the Incarnation, and the Atonement) cannot be fully comprehended or fathomed by human reason; they do not violate reason. The consensus of church history is that truth may range above reason but not against it. Thus, pure rationalism (all truth can be discovered and comprehended through reason) and irrationalism (truth is in conflict with reason) are incompatible with the Christian worldview.

Mystery always accompanies divinely revealed truths, but those truths are not formally at odds with the laws of logic, for God is the source of both. Some specific doctrines, however, face charges of alleged incoherence. These include the Trinity, the Incarnation, and God's specific relationship to evil.

The doctrine of the Trinity. Some critics declare that the doctrine of the Trinity violates the law of noncontradiction (two statements that negate or deny one another cannot both be true at the same time and in the same respect). The incoherence charge stems from the supposition that the Trinity doctrine claims both that God is one and not one and that God is three and not three. This criticism is a straw man argument or misrepresentation (see chapter 4), however, for orthodox Trinitarianism states no such thing.

Trinitarian belief insists on the necessity of distinguishing between God's essence and his subsistence. This doctrine asserts that in the way God is one (in essence or being), he is not three, and in the way God is three (in subsistence or personhood), he is not one. Logically speaking, the Trinity avoids incoherence, for God is one in a *different respect* from the way he is three, and three in a *different respect* from the way he is one. Thus the Trinity, as one What (essence) and three Whos (subsistence), is not a formal contradiction (for more on the Trinity see chapter 8).[4]

The doctrine of the Incarnation. Some skeptics argue that the Christian doctrine of the Incarnation is logically contradictory because it asserts that the finite (Christ's human nature) contains the infinite (Christ's divine nature). But the orthodox view of the Incarnation does not make this theological assertion; such a criticism is yet another straw man argument. The divine nature of Christ was not confined or limited to his human nature (the physical body of Christ). While the divine nature united with the human nature in one person, historic Christian theology insists that Christ's divinity certainly extends beyond the bounds of his humanity.[5]

The Incarnation is better understood as "God plus" (God the Son plus a human nature), rather than "God minus" (loss of deity or divine attributes) or "God limited" (the infinite limited in the finite).[6] It should be thought of as the divine Logos, a preexistent (eternal) person assuming a human nature unto himself without relinquishing his deity.

Like the Trinity, the Incarnation nevertheless remains a genuine mystery. Just how the person of Christ had a divine consciousness and a human consciousness yet remained a single person cannot be comprehended by the finite mind. Yet church history formulated the doctrine in a way that avoids a formal logical contradiction. The idea of two distinct natures united in one person is not only difficult to conceive but also truly paradoxical, yet it is not an actual logical contradiction.[7]

God is all-powerful and all-good in the midst of evil. Skeptics have long leveled charges that the Christian worldview is incoherent specifically because of the so-called problem of evil. This accusation insists that the presence of evil in the world is inconsistent with the existence and character of the all-powerful and completely good Christian God. It asserts that such a God would possess both the desire and ability to eliminate evil, thus evil could not exist.

While admitting that evil is in some respects a deep mystery, Christian philosophers and theologians through the centuries have responded with viable attempts at theodicy[8] (justifying the presence of evil in a world made by a sovereign and completely benevolent God). For example, the concept of evil necessarily presupposes an ultimate standard of goodness. By definition evil is the profound violation of the moral good. But the very existence of this standard fits the context of a theistic worldview better than it does any other metaphysical perspective.

By raising the problem of evil as an objection to the Christian view of God, the critic must account for a bigger problem——the good that makes malevolence even possible. An ultimate standard of goodness, beyond the mere conventions of man, appears inexplicable from a purely secular perspective.[9]

Christian apologists have also argued that an omnipotent and omnibenevolent God might allow evil for substantial reasons—perhaps for purposes of a greater good (human free agency, the transformation of human moral and spiritual character, God's ultimate glory, etc.). According to historic Christianity, the greatest act of evil on humanity's part (the crucifixion of God in human flesh) resulted in the greatest good for humankind (redemption; see Acts 2:22–23). Because God is sovereign, wise, and loving—he ultimately brings good out of the evil that his creatures perform (Gen. 50:20; Rom. 8:28). The historic Christian worldview proclaims that God has a morally adequate, though not yet fully revealed, reason for allowing evil (see chapter 9).

This view stands as far more coherent than naturalism, postmodernism, and pantheistic monism. Christianity provides a solid basis for human rationality, while these other positions struggle to make sense of human cognitive faculties. This historic perspective also provides the best and most plausible explanation for all the wondrous conceptual realities that a person encounters in life. In addition, while God's relationship to evil remains to be fully revealed, God promises that the day will come when he will do away with all evil, pain, and suffering on behalf of his people (Rev. 21:3–4).

2. Balance Test: Is the worldview properly balanced between simplicity and complexity?

The Christian world-and-life view strikes a better balance between metaphysical simplicity and complexity than its major rivals. Explaining the need for a simple system, philosopher William J. Wainwright said that "a system may be simpler because it employs fewer basic concepts or makes fewer basic assumptions, or because it uses fewer explanatory principles or isn't committed to as many kinds of reality."[10]

The Christian theistic vision of reality consists of a single, infinite, eternal, immutable, and tripersonal spiritual God who creates the totality of all finite things. This perspective is more metaphysically economical than the prevalent religious worldview of paganism with its accompanying polytheism and animism. And yet while Christianity's dualism (belief in two realms of reality) isn't as simple as monism (belief in one realm of reality), the monistic-oriented worldviews of naturalism and pantheism aren't really all that simple or precise.

Positing everything as nature or everything as divine involves incredibly complicated states of affairs (even evolutionary or mystical leaps in ontological categories) to account for the explanatory mechanisms that stand behind these worldview systems (see chapters 12 and 14). Therefore, even granting Christian theism's basic dualistic nature, its view of reality seems distinctly clear and uncomplicated especially when compared with worldview competitors.

Christian theism also has the necessary metaphysical complexity to account for the far-ranging phenomena found in nature and life (for example, the material and immaterial aspects of reality). In contrast, naturalism strains to account for nonempirical abstract entities such as logic, propositions, universals, mathematics, values, and so forth. Pantheism engages in philosophical gymnastics to explain away the physical universe. And the explanatory power of Christian theism over Islamic theism is evident in the Trinitarian (plurality of personhood within the one Godhead) capacity to account for God's ability to love before creation—something Islamic unitarianism cannot explain.

3. Explanatory Power and Scope Test: How well does a worldview explain the facts of reality ("power"), and how wide is the range of its explanation ("scope")?

Philosopher William Wainwright describes the importance of this test: "Metaphysical theories are better when they explain a wider range of phenomena. A system that illuminates humanity's scientific, moral, aesthetic, and religious experience, for example, is superior to one that only illuminates science."[11]

One of Christian theism's greatest worldview strengths is the scope of its explanatory power (though admittedly other theistic systems, such as Judaism, share some of this ability). The historic Christian viewpoint accounts for the vast array of realities in nature and in human experience, including:

- *the universe*—its source and singular beginning, order, regularity, and fine-tuning (see chapter 9)
- *abstract entities*—the existence and validity of mathematics, the laws of logic, and scientific models (which include their correspondence to the time-space-matter universe as conceived in the mind of human beings, see chapter 12)
- *ethics*—the existence of universal, objective, and prescriptive moral values (see chapter 11)
- *human beings*—their existence, consciousness, rationality, free agency, enigmatic nature, moral and aesthetic impulse, and their need for meaning and purpose in life (see chapter 10)

- *religious phenomena*—humankind's spiritual nature and religious experience; the miraculous events of Christianity; the unique character, claims, and credentials of Jesus Christ (see chapters 8 and 10)

The realities of the world and life match what the Bible teaches about God's creating the universe (particularly his creation of human beings in his own image and likeness; see the discussion of *imago Dei* in chapter 10). Some Christian philosophers argue that God's existence can be legitimately inferred as a necessary causal explanation.[12] However, the Christian worldview overall does not naively assume divine activity or intervention as an explanation for whatever humans cannot yet explain (god-of-the-gaps presumption), but rather offers a genuine and valid explanatory theory for the nature of life's realities. Skeptical philosophies of life such as naturalism and postmodernism have real difficulty trying to justify these wondrous truths. On this basis, Christian theism's explanatory scope appears far superior to that of secularism.

4. Correspondence Test: Does a particular worldview correspond with well-established, empirical facts, and with a person's experiences in the world?

Christian theism scores well on the basic correspondence test for several reasons. First, when the Bible discusses truth (see chapter 5) it generally incorporates a correspondence theory (truth equals that which matches reality). Therefore, according to historic Christianity, beliefs that conform to reality must be embraced. Truth cannot be separated from reality.

Second, the Christian theistic worldview affirms a type of scientific realism (believing the time-space-matter universe to be an authentic objective reality). Moreover, history proclaims Christianity's respect for the empirical facts of nature. Modern science even owes its emergence to the powerful influence of Christian theism.[13] This connection makes sense given that the God of the Bible created the world and humanity's cognitive faculties and sensory organs in such a way as to allow the inductive process to reveal genuine knowledge about the universe.

Third, in the Christian faith, unlike Eastern mystical religions, people can generally trust their experiences in life and in the world. And the encounters characteristic of human existence are consistent with, not contrary to, the faith. The Christian worldview doesn't separate faith from real-life experience.

5. Verification Test: Can the central truth-claims of the worldview be verified or falsified?

The Christian world-and-life view is one of the few perspectives that passes the verification test with flying colors. According to the New

Testament, Christianity's origins and its central truth-claims are rooted in historical fact (Luke 2:1; Matt. 26:57; Mark 15:1).[14] Therefore the truth-claims of Christianity are open to, and even invite, historical investigation. The key events of the life, death, and resurrection of Jesus Christ, the historical person, can be examined and thus are subject to verification or falsification.

There is a way, theoretically, to falsify the Christian religion. For example, if Jesus Christ's bodily resurrection from the dead could be convincingly disproved, then the Christian faith would be, for all intents and purposes, falsified. The apostle Paul asserts this possibility in his writings about the importance of Jesus's resurrection (1 Cor. 15:14).

The resurrection of Christ can also verify Christianity. Christian apologists through the centuries have appealed to six primary strands of evidence to support the historical and factual nature of the bodily resurrection of Jesus:[15]

- the empty tomb
- Christ's postcrucifixion appearances
- the transformation of the apostles
- the conversion and transformation of Saul of Tarsus to become the apostle Paul
- the emergence of the Christian church
- the day of worship shifted from the seventh to the first day of the week

The ability to objectively test a worldview's truth-claims is critically important in the overall consideration of truth. Historic Christianity invites that type of investigation and scrutiny. When the apostle Paul spoke before government officials about Christ's resurrection, he told them: "What I am saying is true and reasonable. The king is familiar with these things, and I can speak freely to him. I am convinced that none of this has escaped his notice, because it was not done in a corner" (Acts 26:25–26).

6. Pragmatic Test: Does the worldview promote relevant, practical, and workable results?

Christianity works and bears good fruit on behalf of individuals, families, cultures, and civilizations. Believing the gospel of Jesus Christ and embracing the Christian world-and-life view dramatically changes the lives of individual people for the good. The love and forgiveness of God found in knowing Jesus Christ as Savior and Lord have transformed the lives of both men and women who have suffered from the depths of human depravity. They have also changed cowards into heroes.

The Christian worldview provides the educational, economic, legal, political, moral, and spiritual framework and incentives (as well as safeguards) necessary to promote a healthy and thriving culture. It considers marriage and family (the pillars of civilization) as sacred institutions established by God (Eph. 6:1–3; Heb. 13:4). Christians are taught to respect, honor, and appropriately participate in the legal and governmental institutions ordained by God (Rom. 13:1–7). Believers in Christ thus possess a dual citizenship, as Augustine described it, in both the city of man and the city of God (see chapter 5).

And while dark periods occurred in cultures where Christian theism was the dominant worldview (for example: during the Crusades, the Inquisitions, and Catholic-Protestant wars),[16] the darkness arose from distortions of Christian doctrine, not from its rightful application. If Christianity were judged according to the moral and ethical fruit it has produced, all of the good for which it has been responsible over the past two millennia would need to be considered.

In fact, many of today's views concerning social justice find their roots and moral justification in the Judeo-Christian religious tradition.[17] For example, the belief that all human beings are endowed with inherent dignity and moral worth is grounded in the enduring biblical truth that people are created in and bear the image of God. Such moral prescriptions as "the strong should help the weak" and "the rich should help the poor" and "treat others as you would like to be treated" are grounded in the Christian moral tradition.[18]

The idea of granting each individual intrinsic worth is central to the Bible and has seldom been avowed or followed by other cultures and religious traditions. By virtue of this high value placed upon human beings, it is not surprising that religious groups have started the vast majority of the world's charitable organizations, with Christians clearly leading the way. In contrast, secular organizations and individuals have started relatively few charities.

The Christian theistic worldview was also the catalyst behind the great advancement of Western civilization. Christianity's implications led to the founding of the great European university system and the creativity that stimulated the growth of the arts. Its petrol fueled the age of exploration, ignited the flame that sparked the Reformation in theology, and kindled the growth of capitalism (an imperfect but successful economic system). In the process, Christianity's regard for creation supported the launch of science.

When embraced and lived out, the Christian worldview produces relevant, practical, and workable results for individuals, families, cultures, and civilizations.

7. Existential Test: Does the worldview address the internal needs of humanity?

One profound difference between the Christian world-and-life view and the other worldview systems evaluated in this book—especially pantheism and Islam—is that human beings can enjoy a relationship with a loving, caring, personal God who is knowable, reachable, and accepting. Christian theism offers an intimate, redemptive relationship with the God who came to Earth in the person of Jesus. The Christian God came personally in the flesh to suffer and die and rise again in order to resolve humankind's greatest predicament—he came to reconcile lost sinners separated from a holy God.

Historic Christianity's gospel message offers people genuine hope, purpose, and meaning in this life and indescribable goodness in the next. Further, the biblical view of humankind as both great and fallen possesses a stronger and more realistic accounting of the human condition than do the religious worldviews of pantheistic monism and Islamic theism or the secular naturalist position.

8. Cumulative Test: Is the worldview supported by multiple lines of converging evidence that together add increasing support for its truth-claims and extend the breadth of its explanatory power?

An array of data from various fields of inquiry illustrates the historic Christian worldview's explanatory power and makes its case for truthfulness even stronger. Table 16.1 lists a few examples that correspond with or corroborate this position:

Table 16.1
Cumulative Case for Christian Theism's Explanatory Power

Field	Data
Cosmology	The universe had a singular beginning (big bang cosmology); there was a beginning of time.
Astrophysics	Nature's laws appear fine-tuned to allow for human life (anthropic principle); so do the universe's content and systems (galaxy, stars, planets, etc.).
Biology/Chemistry	Life systems yield evidence of having been intelligently designed.
Anthropology/Psychology	Human beings are richly endowed intellectually but morally flawed.
Neuroscience	Humans possess consciousness and a capacity for intentionality and rational reflection.
Math	Mathematical theories correspond with physical reality.
Logic	As abstract entities the laws of logic are universal, invariant, and independent of human conventions.
Ethics	Moral absolutes seem intuitively authentic, and moral relativism is self-defeating.
Religion	Religion is a universal phenomenon, and religious experience seems intuitively real and consistent with biblical revelation.

Field	Data
History	Credible historical reports corroborate the life, death, and resurrection of Jesus Christ.
Philosophy	Human beings crave meaning, purpose, and immortality.

These multiple lines of converging evidence support and verify the Christian worldview's basic truth-claims.

9. Competitive Competence Test: Can the worldview successfully compete in the marketplace of ideas?

Christian theism surpasses its skeptical challengers in the intellectual coliseum. It scores high on a battery of worldview tests and therefore remains a competitive, robust, and viable position for those contemplating the question of truth. Christianity answers the crucial questions of human existence far better than its rivals. Explanatory power and scope are much broader for this worldview than for any alternative.

Its capacity to fulfill mankind's deepest existential needs makes Christianity vastly superior to its religious rivals. Because God the Son entered the time-space-matter world to suffer and die, thereby reconciling sinners to himself, God can be known personally in the Christian faith. Genuine forgiveness and enduring hope are found in the gospel—the heart of this historic world-and-life view. As summarized in the Apostles' Creed and explained in Scripture, Christian theism supplies a lens through which to view the world that is uniquely reasonable, testable, viable, workable, liveable, and highly competitive in the marketplace of ideas.

In A.D. 430, with the mighty Roman Empire beginning to crumble, Augustine succumbed to illness. He died in his midseventies while reciting the Penitential Psalms written on the ceiling above his deathbed. The Christian world-and-life view—with Jesus Christ's life, death, and resurrection at its center—had provided him a genuine reason to live and to die.

The same historic Christian worldview that sustained Augustine also sustained me during my close brush with death. That illness forced me to reevaluate my deepest beliefs and commitments. Staring death in the face in midlife is a chilling experience, but my faith in the Triune God—Father, Son, and Holy Spirit—genuinely sustained me.

The broad Christian theistic perspective that I embrace and have explained and defended in this book shows itself to be the most reasonable explanation of life and reality. "The faith that was once for all entrusted to the saints" (Jude 3) supplies a rational hope to all people wrestling with the questions of life.

Like Augustine and so many other believers before me, I can testify that the Christian world-and-life view remains viable regardless of how much pressure life applies.

Discussion Questions

1. List and explain two important strengths of the historic Christian worldview with respect to logical coherence.
2. In what ways is the explanatory scope of Christian theism superior to that of its worldview rivals?
3. Explain how the Christian worldview passes the pragmatic test.
4. In what ways does Christian theism uniquely meet humankind's greatest existential needs? What does Christianity have to offer that pantheism and Islam cannot?
5. Explain why approaching Christianity from a worldview perspective offers unique apologetic advantages.

For Further Study

Augustine. *Confessions.* Translated by R. S. Pine-Coffin. New York: Penguin, 1961.

Corduan, Winfried. *No Doubt about It: The Case for Christianity.* Nashville: Broadman & Holman, 1997.

Davis, John Jefferson. *Foundations of Evangelical Theology.* Grand Rapids: Baker, 1984.

Moreland, J. P., and William Lane Craig. *Philosophical Foundations for a Christian Worldview.* Downers Grove, IL: InterVarsity, 2003.

Nash, Ronald H. *Worldviews in Conflict: Choosing Christianity in a World of Ideas.* Grand Rapids: Zondervan, 1992.

Samples, Kenneth Richard. *Without a Doubt: Answering the 20 Toughest Faith Questions.* Grand Rapids: Baker, 2004.

APPENDIX

WORLDVIEW CHARTS

The following tables are intended as helpful models of the distinctive worldview perspectives. Though simplified for the sake of brevity and comparison, each summary addresses six fundamental components of a worldview.

A Worldview Model for Christian Theism

God	God is an infinite, eternal, immutable, morally perfect, and tripersonal spiritual being (Triune)—the transcendent Creator and sovereign Sustainer of all things.
World	The time-space-matter universe was created by God *ex nihilo* and thus has a real existence, yet is dependent upon God's providential power, control, and guidance.
Knowledge	Authentic knowledge (of God, the self, and the world) is available to man through God's general and special revelation (via the created order and redemptive actions).
Ethics	Objective, universal, unchanging, and prescriptive moral values exist (absolutes) and find their source and ground in God's perfect and immutable moral character.
Human beings	Human beings were created in the image of God (as rational, moral, and spiritual beings) but have misused their freedom in order to sin and thus need redemption in Christ.
History	The linear direction of historical events is ordained by God and unfolds according to his sovereign will (including creation, Fall, redemption, glorification, new creation).

A Worldview Model for Naturalism

God	No supernatural entities are real thus no God or gods exist (atheism) in or beyond the natural, physical, and material universe (humans invented the concept of God).
World	The time-space-matter universe is the sole reality (thus the cosmos as a closed and uniform natural system stands as complete, self-contained, and self-sufficient).
Knowledge	Science is viewed as the only reliable method (strong scientism) or the best method (weak scientism) for obtaining genuine knowledge about the cosmos.
Ethics	Moral values arose via man's evolutionary need for survival (ethics are thus subjective, invented, conventional, relative, and descriptive in nature).
Human beings	Human beings evolved from the lower primates through purely natural processes and since man has reached the highest tier on the evolutionary ladder he has value.
History	History unfolds according to purely natural processes that include materialistic forces but also human societal influences such as science and technology.

A Worldview Model for Postmodernism
(Secular)

God	No supernatural God or gods exist (atheism) and even if a deity did exist it could not be known objectively (all religions are on equal subjective ground).
World	Unlike other worldviews, this perspective is not centered upon questions of ultimate reality and being (but secular postmodernists embrace naturalism).
Knowledge	There is no objective, universal, and unbiased knowledge and truth (truth is solely a matter of context or perspective that is invented or socially constructed).
Ethics	Moral values are relative to their cultural context so moral absolutes are rejected (though pluralism, tolerance, relativism, and inclusivism are virtual absolutes).
Human beings	This perspective is suspicious of the very concept of an objective "human nature," but secular postmodernists generally embrace naturalistic evolutionary theory.
History	The concept of "historical progress" is viewed as concealing an oppressive agenda on the part the modernists who embrace a failed metanarrative encapsulating history.

A Worldview Model for Pantheistic Monism

God	All reality is an undifferentiated one (monism) and that one is God or Ultimate Reality (pantheism); this reality is beyond personal, rational, and moral categories.
World	The physical universe is either apparently real (an actual illusion) or it somehow emanates from God or is created out of God's being (*ex Deo* instead of *ex nihilo*).
Knowledge	Truth is beyond rational apprehension and description, and Western notions of knowledge, reason, and logic are illusory and interfere with mystical enlightenment.
Ethics	The law of karma is a cosmic principle of justice or a universal moral law of cause and effect that is operative in the universe (Ultimate Reality is, however, amoral).
Human beings	The true human "self" (*atman*) is identical in essence to Ultimate Reality or God (world soul); however, man mistakenly perceives himself as distinct from God.
History	Eastern philosophy and religion embrace a cyclical and mystical view of history that rejects the Western linear viewpoint with its singular beginning and climactic end.

A Worldview Model for Islamic Theism

God	God ("Allah") is a single, solitary personal divine being, the sovereign, transcendent, all-powerful, and all-knowing Creator, Sustainer, Ordainer, and Judge of all.
World	The time-space-matter universe was created by God and thus has an authentic existence, yet is dependent upon God's determined power, rule, and direction.
Knowledge	Genuine knowledge is available to humankind through both man's created faculties and through special divine revelation (especially that in the Qur'an).
Ethics	Ethics flow from God's expressed will as revealed in the Qur'an and Hadith; practical moral conduct for Muslims is connected to the practice of Sharia Law.
Human beings	God created human beings good and with free agency (but not in the divine image); humans as limited and weak creatures (but not fallen sinners) will face judgment.
History	History unfolds according to Allah's sovereign will and moves in a linear direction (passing through the stages of creation, final revelation, and judgment).

NOTES

Introduction

1. Ronald H. Nash, *Worldviews in Conflict: Choosing Christianity in a World of Ideas* (Grand Rapids: Zondervan, 1992), 18.

2. "Church Doesn't Think Like Jesus," WorldNetDaily, www.worldnetdaily.com/news/ article (accessed December 3, 2003). See also John Piper, "The Doctrine Difference," *World Magazine*, March 5, 2005, 51.

Chapter 1 Shades of Reality

1. See Norman L. Geisler and William D. Watkins, *Worlds Apart: A Handbook on World Views*, 2nd ed. (Eugene, OR: Wipf and Stock, 2003), 11–12; and Nash, *Worldviews in Conflict*, 17–18.

2. For a thorough historical and philosophical analysis of the term *Weltanschauung* (worldview), see David K. Naugle, *Worldview: The History of a Concept* (Grand Rapids: Eerdmans, 2002).

3. Ronald H. Nash, *Faith and Reason: Searching for a Rational Faith* (Grand Rapids: Zondervan, 1988), 24. My thinking about the subject of worldviews, and the Christian worldview in particular, has been especially influenced by the writings of Ronald Nash.

4. Geisler and Watkins, *Worlds Apart*, 11.

5. Michael D. Palmer, comp. and ed., *Elements of a Christian Worldview* (Springfield, MO: Logion, 1998), 24.

6. Albert M. Wolters, *Creation Regained: Biblical Basics for a Reformational Worldview* (Grand Rapids: Eerdmans, 1985), 4.

7. Brian J. Walsh and J. Richard Middleton, *The Transforming Vision: Shaping a Christian Worldview* (Downers Grove, IL: InterVarsity, 1984), 35; David S. Dockery and Gregory Alan Thornbury, eds., *Shaping a Christian Worldview: The Foundation of Christian Higher Education* (Nashville: Broadman & Holman, 2002), 3.

8. Patrick J. Hurley, *A Concise Introduction to Logic*, 8th ed. (Belmont, CA: Wadsworth, 2003), 173.

9. In terms of the orthodox Christian theistic view of God, I recommend the following two sources on the subject of philosophical theology: Ed L. Miller, *God and Reason: An Invitation to Philosophical Theology*, 2nd ed. (Upper Saddle River, NJ: Prentice Hall, 1995); Thomas V. Morris, *Our Idea of God: An Introduction to Philosophical Theology* (Downers Grove, IL: InterVarsity, 1991).

10. In terms of an orthodox Christian theistic view of metaphysics, see J. P. Moreland and William Lane Craig, *Philosophical Foundations for a Christian Worldview* (Downers Grove, IL: InterVarsity, 2003), chaps. 8–14. As an Augustinian-Reformed Christian, I disagree with the more Arminian theological views expressed by these two authors, yet the book has excellent overall content.

11. For a basic discussion of metaphysics, see Ed L. Miller, *Questions That Matter: An Invitation to Philosophy*, 4th ed. (New York: McGraw-Hill, 1996), chaps. 3–7.

12. In terms of an orthodox Christian theistic view of epistemology, see Moreland and Craig, *Philosophical Foundations for a Christian Worldview*, chaps. 3–7.

13. For a basic discussion of epistemology, see Miller, *Questions That Matter*, chaps. 8–11.

14. For a basic discussion of axiology, see Miller, *Questions That Matter*, 6.

15. In terms of an orthodox Christian theistic view of ethics, see Moreland and Craig, *Philosophical Foundations for a Christian Worldview*, chaps. 19–22.

16. For a discussion of the problem of evil, see Kenneth Richard Samples, "How Can a Good and All-Powerful God Allow Evil?" in *Without a Doubt: Answering the 20 Toughest Faith Questions* (Grand Rapids: Baker, 2004), 239–54.

17. For an evangelical assessment of various views about the meaning of history, see Ronald H. Nash, *The Meaning of History* (Nashville: Broadman & Holman, 1998).

18. To educate oneself in the field of Christian eschatology, I recommend the following sources: for a premillennial perspective, see George Eldon Ladd, *The Last Things: An Eschatology for Laymen* (Grand Rapids: Eerdmans, 1978); for an amillennial perspective, see Anthony A. Hoekema, *The Bible and the Future* (Grand Rapids: Eerdmans, 1979); and for a postmillennial perspective, see John Jefferson Davis, *Christ's Victorious Kingdom: Postmillennialism Reconsidered* (Grand Rapids: Baker, 1986).

Chapter 2 Testable Truth

1. The following sources influenced my development of these nine worldview tests: William J. Wainwright, *Philosophy of Religion* (Belmont, CA: Wadsworth, 1988), 171–75; Robert A. Harris, *The Integration of Faith and Learning: A Worldview Approach* (Eugene, OR: Cascade, 2004), 187–206; James W. Sire, *The Universe Next Door: A Basic Worldview Catalog*, 3rd ed. (Downers Grove, IL: InterVarsity, 1997), 195–98; Winfried Corduan, *No Doubt about It: The Case for Christianity* (Nashville: Broadman & Holman, 1997), 74–77; Nash, *Worldviews*

in Conflict, 54–63; L. Russ Bush, *A Handbook for Christian Philosophy* (Grand Rapids: Zondervan, 1991), 81–91; and A. J. Hoover, *The Case for Christian Theism: An Introduction to Apologetics* (Grand Rapids: Baker, 1976), 41–53.

2. Hoover, *Case for Christian Theism*, 49.

3. Bush, *Handbook for Christian Philosophy*, 85.

4. Hoover, *Case for Christian Theism*, 51.

5. William of Ockham (ca. 1285–1349), a Franciscan monk and philosopher, is remembered for his principle of parsimony or simplicity, popularly called "Ockham's Razor." For a detailed discussion of William of Ockham's philosophical and theological views, see Frederick Copleston, *A History of Philosophy*, vol. 3 (New York: Doubleday, 1993), 43–152; and Paul Edwards, ed., *The Encyclopedia of Philosophy*, vols. 7 and 8 (New York: Macmillan, 1967), s.v. "William of Ockham."

6. Harris, *Integration of Faith and Learning*, 197.

7. For an explanation and defense of the correspondence view of truth including its biblical basis, see Douglas Groothuis, *Truth Decay: Defending Christianity against the Challenges of Postmodernism* (Downers Grove, IL: InterVarsity, 2000), see chaps. 3–4.

8. Nash, *Worldviews in Conflict*, 59.

9. Groothuis, *Truth Decay*, 81.

10. Hoover, *Case for Christian Theism*, 51–52.

11. C. S. Lewis, *The Weight of Glory and Other Addresses*, rev. ed. (New York: Macmillan, 1965), 92.

12. For the fundamental problem with deism, see Corduan, *No Doubt about It*, 90–92.

13. Ravi Zacharias, *A Shattered Visage: The Real Face of Atheism* (Grand Rapids: Baker, 1990), 191.

14. Hoover, *Case for Christian Theism*, 52.

Chapter 3 Logic 101 and Christian Truth-Claims

1. I have had subsequent discussions with atheists who have disputed my reasoning in critiquing atheism on this point. However, according to the logical rules relating to categorical propositions, to say "no gods are real" by necessity makes reference to all members of the predicate class, namely, all that is "real." In other

words, the statement "no gods are real" means "no gods are among the class of all real things." In the universal negative proposition (form E: No S are P ["No God or gods are real"]) the predicate term is distributed. An assertion is being made about every member of the class denoted by the predicate term. Consider the explanation offered by logician Patrick Hurley:

"Let us now consider the universal negative (E) proposition. "No S are P" states that the S and P classes are separate. . . . This statement makes a claim about every member of S and every member of P. It asserts that every member of S is separate from every member of P, and also that every member of P is separate from every member of S. Accordingly, by the definition above, both the subject and predicate terms of universal negative (E) propositions are distributed." Patrick J. Hurley, A Concise Introduction to Logic, 8th ed. (Belmont, CA: Wadsworth, 2000), 192–93.

A skeptical response to my argument is found in Jeffrey Jay Lowder, "Is a Sound Argument for the Nonexistence of a God Even Possible?" 3rd ed. (paper, Internet Infidels, 1998). Paper available online from www.infidels.org/library/modern/jeff_lowder/ipnegep.html (accessed May 2, 2005).

2. For a discussion of God's relationship to logic, see Ronald H. Nash, The Word of God and the Mind of Man (Grand Rapids: Zondervan, 1982), 107–11; Norman L. Geisler and Ronald M. Brooks, Come, Let Us Reason: An Introduction to Logical Thinking (Grand Rapids: Baker, 1990), 15–20; Gordon H. Clark, A Christian View of Men and Things: An Introduction to Philosophy (Grand Rapids: Eerdmans, 1952).

3. Genesis 1:26–27.

4. Genesis 5:1–2; 9:4–7; Psalm 8:3–8.

5. Deuteronomy 6:5, Matthew 22:37.

6. Job 28:28; 34:4; Psalm 111:10; Proverbs 1:7; 9:10.

7. Acts 17:11; Romans 12:2; 1 Corinthians 14:29; Colossians 2:8; 1 Thessalonians 5:21.

8. For more about the Christian's need to cultivate the life of the mind to the glory of God in an apologetics context, see Samples, "How Should a Christian Prepare to Give Reasons for Faith?" in Without a Doubt, 255–59.

9. My thinking about the three fundamental laws of logic has been influenced by the following sources: Nash, The Word of God and the Mind of Man, 103–12; Miller, Questions That Matter, 31–54.

10. Miller, Questions That Matter, 32–33.

11. See Peter A. Angeles, The HarperCollins Dictionary of Philosophy, 2nd ed. (New York: HarperCollins, 1992), s.v. "laws of thought, the three"; Ronald H. Nash, Life's Ultimate Questions: An Introduction to Philosophy (Grand Rapids: Zondervan, 1999), 193–208.

12. Geisler and Brooks, Come, Let Us Reason, 14.

13. Hurley, Concise Introduction to Logic, 1. I use Hurley's excellent book as one of my required textbooks when I teach college courses in logic and critical thinking.

14. T. Edward Damer, Attacking Faulty Reasoning: A Practical Guide to Fallacy-Free Arguments, 4th ed. (Belmont, CA: Wadsworth, 2001), 12. I use Damer's excellent book as one of my required textbooks when I teach college courses in logic and critical thinking.

15. The construction of my TRACK acrostic was influenced by Damer, Attacking Faulty Reasoning, 23–31.

16. Ibid., 24.

17. Ibid., 28.

18. My discussion of the three basic forms of logical arguments was influenced by Miller, Questions That Matter, 35–45; Louis P. Pojman, Philosophy: The Pursuit of Wisdom, 3rd ed. (Belmont, CA: Wadsworth, 2001), see chap. 2, "A Little Bit of Logic," 16–23. I use both of these fine books as textbooks in the college courses I teach on philosophy.

19. For more discussion of these deductive arguments, see Pojman, Philosophy, 17–20.

20. My comparison of deductive and inductive arguments was influenced by Hurley, Concise Introduction to Logic, 48.

21. My comparison of deductive and inductive arguments was influenced by Geisler and Brooks, Come, Let Us Reason, 23.

22. An abductive case for accepting Jesus of Nazareth as the divine Messiah is in Samples, Without a Doubt, 109–18.

Chapter 4 Straight Thinking

1. Saint Augustine, Confessions, trans. R. S. Pine-Coffin (New York: Penguin, 1961), 1.6.25.

2. My discussion of informal fallacies was influenced by Damer, *Attacking Faulty Reasoning*, chaps. 5–8; Hurley, *Concise Introduction to Logic*, 114–162; and Geisler and Brooks, *Come, Let Us Reason*, 90–118.

3. Hurley, *Concise Introduction to Logic*, 114.

4. Ibid., 147–48.

5. Ibid., 135–38.

6. Ibid., 468.

7. Ibid., 130–32.

8. Alvin Plantinga and Nicholas Wolterstorff, eds., *Faith and Rationality: Reason and Belief in God* (Notre Dame: University of Notre Dame Press, 1983), 25–28.

9. Two of evangelicalism's best contemporary theologians who also have degrees in science think that old earth creationism is in accord with sound biblical exegesis, see, for example, John Jefferson Davis, *The Frontiers of Science and Faith: Examining Questions from the Big Bang to the End of the Universe* (Downers Grove, IL: InterVarsity, 2002); see also the responses of Vern Poythress and John Jefferson Davis in J. P. Moreland and John Mark Reynolds, eds., *Three Views on Creation and Evolution* (Grand Rapids: Zondervan, 1999).

10. Hurley, *Concise Introduction to Logic*, 122–23.

11. Damer, *Attacking Faulty Reasoning*, 29–31.

Chapter 5 A Christian Vision of Truth, Knowledge, and History

1. For a critique of moral relativism, see Samples, "Isn't Morality Simply in the Eye of the Beholder?" in *Without a Doubt*, 229–38.

2. John Jefferson Davis, *Handbook of Basic Bible Texts: Every Key Passage for the Study of Doctrine and Theology* (Grand Rapids: Zondervan, 1984), 35.

3. Groothuis, *Truth Decay*, 62–64.

4. Ibid., 63.

5. Moreland and Craig, *Philosophical Foundations for a Christian Worldview*, 130.

6. D. A. Carson and Douglas J. Moo, *An Introduction to the New Testament*, 2nd ed. (Grand Rapids: Zondervan, 2005), 65.

7. My seven points concerning a Christian view of truth were influenced by the outstanding discussion by Douglas Groothuis, "The

Biblical View of Truth," in Groothuis, *Truth Decay*, 60–82.

8. Isaiah 43:10–13.

9. Jeremiah 10:6–16.

10. See the discussion of God's attribute of "Truthfulness," in Wayne Grudem, *Systematic Theology: An Introduction to Biblical Doctrine* (Grand Rapids: Zondervan, 1994), 195–97. See also Numbers 23:16–19; 2 Timothy 2:13.

11. John 17:17; 2 Timothy 3:15–16.

12. This point is taken from Davis, *Handbook of Basic Bible Texts*, 35.

13. John 1:14; Philippians 2:6–7; Colossians 2:9.

14. John 5:26; 17:3.

15. Psalm 31:5; Isaiah 65:16.

16. Harris, *Integration of Faith and Learning*, 182.

17. Psalm 19:1–11; Romans 1:18–21.

18. "Common grace" is made available to all people by God (the Holy Spirit) and includes physical, intellectual, and moral blessings that come through such means as general revelation, human government, and societal laws. Common grace serves to restrain sin and reinforce man's original rational and moral nature, though it does not produce salvation. For more on the importance of common grace, see Louis Berkhof, *Summary of Christian Doctrine* (Grand Rapids: Eerdmans, 1947), 121–24.

19. John 8:32; 2 Timothy 3:15–17.

20. John 20:28; Romans 10:9–13; Philippians 2:11.

21. Matthew 28:18; Romans 9:5; Colossians 1:16; Revelation 1:5.

22. Groothuis, *Truth Decay*, 69.

23. Cf. Matthew 24:23–24; John 10:8.

24. For a discussion concerning the issue of tolerance within the Christian worldview, see Samples, "Doesn't Christianity Promote Intolerance?" in *Without a Doubt*, 222–28.

25. Clark, *Christian View of Men and Things*, 30.

26. Psalm 58:3; Romans 1:18.

27. See Philippians 3:10.

28. Carson and Moo, *Introduction to the New Testament*, 64. (See also John 8:32.)

29. Christian philosopher Ronald H. Nash provides an overview of how epistemological issues might be approached within the Christian worldview in his book *Faith and Reason*,

chaps. 3–7. Christian philosophers J. P. Moreland and William Lane Craig discuss a variety of epistemological issues that impact the Christian worldview in their book *Philosophical Foundations for a Christian Worldview*, chaps. 3–7.

30. Psalm 19:1–4; Acts 17:27–28; Romans 1:18–21.

31. Genesis 1:26–27.

32. Geoffrey W. Bromiley, ed., *The International Standard Bible Encyclopedia*, vol. 3, rev. ed. (Grand Rapids: Eerdmans, 1986), s.v. "Know, Knowledge" by Carl F. H. Henry.

33. For a definition of this "sense of the divine," see Richard A. Muller, *Dictionary of Latin and Greek Theological Terms: Drawn Principally from Protestant Scholastic Theology* (Grand Rapids: Baker, 1985), s.v. "*sensus divinitatis*." For an advocate of this position, see John Calvin, *Institutes of the Christian Religion*, 1.3.1, ed. John T. McNeill, trans. Ford Lewis Battles, Library of Christian Classics (Philadelphia: Westminster Press, 1960), 1:43.

34. For a clear and thoughtful discussion of knowledge defined as "properly justified true belief," see Tom Morris, *Philosophy for Dummies* (Foster City, CA: IDG Books Worldwide, 1999), 44–49. Morris's discussion of knowledge influenced my thinking on this point.

35. See Moreland and Craig, *Philosophical Foundations for a Christian Worldview*, 112–121.

36. Robert Audi, ed., *The Cambridge Dictionary of Philosophy*, (Cambridge: Cambridge University Press, 1995), s.v. "foundationalism."

37. Plantinga, "Reason and Belief in God," in Plantinga and Wolterstorff, *Faith and Rationality*, 16–93; see also Nash, *Faith and Reason*, 69–92.

38. Psalm 8:3–6.

39. Psalms 139:1–6; 147:5.

40. Romans 11:33–36.

41. Ephesians 2:1–3; 4:17–19.

42. Acts 16:14; 1 Corinthians 2:14–16; 2 Corinthians 4:4–6.

43. Some of the diverse views in Christian church history regarding the relationship between faith and reason are reflected in the following four approaches: *Crede, ut intelligas*: "Believe in order that you may understand" (Augustine A.D. 354–430); *Credo, ut intelligam*: "I believe in order that I might understand"

(Anselm A.D. 1033–1109); *Intelligo et credo*: "I understand and I believe" (Thomas Aquinas A.D. 1225–1274); *Credo quia absurdum est*: "I believe because it is absurd" (Søren Kierkegaard 1813–1855). These approaches to faith and reason are explored and explained in Miller, *God and Reason*, 129–53, and in Kenneth D. Boa and Robert M. Bowman Jr., *Faith Has Its Reasons: An Integrative Approach to Defending Christianity* (Colorado Springs: NavPress, 2001).

44. Sinclair B. Ferguson, J. I. Packer, and David F. Wright, eds., *New Dictionary of Theology* (Downers Grove, IL: InterVarsity, 1988), s.v. "Faith and reason."

45. These two New Testament Greek words can be defined accordingly: *pisteuō*: "I have faith (in), believe" (Metzger); "believe in, be convinced of, give credence to, trust in" (Gingrich); *pistis*: "faith, belief, trust" (Metzger), "faith, trust, commitment" (Gingrich). See Bruce M. Metzger, *Lexical Aids for Students of New Testament Greek*, 3rd ed. (Grand Rapids: Baker, 1998), 9; and F. Wilber Gingrich, *Shorter Lexicon of the Greek New Testament*, revised by Frederick W. Danker, 2nd ed. (Chicago: University of Chicago Press, 1983), 159.

46. Saving faith is the sovereign gift of God (John 6:65; Acts 13:48, 16:14; Romans 12:3; 1 Corinthians 12:3; 2 Corinthians 4:13; Ephesians 2:8–9, 6:23; Philippians 1:29; 1 Thessalonians 2:13; Hebrews 12:2; 1 John 5:1). For a helpful biblical discussion of how faith is a sovereign gift of God, see Anthony A. Hoekema, *Saved by Grace* (Grand Rapids: Eerdmans, 1989), 143–45.

47. The apostle Paul describes this action in Romans 12:2.

48. For a discussion of Augustine's expression of "faith seeking understanding" (Latin: *fides quaerens intellectum*), see Miller, *God and Reason*, 134–37.

49. Matthew 22:37.

50. Daniel 2:21; Acts 17:25–27.

51. Psalm 147:8–9.

52. Job 12:23–24.

53. Genesis 50:20.

54. Romans 8:28.

55. Hebrews 9:27.

56. John 1:14; Philippians 2:5–7.

57. Luke 2:1–7.

58. Luke 3:1; 23:1–24.

59. 1 Corinthians 15:5–8.

60. Written over a thirteen-year period, *The City of God* (the title is taken from Psalm 87:3) stands as Augustine's *magnum opus*. It is his longest and most comprehensive work and is considered by some to be his most significant contribution to Western thought. In this book, Augustine laid new foundations in the fields of Christian apologetics and in the analysis of Christian history. For more about this work and Augustine's life and thought, see *Augustine through the Ages: An Encyclopedia*, ed. Allan D. Fitzgerald (Grand Rapids: Eerdmans, 1999).

61. Augustine's use of Babylon and Jerusalem as types of these two "cities" derives from chapters 17–22 of the book of Revelation.

62. Acts 1:9–11; 2 Timothy 4:1; Hebrews 9:26–28.

63. Revelation 20–22.

64. Genesis 3.

65. In terms of Christian eschatology (last things), I recommend the following sources: for a premillennial perspective, see Ladd, *Last Things*; for an amillennial perspective, see Hoekema, *Bible and the Future*; and for a postmillennial perspective, see Davis, *Christ's Victorious Kingdom*.

66. 2 Peter 3:7, 10, 12.

67. Revelation 21:1–5.

Chapter 6 A Soldier's Creed

1. Not every usage of the word "Lord" (*kyrios*) in specific application to Jesus in the New Testament implies deity; however, in context, the four scriptural references cited above clearly do. See F. F. Bruce, *Jesus: Lord and Savior* (Downers Grove, IL: InterVarsity, 1986), 203.

2. Alister E. McGrath, *I Believe: Understanding and Applying the Apostles' Creed* (Grand Rapids: Zondervan, 1991), 44.

3. Peter Kreeft, *Fundamentals of the Faith: Essays in Christian Apologetics* (San Francisco: Ignatius, 1988), 107.

4. Ibid.

5. McGrath, *I Believe*, 41.

6. Ibid.

7. On the subject of sin, see Samples, "Why Did Jesus Christ Have to Die?" in *Without a Doubt*, 149–52.

8. For a critical analysis of this phrase "he descended to hell," even arguing that it is patently

unbiblical and should be eliminated from the Apostles' Creed, see Wayne Grudem, *Systematic Theology*, 586–94.

9. Ibid., 586–87.

10. McGrath, *I Believe*, 77–82.

11. Both Reformed catechisms connect the phrase "he descended to hell" to Jesus Christ suffering the wrath of God on the cross; see the Heidelberg Catechism, Question and Answer 44, in *Ecumenical Creeds and Reformed Confessions* (Grand Rapids: CRC Publications, 1988), 29, and the Westminster Larger Catechism, Question and Answer 50, in *Reformed Confessions Harmonized*, ed. Joel R. Beeke and Sinclair B. Ferguson (Grand Rapids: Baker, 1999), 77.

12. On Jesus's resurrection, see Samples, "Did Jesus Christ Actually Rise from the Dead?" in *Without a Doubt*, 134–47.

13. Jim Morrison, "Five to One," *The Best of the Doors*, disc 1, compact disc, Elektra/Asylum Records, 60345–2, 1985.

14. J. I. Packer, *Concise Theology: A Guide to Historic Christian Beliefs* (Wheaton: Tyndale, 1993), 128.

15. McGrath, *I Believe*, 126.

16. Ibid., 147.

Chapter 7 God's Written Word— Scripture

1. *Great Books of the Western World*, 60 vols., ed. Mortimer J. Adler (Chicago: Encyclopaedia Britannica, 1994).

2. Mortimer J. Adler and Charles Van Doren, *How to Read a Book*, rev. ed. (New York: Simon & Schuster, 1972), 343.

3. Roman Catholicism and historic Protestantism agree with regard to the extent of the New Testament canon, but they are divided over the question of the Old Testament apocryphal books (or, as Catholics refer to them, deuterocanonical books). For a defense of the evangelical Protestant view of the canon, see F. F. Bruce, *The Canon of Scripture* (Downers Grove, IL: InterVarsity, 1988).

4. My discussion of the doctrine of Scripture in this chapter was influenced by the following sources: Davis, *Handbook of Basic Bible Texts*, 13–19; Bruce Milne, *Know the Truth: A Handbook of Christian Belief* (Downers Grove, IL: InterVarsity, 1982), 27–51; Berkhof, *Summary*

of Christian Doctrine, 18–23; Packer, *Concise Theology*, 16–18; Ferguson, Wright, and Packer, *New Dictionary of Theology*, s.v. "Scripture"; Grudem, *Systematic Theology*, chaps. 2–8; John W. Wenham, "Christ's View of Scripture," in *Inerrancy*, ed. Norman L. Geisler, (Grand Rapids: Zondervan, 1980), 3–36.

5. For further discussion of the historic Christian doctrine of revelation, see Samples, "How Has God Revealed Himself?" in *Without a Doubt*, 42–51.

6. Belgic Confession (Art. 2), in *Ecumenical Creeds and Reformed Confessions*, 79.

7. For the Bible's reliability, see K. A. Kitchen, *On the Reliability of the Old Testament* (Grand Rapids: Eerdmans, 2003) and Craig Blomberg, *The Historical Reliability of the Gospels* (Downers Grove, IL: InterVarsity, 1987).

8. Genesis 2:7; Job 33:4; Psalm 33:6.

9. Milne, *Know the Truth*, 37.

10. Berkhof, *Summary of Christian Doctrine*, 20.

11. "The Chicago Statement on Biblical Inerrancy, A Short Statement," points 2 and 4, as quoted in Geisler, *Inerrancy*, 494.

12. Davis, *Handbook of Basic Bible Texts*, 18.

13. For popular hermeneutics texts, see R. C. Sproul, *Knowing Scripture* (Downers Grove, IL: InterVarsity, 1977) and Robert H. Stein, *A Basic Guide to Interpreting the Bible: Playing by the Rules* (Grand Rapids: Baker, 1994); for a more technical work, see Bernard Ramm, *Protestant Biblical Interpretation: A Textbook of Hermeneutics*, 3rd ed. (Grand Rapids: Baker, 1970).

14. Concerning the canon of Scripture, see F. F. Bruce, *The Books and the Parchments: How We Got Our English Bible* (Old Tappan, NJ: Revell, 1984), and the more extensive work by Bruce, *The Canon of Scripture*.

15. Bruce, *Canon of Scripture*, see chaps. 2–7.

16. Bruce, *Books and the Parchments*, 88–89.

17. Deuteronomy 4:2; 12:32; Proverbs 30:6.

18. Bruce, *Books and the Parchments*, 161–63; Bruce M. Metzger, *An Introduction to the Apocrypha* (Oxford: Oxford University Press, 1957).

19. Bruce, *Canon of Scripture*, see chaps. 8–20; Bruce, *Books and the Parchments*, chaps. 14–16.

20. For an evangelical introduction to the New Testament, see Donald Guthrie, *New Testament Introduction*, 4th ed. (Downers Grove, IL: InterVarsity, 1990) and Carson and Moo, *Introduction to the New Testament*.

21. For a list and evaluation of these writings from an evangelical Christian perspective, see Norman L. Geisler and William E. Nix, *A General Introduction to the Bible*, rev. ed. (Chicago: Moody, 1986), 301–12.

22. Bruce, *Canon of Scripture*, 255–69.

23. Bruce, *Books and the Parchments*, 103–4.

24. Milne, *Know the Truth*, 33.

25. Muller, *Dictionary of Latin and Greek Theological Terms*, s.v. "sola Scriptura"; J. I. Packer, "'Sola Scriptura' in History and Today," in *God's Inerrant Word: An International Symposium on the Trustworthiness of Scripture*, ed. John Warwick Montgomery (Minneapolis: Bethany, 1974), 43–62.

26. This quote is taken from Robert M. Bowman Jr.'s excellent unpublished study outline entitled: "*Sola Scriptura*: The Protestant Doctrine of the Authority of Scripture," n.d., (available by request from http://www.biblicalapologetics.net). My discussion of the Protestant principle of *sola Scriptura* in this chapter was influenced by Bowman's study outline.

27. Belgic Confession (Art. 7), in *Ecumenical Creeds and Reformed Confessions*, 82.

28. The 39 Articles of the Church of England, http://anglicansonline.org/basics/thirtynine_articles.html (accessed July 19, 2006).

29. The Formula of Concord, http://www.bookofconcord.org/fc-ep.html#Comprehensive%20Summary,%20%20Rule%20and%20Norm (accessed July 31, 2006).

30. Westminster Confession of Faith, chap. 1, sec. 10 (Norcross, GA: Great Commission, 1992).

31. "The Chicago Statement on Biblical Inerrancy," Articles 1 and 2, reprinted in Geisler, *Inerrancy*, 494.

32. John 14:26; 2 Peter 1:21.

33. See Norman L. Geisler and Ralph E. Mackenzie, *Roman Catholics and Evangelicals: Agreements and Disagreements* (Grand Rapids: Baker, 1995), chap. 10 (177–201).

34. Bowman, "*Sola Scriptura*."

35. Deuteronomy 4:2; 12:32; Proverbs 30:6; Revelation 22:18–19.

36. Geisler and Mackenzie, *Roman Catholics and Evangelicals*, chap. 10.

37. Deuteronomy 6:6–7; Psalms 1:2; 19:7; 119:130; Matthew 12:3; 5, 21:42; 22:29; 2 Timothy 3:15.

38. Muller, *Dictionary of Latin and Greek Theological Terms*, s.v. "sola Scriptura"; Ferguson, Wright, and Packer, *New Dictionary of Theology*, s.v. "Scripture and Tradition."

39. For a summary of Roman Catholic criticisms of *sola Scriptura*, see Kreeft, *Fundamentals of the Faith*, 274–75.

40. Bowman, "*Sola Scriptura*."

41. J. I. Packer, *"Fundamentalism" and the Word of God: Some Evangelical Principles* (Grand Rapids: Eerdmans, 1958), 55.

42. Wenham, "Christ's View of Scripture," 12–14; see also Matthew 19:18–19; Mark 10:19; Luke 18:20.

43. Matthew 26:54; Luke 24:44; John 19:28.

44. See Bruce, *Books and the Parchments*, 96.

45. Acts 4:25; 28:25; Romans 3:2; 9:27, 29; 2 Timothy 3:15–16; 2 Peter 1:20–21.

46. John 21:22–23.

47. Bowman, "*Sola Scriptura*."

48. Muller, *Dictionary of Latin and Greek Theological Terms*, s.v. "sola Scriptura."

49. Reinhold Seeberg, *Text-book of the History of Doctrines*, trans. Charles E. Hay, vol. 1, *History of Doctrines in the Ancient Church* (1895; repr., Grand Rapids: Baker, 1964), 358; J. N. D. Kelly, *Early Christian Doctrine*, rev. ed. (San Francisco: HarperSanFrancisco, 1978), 42–43.

50. Augustine, *Letters of St. Augustin*, 82.3.24—To Jerome, trans. J. G. Cunningham, vol. 1 of *Nicene and Post-Nicene Fathers*, first series, ed. Philip Schaff (1886; repr., Peabody, MA: 1994), 358.

51. Augustine, *The City of God*, 11.3, trans. Marcus Dods, vol. 2 of *Nicene and Post-Nicene Fathers*, first series, ed. Philip Schaff (1887; repr., Peabody, MA: Hendrickson, 1994), 206.

52. Augustine, *Reply to Faustus the Manichaean*, 11.5, trans. Richard Stothert, vol. 4 of *Nicene and Post-Nicene Fathers*, first series, ed. Philip Schaff (1887; repr., Peabody, MA: Hendrickson, 1994), 180.

53. Thomas Aquinas, *Truth*, trans. James V. McGlynn, vol. 2, Questions 10–20 (Chicago: Henry Regnery, 1953), question 14, art. 10.11, p. 258.

54. Thomas Aquinas, *Summa Theologiae*, vol. 1 of *Christian Theology* (1a.1), trans. Victor White, ed. Thomas Gilby (Cambridge: Blackfriars / New York: McGraw-Hill, 1964), question 1, pt. 8, p. 33. Aquinas is quoting Augustine's letter to Jerome (*Letters of St. Augustin*, 82.3, 350).

55. Packer, "'Sola Scriptura' in History and Today," 55.

56. Ibid., 55–56.

57. For a defense of the Roman Catholic view of the papacy, see Scott Butler, Norman Dahlgren, David Hess, *Jesus, Peter and the Keys: A Scriptural Handbook on the Papacy* (Santa Barbara, CA: Queenship, 1997). For a Protestant critique of the papacy, see Geisler and Mackenzie, *Roman Catholics and Evangelicals*, and James R. White, *Scripture Alone: Exploring the Bible's Accuracy, Authority, and Authenticity* (Minneapolis: Bethany, 2004). For audiotapes of a Protestant-Catholic dialogue between Kenneth Samples and Father Mitchell Pacwa, SJ, on the question of religious authority, contact St. Joseph Communications, Inc., PO Box 720, W. Covina, CA 91793, 1-818-331-3549.

58. For a discussion of the broad diversity that exists within the Roman Catholic church, see Kenneth Richard Samples, "What Think Ye of Rome? An Evangelical Appraisal of Contemporary Catholicism," pt. 1, *Christian Research Journal* (Winter 1993), 32–42.

Chapter 8 The Historic Christian View of God

1. For a helpful discussion of the historic Christian view of God, see Gerald Bray, *The Doctrine of God* (Downers Grove, IL: InterVarsity, 1993); Louis Berkhof, *Systematic Theology*, new combined ed. (Grand Rapids: Eerdmans, 1996); Grudem, *Systematic Theology*.

2. For discussion on the doctrine of the Trinity, see Samples, "How Can God Be Three and One?" in *Without a Doubt*, 63–76; Robert M. Bowman Jr., *Why You Should Believe in the Trinity: An Answer to Jehovah's Witnesses* (Grand Rapids: Baker, 1989); Millard J. Erickson, *Christian Theology*, 2nd ed. (Grand Rapids: Baker,

1998), 321–42; Muller, *Dictionary of Latin and Greek Theological Terms*, s.v. "Trinitas," 306–10; Grudem, *Systematic Theology*, 226–61; Bray, *Doctrine of God*, 111–51; Milne, *Know the Truth*, 59–64; Berkhof, *Summary of Christian Doctrine*, 42–45; Packer, *Concise Theology*, 40–42.

3. Ferguson, Wright, and Packer, *New Dictionary of Theology*, s.v. "God."

4. For extensive scriptural support for the doctrine of the Trinity, see Robert M. Bowman Jr., "The Biblical Basis of the Doctrine of the Trinity: An Outline Study," Center for Biblical Apologetics, http://www.biblicalapologetics .net/Subjects/T/Trinity_Outline.htm (accessed February 12, 2006).

5. For a list and description of heretical views concerning the nature of God, see Samples, *Without a Doubt*, 71–72.

6. See the evangelical critique of polytheism in Geisler and Watkins, *Worlds Apart*, 217–53.

7. See the evangelical critique of a contemporary form of polytheism in James R. White, *Is the Mormon My Brother? Discerning the Differences between Mormonism and Evangelical Christianity* (Minneapolis: Bethany, 1997); Kurt Van Gorden, *Mormonism* (Grand Rapids: Zondervan, 1995), 31–47.

8. Monarchianism is the view that God is a single solitary being and person, stressing the absolute unity of God.

9. See the evangelical critique of a contemporary form of Unitarianism in Alan W. Gomes, *Unitarian Universalism* (Grand Rapids: Zondervan, 1998).

10. Deism is the view that God created the universe but does not intervene within it; thus no miracles. For a clear and thoughtful Christian critique of deism, see Corduan, *No Doubt about It*, 90–92; and Geisler and Watkins, *Worlds Apart*, 147–85.

11. For an evangelical Christian assessment of the religions of Jainism and Buddhism, see Winfried Corduan, *Neighboring Faiths: A Christian Introduction to World Religions* (Downers Grove, IL: InterVarsity, 1998), 220–61.

12. See the evangelical critique of a contemporary form of modalism in Gregory A. Boyd, *Oneness Pentecostals and the Trinity* (Grand Rapids: Baker, 1992).

13. See the evangelical critique of a contemporary form of Arianism in Robert M. Bowman

Jr., *Jehovah's Witnesses* (Grand Rapids: Zondervan, 1995), 20–30.

14. Augustine of Hippo (A.D. 354–430) was a member of the sect of the Manichees for several years before his conversion to Christianity. He writes about this group and their beliefs in his autobiography titled *Confessions* (A.D. 400); see bk. 5, 91–109. For an assessment of the ancient Persian religion of Zoroastrianism, which has some similarities to Manichaeism, see Corduan, *Neighboring Faiths*, 113–34.

15. For discussion of the doctrine of the Incarnation, see Samples, "How Can Jesus Christ Be Both God and Man?" in *Without a Doubt*, 120–33.

16. For other passages that imply the truth of the Incarnation, see 1 Timothy 3:16; Hebrews 2:14; 5:7; 1 John 1:1–3.

17. John 1:1.

18. Gnostic-oriented groups viewed matter as evil, thus God could not become flesh. See the evangelical critique of the contemporary form of Gnosticism in Douglas Groothuis, *Revealing the New Age Jesus* (Downers Grove, IL: InterVarsity, 1990). See the evangelical critique of the contemporary form of Gnosticism in mind-science groups in Todd Ehrenborg, *Mind Sciences: Christian Science, Religious Science, and Unity School of Christianity* (Grand Rapids: Zondervan, 1995).

19. Isaiah 11:1.

20. For more detailed biblical support for Jesus Christ's human nature, see Samples, *Without a Doubt*, 126–27.

21. For a list and description of ancient Christological heresies, see Samples, *Without a Doubt*, 131.

22. My discussion of how the various religious and secular views of Jesus contradict the historic Christian claim of him being God Incarnate was inspired by the analysis in Groothuis, *Truth Decay*, 166.

23. The lordship of Jesus Christ is discussed in Bromiley, *International Standard Bible Encyclopedia*, vol. 3, s.v. "LORD," and Walter A. Elwell, ed., *Evangelical Dictionary of Theology* (Grand Rapids: Baker, 1984), s.v. "Lord, Jesus as."

24. 1 Corinthians 12:3.

25. John 1:3.

26. Colossians 1:17.

27. Revelation 1:5.

28. Mark 2:5–7.

29. Matthew 28:16–17.

30. John 5:21.

31. John 5:22.

32. Acts 10:36.

33. Romans 14:8; 1 Corinthians 8:6; Colossians 1:15–17; James 4:15.

34. Abraham Kuyper, "Sphere Sovereignty," in *Abraham Kuyper: A Centennial Reader* (Grand Rapids: Eerdmans, 1998), 488.

35. Protestant evangelical scholars (principally of the Reformed theological tradition) who have held the highest view of Christ's lordship and of the authority of Scripture have largely been responsible for the movement to think of Christianity in worldview terms or as the faith encompassing a worldview. David Naugle identifies the likes of James Orr, Abraham Kuyper, Herman Dooyeweerd, Gordon H. Clark, Carl F. H. Henry, and Francis A. Schaeffer as playing a significant role in this regard. See David K. Naugle, *Worldview: The History of a Concept* (Grand Rapids: Eerdmans, 2002), chap. 1. Scholars today who are carrying on that same worldview emphasis include Ronald H. Nash, Arthur F. Holmes, Richard J. Mouw, James W. Sire, Charles Colson, Albert M. Wolters, and Nancy R. Pearcey.

36. For a study of pneumatology, see Michael Green, *I Believe in the Holy Spirit*, rev. ed. (Grand Rapids: Eerdmans, 2004).

37. For a discussion of the attributes of God, see Davis, *Handbook of Basic Bible Texts*, 23–37; Berkhof, *Systematic Theology*, 29–81; Berkhof, *Summary of Christian Doctrine*, 34–41; Grudem, *Systematic Theology*, 156–225; Millard J. Erickson, *Introducing Christian Doctrine*, ed. L. Arnold Hustad (Grand Rapids: Baker, 1992), 88–95; Packer, *Concise Theology*, 23–36, 43–50.

38. Genesis 1:26–27.

39. There is no universally accepted list of divine attributes presented by Christian theologians. Those attributes mentioned here are some of the most important, but the list is certainly not exhaustive.

40. Packer, *Concise Theology*, 26.

41. Exodus 3:14; Isaiah 40:13–14; 44:24; Jeremiah 10:10; John 5:26; Romans 11:34–35; Revelation 4:11.

42. For a source that compares and contrasts the Christian theistic view of the origin of humanity with that of Darwinian evolution, see Fazale Rana with Hugh Ross, *Who Was Adam? A Creation Model Approach to the Origin of Man* (Colorado Springs: NavPress, 2005). For a work that does the same concerning the origin of life on earth, see Fazale Rana and Hugh Ross, *Origins of Life: Biblical and Evolutionary Models Face Off* (Colorado Springs: NavPress, 2004).

43. Evangelical theologians have different views on the question of whether God has emotions. The "classical theism" position is that God does not have emotions. Much depends, however, on how one defines emotion.

44. Numbers 23:19; Psalms 33:11; 102:27; Malachi 3:6; Hebrews 6:17; 13:8.

45. Titus 1:2; 2 Timothy 1:9.

46. Deuteronomy 33:27; Psalms 90:2; 102:27; Isaiah 57:15.

47. Grudem, *Systematic Theology*, 180.

48. Exodus 34:6–7; Isaiah 43:10; 44:6; 1 Corinthians 8:4–6.

49. Exodus 20:4–6; 33:20; 1 Timothy 1:17; 6:15–16; 1 John 4:12.

50. For an evangelical critique of animism, see Gailyn Van Rheenen, *Communicating Christ in Animistic Contexts* (Grand Rapids: Baker, 1991).

51. For an evangelical critique of folk and/or basic religions, see Corduan, *Neighboring Faiths*, chaps. 5 and 6.

52. Titus 1:2; Hebrews 6:17–18; James 1:13.

53. Genesis 18:14; 2 Chronicles 20:6; Isaiah 14:27; Matthew 19:26; Mark 10:27; Luke 1:37; Ephesians 1:11.

54. 1 Kings 8:27.

55. Genesis 1:1.

56. Psalm 139:7–10; Isaiah 66:1; Jeremiah 23:23–24; Acts 7:48–49; Ephesians 4:10.

57. Isaiah 46:9–10.

58. Matthew 11:21–23.

59. Hebrews 4:13.

60. 1 Corinthians 2:10–11.

61. Psalm 139:1–4.

62. Psalm 90:4.

63. Job 37:16; Psalm 139:1–6; Isaiah 40:28; Romans 11:33.

64. 1 Kings 8:27; Psalm 102:25–27; Isaiah 40:22; 42:5; 66:1–2; Acts 7:48–49.

65. Deuteronomy 4:7; Psalm 139:7–10; Jeremiah 23:23; Acts 17:27–28.

66. Deuteronomy 10:14; Psalms 103:19; 135:6; Proverbs 16:33; Acts 16:14; Ephesians 1:11, 21.

67. Psalms 104:24; 147:5; Daniel 2:20–21; Romans 16:27; Colossians 2:2–3.

68. Job 15:8; Isaiah 40:13–14; Jeremiah 23:18; Romans 11:34; 1 Corinthians 2:11.

69. Exodus 15:11; Leviticus 11:44; Psalm 22:3; Isaiah 57:15; 1 Peter 1:15–16; Revelation 4:8.

70. Genesis 18:25; Deuteronomy 32:4; Psalms 36:6; 98:9; Acts 17:31; Romans 3:25–26.

71. Exodus 32:9–10; 2 Kings 22:13; Psalm 103:8–9; John 3:36; Romans 2:5; Hebrews 10:31.

72. Jeremiah 10:6–16; 1 Thessalonians 1:9; 1 John 5:20; Revelation 3:7; 6:10.

73. Numbers 23:19; Deuteronomy 7:9; 1 Corinthians 1:9; 2 Corinthians 1:18–22; 2 Timothy 2:13; 1 John 1:9.

74. Numbers 23:19; Psalms 33:4; 119:160; John 17:17; Titus 1:1–2; Hebrews 6:18.

75. Deuteronomy 33:12; Psalm 42:8; Jeremiah 31:3; John 3:16; Romans 5:8; Ephesians 2:4–5; Galatians 2:20.

76. Exodus 33:19; Psalm 103:8; Nehemiah 9:17; Romans 3:23–24; Ephesians 1:6; 2:8–9.

77. Exodus 34:6; 2 Samuel 24:14; Romans 9:16; Ephesians 2:4–5; Hebrews 4:16; James 5:11.

Chapter 9 God's World—Creation and Providence

1. See, for example, *Ecumenical Creeds and Reformed Confessions*.

2. My discussion of the doctrine of creation in this chapter was influenced by the following sources: Davis, *Handbook of Basic Bible Texts*, 45–47; C. John Collins, *Science and Faith: Friends or Foes?* (Wheaton: Crossway, 2003); Milne, *Know the Truth*, 72–81; Berkhof, *Summary of Christian Doctrine*, 51–58; Berkhof, *Systematic Theology*, 126–64; Grudem, *Systematic Theology*, 262–314; Robert L. Reymond, *A New Systematic Theology of the Christian Faith* (Nashville: Nelson, 1998), 383–414; Erickson, *Christian Theology*, 391–411; Erickson, *Introducing Christian Doctrine*, 120–27; Packer, *Concise Theology*, 21–22.

3. Creation events (Genesis 1–2); creation's power and complexity (Job 9, 34–41); creation

psalms (Psalms 8, 19, 65, 102, 104, 139, 147–48); Israel's Creator (Isaiah 40, 44, 48).

4. John 1:1–3; Acts 14:15–17; 17:24–28; Romans 1:18–23; 2:14; 4:17; 5:12, 18–19; 1 Corinthians 8:6; 11:7–9; Colossians 1:15–17; Hebrews 1:2–3; 11:3; Revelation 4:11; 10:6.

5. For a discussion of the doctrine of the Trinity, see Samples, "How Can God Be Three and One?" 63–76.

6. Erickson, *Introducing Christian Doctrine*, 123.

7. For a book-length defense of the historic Christian doctrine of creation *ex nihilo*, see Paul Copan and William Lane Craig, *Creation out of Nothing: A Biblical, Philosophical, and Scientific Exploration* (Grand Rapids: Baker, 2004).

8. Muller, *Dictionary of Latin and Greek Theological Terms*, s.v. "ex nihilo."

9. Copan and Craig, *Creation out of Nothing*, 43.

10. Ibid., 78–83.

11. Ibid., 82.

12. For eight such biblical expressions, see Erickson, *Introducing Christian Doctrine*, 122.

13. Copan and Craig, *Creation out of Nothing*, 27.

14. Exodus 20:3–6; Romans 1:18–23.

15. Genesis 1:26–27.

16. 2 Peter 3:7, 10, 13; Revelation 21:1.

17. Cornelius Plantinga Jr., *Engaging God's World: A Christian Vision of Faith, Learning, and Living* (Grand Rapids: Eerdmans, 2002), 20, 22.

18. Samples, *Without a Doubt*, 75.

19. Copan and Craig, *Creation out of Nothing*, 16.

20. Ibid., 25.

21. For clear and thoughtful Christian critiques of pantheism and panentheism, see Corduan, *No Doubt about It*, 92–99; and Geisler and Watkins, *Worlds Apart*, 75–146.

22. For a clear and thoughtful Christian critique of the metaphysical concept of monism (as expressed in Eastern mysticism and metaphysical naturalism), see Dean C. Halverson, ed., *The Compact Guide to World Religions* (Minneapolis: Bethany, 1996), 30–31, 160–97.

23. For clear and thoughtful Christian critiques of some of these religious philosophies, see Corduan, *Neighboring Faiths*; and Halverson, *Compact Guide to World Religions*.

24. For clear and thoughtful Christian critiques of some of these basic or folk religions, see Corduan, *Neighboring Faiths*; and Halverson, *Compact Guide to World Religions.*

25. For clear and thoughtful Christian critiques of secularism, materialism, and atheism from a Christian theistic perspective, see Corduan, *No Doubt about It*, 83–88; and Halverson, *Compact Guide to World Religions*, 144–59, 182–97.

26. For a summary of the problems associated with the naturalistic worldview, see Nash, *Worldviews in Conflict*, 116–29; for a Christian critique of naturalistic explanations for the emergence of the cosmos, see Copan and Craig, *Creation out of Nothing*, 249–66.

27. For a clear and thoughtful Christian critique of nihilism, see Sire, *Universe Next Door*, 74–93.

28. For a Christian critique of methodological naturalism, see Alvin Plantinga, "Methodological Naturalism?" Access Research Network, http://www.arn.org/docs/odesign/od181/methnat181.htm, pt. 1, and http://www.arn.org/docs/odesign/od182/methnat182.htm, pt. 2 (accessed August 7, 2006).

29. For a clear and thoughtful Christian critique of finite godism and process theology, see Geisler and Watkins, *Worlds Apart*, chaps. 4 and 6; for the same on open theism, see John M. Frame, *No Other God: A Response to Open Theism* (Phillipsburg, NJ: P & R Publishing, 2001).

30. For a clear and thoughtful Christian critique of deism, see Corduan, *No Doubt about It*, 90–92; and Geisler and Watkins, *Worlds Apart*, 147–85; for the same on Islam, see Corduan, *Neighboring Faiths*, 77–112; and Halverson, *Compact Guide to World Religions*, 103–20.

. 31. For introductory articles on the life and thought of Augustine, which includes his interaction with Manichaeism, see Kenneth Richard Samples, "Augustine of Hippo: From Pagan, to Cultist, to Skeptic, to Christian Sage," *Facts for Faith*, no. 5 (Q 1 2001), 36–41; "Augustine of Hippo: Rightly Dividing the Truth," *Facts for Faith*, no. 6 (Q 2 2001), 34–39. These articles can be accessed on the Internet at Augustine Fellowship Study Center, http://www.augustinefellowship.org/. For an evangelical assessment of Zoroastrianism, see Corduan, *Neighboring Faiths*, 113–34; for a critique of Gnosticism, see N. T.

Wright, *Judas and the Gospel of Jesus* (Grand Rapids: Baker, 2006), 29–41.

32. For a philosophical and theological critique of the Mormon view of God, see *The New Mormon Challenge: Responding to the Latest Defenses of a Fast-Growing Movement*, ed. Francis J. Beckwith, Carl Mosser, and Paul Owen (Grand Rapids: Zondervan, 2002).

33. Gottfried Wilhelm Leibniz, "The Principles of Nature and of Grace, Based on Reason," in *Philosophic Classics: Bacon to Kant*, vol. 2, ed. Walter Kaufmann (Englewood Cliffs, NJ: Prentice-Hall, 1961), sec. 7, 256.

34. Peter Kreeft and Ronald K. Tacelli, *Handbook of Christian Apologetics: Hundreds of Answers to Crucial Questions* (Downers Grove, IL: InterVarsity, 1994), 58. For discussion of the *kalam* cosmological argument, see J. P. Moreland, *Scaling the Secular City: A Defense of Christianity* (Grand Rapids: Baker, 1987), 18–42.

35. See Copan and Craig, *Creation out of Nothing*, 249–66.

36. For a discussion of multiverse, see Hugh Ross, *The Creator and the Cosmos: How the Greatest Scientific Discoveries of the Century Reveal God*, 3rd ed. (Colorado Springs: NavPress, 2001), 171–74.

37. Copan and Craig, *Creation out of Nothing*, 19.

38. Ezekiel 28:12–19; Isaiah 14:12–20.

39. John 12:31; 2 Corinthians 4:4; Ephesians 2:2; 1 John 5:19.

40. See Kenneth D. Boa and Robert M. Bowman Jr., *Sense and Nonsense about Angels* (Grand Rapids: Zondervan, 2007).

41. Genesis 1:26–27; 2:7; 2:21–22.

42. For a presentation of the position of theistic evolution in an interaction with other evangelical views, see Howard J. Van Till, "The Fully Gifted Creation," in Moreland and Reynolds, *Three Views on Creation and Evolution.*

43. Erickson, *Introducing Christian Doctrine*, 123.

44. My discussion of the doctrine of providence in this chapter was influenced by the following sources: Davis, *Handbook of Basic Bible Texts*, 49–52; Collins, *Science and Faith*, 161–79; Milne, *Know the Truth*, 81–89; Berkhof, *Summary of Christian Doctrine*, 59–63; Berkhof, *Systematic Theology*, 165–78; Grudem, *Systematic Theology*, 315–54; Reymond, *New Systematic*

Theology of the Christian Faith, 398–414; Erickson, *Christian Theology*, 412–35; Erickson, *Introducing Christian Doctrine*, 128–37; Packer, *Concise Theology*, 54–56.

45. Davis, *Handbook of Basic Bible Texts*, 49.

46. Berkhof, *Summary of Christian Doctrine*, 59–63; Grudem, *Systematic Theology*, 316–36; Erickson, *Introducing Christian Doctrine*, 128–37.

47. Psalms 136:25; 145:15; Nehemiah 9:6; Acts 17:28; Colossians 1:17; Hebrews 1:3.

48. Deuteronomy 8:18; Psalm 104:20–21, 30; Amos 3:6; Matthew 5:45; 10:29; Acts 14:17; Philippians 2:13.

49. Genesis 50:20; cf. 45:5–8; Psalm 103:19; Proverbs 16:33; Daniel 4:34–35; Matthew 10:29–31; Acts 16:14; Ephesians 1:11.

50. Davis, *Handbook of Basic Bible Texts*, 49–52; Packer, *Concise Theology*, 54–55.

51. Daniel 4:35; Ephesians 1:11.

52. Psalm 104:14; Matthew 5:45.

53. Job 12:23–24; Acts 4:27–28.

54. Job 14:5; Galatians 1:15–16.

55. Proverbs 16:33; Romans 8:28.

56. Genesis 22:8; 2 Corinthians 9:8.

57. 2 Chronicles 33:13; Matthew 7:7.

58. Erickson, *Introducing Christian Doctrine*, 128–29.

59. See Samples, "Aren't Christianity and Science Enemies?" in *Without a Doubt*, 187–200.

60. For further discussion on the problem of evil in relationship to historic Christianity, see Samples, "How Can a Good and All-Powerful God Allow Evil?" 239–54.

61. See Packer, *Concise Theology*, 56; Grudem, *Systematic Theology*, 322–30.

62. Grudem, *Systematic Theology*, 271.

Chapter 10 The Historic Christian View of Man

1. William Hasker, *Metaphysics: Constructing a Worldview* (Downers Grove, IL: InterVarsity, 1983), 72.

2. Genesis 5:1; 9:6; 1 Corinthians 11:7; Colossians 3:10; James 3:9.

3. Grudem, *Systematic Theology*, 442–50. Grudem's discussion of the *imago Dei* is clear and thoughtful.

4. Geoffrey W. Bromiley, ed., *The International Standard Bible Encyclopedia*, vol. 2 rev. ed. (Grand Rapids: Eerdmans, 1982), s.v. "Image of God."

5. Grudem, *Systematic Theology*, 443.

6. Muller, *Dictionary of Latin and Greek Theological Terms*, s.v. "imago Dei."

7. Erickson, *Christian Theology*, 513.

8. Berkhof, *Summary of Christian Doctrine*, 69–70.

9. Grudem, *Systematic Theology*, 445–48; Berkhof, *Summary of Christian Doctrine*, 69–70.

10. Plantinga, *Engaging God's World*, x.

11. It appears that there are two types of "immortality" implied in Scripture. First, through being made in the image of God, human beings have a derived or created immortality which means that the soul will survive the death of the body. This "consciousness" in the intermediate state following death is true for believers (Luke 23:43; 2 Cor. 5:6–8; Phil. 1:21, 23–24; Heb. 12:23; Rev. 6:9–10; 14:13) and nonbelievers (Eccles. 12:7; Luke 16:22–23; 2 Peter 2:9). Second, immortality is spoken of as being the gift of God through redemption in Jesus Christ (Rom. 2:7; 2 Tim. 1:10). Of course, only God alone has an inherent immortality (1 Tim. 1:17; 6:16).

12. Ecclesiastes 7:29.

13. Genesis 1–2.

14. Charles Hodge, *Systematic Theology*, vol. 2 (1873; repr., Grand Rapids: Eerdmans, 1986), 97.

15. Herman Bavinck, *Gereformeerde Dogmatiek*, 3rd ed. (Kampen, Netherlands: Kok, 1918), 2:595–96, as quoted and translated by Anthony A. Hoekema in *Created in God's Image* (Grand Rapids: Eerdmans, 1986), 65.

16. Hoekema, *Created in God's Image*, 5–10.

17. Romans 11:33–36.

18. Genesis 3.

19. Romans 5:12–21.

20. Psalms 51:5; 58:3; Romans 1:18–21; 6:23; 8:7–8; Ephesians 2:1–3; 4:17–19.

21. Romans 3:23; Galatians 5:19–21.

22. Genesis 9:6; James 3:9.

23. Genesis 6:5; Romans 1:18–21; Ephesians 2:1–3; 4:17–19.

24. Davis, *Handbook of Basic Bible Texts*, 53.

25. Hoekema, *Created in God's Image*, 22.

26. John 1:14; Philippians 2:6–11; Colossians 2:9.

27. Hoekema, *Created in God's Image*, 22.

28. Ephesians 1:4; 2 Timothy 1:9–10; 1 Peter 1:18–21; Revelation 13:8.

29. John 14:8–9.

30. Davis, *Handbook of Basic Bible Texts*, 54.

31. Grudem, *Systematic Theology*, 449–50; Erickson, *Christian Theology*, 516.

32. Davis, *Handbook of Basic Bible Texts*, 54.

33. Hoekema, *Created in God's Image*, 16.

34. See the chapter on capital punishment in J. P. Moreland and Norman L. Geisler, *The Life and Death Debate: Moral Issues of Our Times* (New York: Praeger, 1990), 103–21; see also the chapter on capital punishment in John Jefferson Davis, *Evangelical Ethics: Issues Facing the Church Today*, 2nd ed. (Phillipsburg, NJ: P & R Publishing, 1993), 175–88. The penalty of life imprisonment for murderers is not justice because the punishment (life in confinement) does not match the crime (the taking of an innocent life).

35. Romans 13:1–5.

36. Calvin, *Institutes of the Christian Religion*, 1.1.1.

37. Westminster Shorter Catechism, Q. 1, in *Reformed Confessions Harmonized*, 3.

38. Ibid.

39. Augustine, *Confessions*, bk. 1, 1.

40. Ibid., bk. 1, 20.

41. For a provocative and clear discussion of humankind's fallen condition and how that often leads to the state of the "divided self," see Nash, *Worldviews in Conflict*, 46–53.

42. Plantinga, *Engaging God's World*, 6–7.

43. Blaise Pascal, *Pensées*, trans. A. J. Krailsheimer, rev. ed. (New York: Penguin, 1995), no. 148/428. The *Pensées* have been translated into two basic versions. The numbering of the sections from both translations is provided.

44. Ibid., 417/548.

45. Augustine, *Confessions*, bk. 1, 5.

46. *The NIV Study Bible*, ed. Kenneth Barker (Grand Rapids: Zondervan, 1995), 8.

47. Genesis 1:29–30.

48. Genesis 2:19; cf. 2:7 where the term refers to Adam.

49. Rana with Ross, *Who Was Adam?* 48–49, 199–225.

50. See Harold H. Titus, Marilyn S. Smith, and Richard T. Nolan, *Living Issues in Philosophy*, 9th ed. (Belmont, CA: Wadsworth, 1995), 28–29. This philosophy text lists eight ways in which humans differ from the rest of nature. This chapter utilizes some of that material but also reorganizes and adds to it.

51. Ibid., 29.

52. For a refutation of moral relativism and a defense of moral absolutism, see Samples, "Isn't Morality Simply in the Eye of the Beholder?" in *Without a Doubt*, 229–38.

53. Alvin Plantinga, "Right and Wrong," in *Great Thinkers on Great Questions*, ed. Roy Abraham Varghese (Oxford: Oneworld, 1998), 102.

54. J. P. Moreland, *Christianity and the Nature of Science* (Grand Rapids: Baker, 1989), 11.

55. Titus, Smith, and Nolan, *Living Issues in Philosophy*, 29.

56. Stephen W. Hawking, *A Brief History of Time: From the Big Bang to Black Holes* (New York: Bantam, 1988), 171.

57. Ibid., 175.

58. Pascal, *Pensées*, 114/397.

59. For a discussion of Pascal's view of man and the explanatory power of Christianity, see Samples, "Why Should I Gamble on Faith?" in *Without a Doubt*, 77–87.

60. Thomas V. Morris, *Making Sense of It All: Pascal and the Meaning of Life* (Grand Rapids: Eerdmans, 1992), 129.

61. The discussion of sin in this chapter was modified from Samples, *Without a Doubt*, 150.

62. Erickson, *Christian Theology*, 781–823.

63. For a discussion of the view known as "federalism," see Berkhof, *Summary of Christian Doctrine*, 75–76.

64. Reymond, *New Systematic Theology of the Christian Faith*, 430–36.

65. Romans 5:12, 18–19.

66. Davis, *Handbook of Basic Bible Texts*, 56. See also Psalms 51:5; 58:3; 1 Corinthians 15:22; Ephesians 2:3.

67. Psalms 51:5, 58:3; Proverbs 20:9.

68. Psalm 143:2; Ecclesiastes 7:20; Jeremiah 17:9; Galatians 3:22; James 3:2; 4:4.

69. John 8:45; 2 Corinthians 5:21; Hebrews 4:15; 1 Peter 2:22; 1 John 3:5.

70. Jeremiah 17:9; Matthew 15:19.

71. Ephesians 2:3; 4:17–19.

72. Reymond, *New Systematic Theology of the Christian Faith*, 450–53.

73. Jeremiah 17:9; John 5:42; 6:44; Romans 3:19–20; 7:18; 1 Corinthians 2:14; Titus 1:15.

74. Ecclesiastes 7:20; Matthew 15:19; Romans 3:23.

75. Isaiah 6:3; Deuteronomy 32:4; Psalm 98:9.

76. Romans 1:18; Ephesians 2:3.

77. For a discussion of salvation in and through faith in Jesus Christ, see Samples, "Why Did Jesus Christ Have to Die?" 148–57.

78. See Mark Roseman, *The Wannsee Conference and the Final Solution: A Reconsideration* (New York: Henry Holt and Company, 2002).

79. Hugh Ross conveyed this to me in a private conversation (Glendora, CA, 2001).

Chapter 11 The Historic Christian View of Moral Values

1. For more on the Christian worldview's perspective on ethics and values, see Samples, "Isn't Morality Simply in the Eye of the Beholder?" 235–37.

2. For a brief but clear response to the "Euthyphro Problem," see Paul Copan, "A Moral Argument," in *To Everyone an Answer: A Case for the Christian Worldview: Essays in Honor of Norman L. Geisler*, ed. Francis J. Beckwith, William Lane Craig, and J. P. Moreland (Downers Grove, IL: InterVarsity, 2004), 119–22.

3. Ibid., 113.

4. Miller, *Questions That Matter*, 406.

5. Nash, *Life's Ultimate Questions*, 345–46.

6. For a fuller discussion of moral relativism, see Samples, *Without a Doubt*, 229–38.

7. For more discussion on God and the problem of evil, see Samples, "How Can a Good and All-Powerful God Allow Evil?" 239–54.

8. Morris, *Making Sense of It All*, 56–59.

9. Acts 20:28; Romans 3:24–25; 4:25; 8:2–3; 2 Corinthians 8:9; 9:15.

Chapter 12 Naturalism: A Secular Worldview Challenge

1. According to some figures, secularism could represent 20 percent of the world's population; see Dean Halverson, ed., *The Illustrated Guide to World Religions* (Bloomington, MN: Bethany, 2003), 196.

2. For a popular website that both explains and defends metaphysical or ontological naturalism, see the Center for Naturalism, http://www.centerfornaturalism.org/, and its companion website Naturalism.org, http://www.naturalism.org/. There are two articles on these websites that are quite informative: "Tenets of Naturalism" http://www.naturalism.org/tenetsof.htm and "A Guide to Naturalism" http://www.centerfornaturalism.org/descriptions.htm (accessed November 2, 2005).

3. The following sources have helpful articles on philosophical "naturalism": Angeles, *HarperCollins Dictionary of Philosophy*, s.v. "naturalism"; Audi, *Cambridge Dictionary of Philosophy*, s.v. "naturalism"; Norman L. Geisler, *Baker Encyclopedia of Christian Apologetics* (Grand Rapids: Baker, 1999), s.v. "Naturalism"; Elwell, *Evangelical Dictionary of Theology*, s.v. "Naturalism."

4. *Britannica Concise Encyclopedia* (Chicago: Encyclopaedia Britannica, 2002), s.v. "naturalism."

5. See Audi, *Cambridge Dictionary of Philosophy*, s.v. "naturalism."

6. See Michael Rea, "Naturalism and Material Objects," in *Naturalism: A Critical Analysis*, ed. William Lane Craig and J. P. Moreland (London: Routledge, 2000), 110.

7. There are helpful articles on "monism" in the following sources: Angeles, *HarperCollins Dictionary of Philosophy*; Geisler, *Baker Encyclopedia of Christian Apologetics*; Elwell, *Evangelical Dictionary of Theology*.

8. Audi, *Cambridge Dictionary of Philosophy*, s.v. "naturalism."

9. Ibid.; The *Britannica Concise Encyclopedia's* article on "naturalism" states the following concerning naturalism's relationship to materialism: "While naturalism has often been equated with materialism, it is much broader in scope. Though materialism is naturalistic, the converse is not necessarily true. Strictly speaking, naturalism has no ontological bias toward any particular set of categories of reality."

10. There are helpful articles on philosophical "materialism" in the following sources: Angeles, *HarperCollins Dictionary of Philosophy*, s.v. "materialism"; Audi, *Cambridge Dictionary of Philosophy*, s.v. "metaphysics"; Geisler, *Baker Encyclopedia of Christian Apologetics*, s.v. "Materialism."

11. There are brief but helpful articles on "physicalism" in the following sources: Angeles, *HarperCollins Dictionary of Philosophy*, s.vv. "physicalism," "physicalism (mind/body)"; and Audi, *Cambridge Dictionary of Philosophy*, s.v. "physicalism." For a thorough evaluation of physicalism from a Christian theistic perspective, see Moreland and Craig, *Philosophical Foundations for a Christian Worldview*, chaps. 8–14.

12. There are helpful articles on "scientism" in the following sources: Angeles, *HarperCollins Dictionary of Philosophy*; and Geisler, *Baker Encyclopedia of Christian Apologetics*.

13. "Tenets of Naturalism," http://www.naturalism.org/tenetsof.htm (accessed November 2, 2005).

14. For a fair and objective comparison of the naturalistic models of the origin of life with that of the biblical creation model, see Rana and Ross, *Origins of Life*.

15. Brief but helpful articles on the general theory of evolution are found in the following sources: Angeles, *HarperCollins Dictionary of Philosophy*, s.vv. "evolution," "natural selection (Darwin)"; and *Britannica Concise Encyclopedia*, s.v. "evolution."

16. For a fair and objective comparison of the evolutionary model of human origins with that of the biblical creation model, see Rana with Ross, *Who Was Adam?*

17. Angeles, *HarperCollins Dictionary of Philosophy*, s.v. "naturalism."

18. "A Guide to Naturalism," http://www.centerfornaturalism.org/descriptions.htm (accessed November 2, 2005).

19. For arguments in favor of God's existence, see Samples, "How Can Anyone Know That God Exists?" and "How Can I Believe in a God I Can't See?" in *Without a Doubt*, 21–33 and 34–41, respectively.

20. There are helpful articles on both atheism and agnosticism in the following sources: Angeles, *HarperCollins Dictionary of Philosophy*; Audi, *Cambridge Dictionary of Philosophy*; and

Paul Edwards, ed., *The Encyclopedia of Philosophy*, vol. 1 (New York: Macmillan, 1967).

21. There are helpful articles on secular humanism in the following sources: Angeles, *HarperCollins Dictionary of Philosophy*, s.v. "humanism, philosophical"; Audi, *Cambridge Dictionary of Philosophy*, s.v. "humanism"; and Geisler, *Baker Encyclopedia of Christian Apologetics*, s.v. "Humanism, Secular."

22. Some of the prominent works of contemporary scientists who embrace naturalism include: Carl Sagan, *The Demon-Haunted World: Science as a Candle in the Dark* (New York: Ballantine, 1997); Stephen J. Gould, *Rock of Ages: Science and Religion in the Fullness of Life* (New York: Ballantine, 2002); Richard Dawkins, *The Blind Watchmaker: Why the Evidence of Evolution Reveals a Universe without Design* (New York: Norton, 1987). Works of contemporary philosophers who defend naturalism include: J. L. Mackie, *The Miracle of Theism: Arguments For and Against the Existence of God* (Oxford: Oxford University Press, 1982); Daniel C. Dennett, *Darwin's Dangerous Idea: Evolution and the Meanings of Life* (New York: Simon & Schuster, 1996); Bertrand Russell, *Why I Am Not a Christian: And Other Essays on Religion and Related Subjects*, ed. Paul Edwards (New York: Simon & Schuster, 1957). For some recent works that explain and defend naturalism, see Andrew Melnyk, *A Physicalist Manifesto: Thoroughly Modern Materialism* (New York: Cambridge University Press, 2003); Richard C. Carrier, *Sense and Goodness without God: A Defense of Metaphysical Naturalism* (Bloomington, MN: Authorhouse, 2005); and Jaegwon Kim, *Physicalism, or Something Near Enough* (Princeton, NJ: Princeton University Press, 2005).

23. Hoover, *Case for Christian Theism*, 55.

24. Wainwright, *Philosophy of Religion*, 174.

25. Several thinkers have argued that naturalism in one manner or another involves a fundamental state of epistemological incoherence or is self-defeating in nature. These thinkers include: C. S. Lewis, *Miracles: A Preliminary Study* (New York: Macmillan, 1978), chaps. 1–4, 13; Richard Taylor, *Metaphysics*, 4th ed. (Englewood Cliffs, NJ: Prentice-Hall, 1992), 110–12; Alvin Plantinga, *Warrant and Proper Function* (New York; Oxford University Press,

1993), chaps. 11–12; Victor Reppert, *C. S. Lewis's Dangerous Idea: A Philosophical Defense of Lewis's Argument from Reason* (Downers Grove, IL: InterVarsity, 2003).

26. Copan, "A Moral Argument," 118.

27. See Daniel C. Dennett, *Breaking the Spell: Religion as a Natural Phenomenon* (New York: Viking, 2006); and Michael Shermer, "Believing in Belief," *Science* 311 (2006): 471.

28. For an extensive philosophical discussion of the "argument from reason," see Reppert, *C. S. Lewis's Dangerous Idea*; Victor Reppert, "Several Formulations of the Argument from Reason," *Philosophia Christi* 5, no. 1, (2003): 9–33; see also the following critiques: Theodore M. Drange, "Several Unsuccessful Formulations of the Argument from Reason: A Response to Victor Reppert," *Philosophia Christi*, 35–52; William Hasker, "What about a Sensible Naturalism? A Response to Victor Reppert," *Philosophia Christi*, 53–62; Keith Parsons, "Need Reasons Be Causes? A Further Reply to Victor Reppert's Argument from Reason," *Philosophia Christi*, 63–75; and Victor Reppert's response, "Some Supernatural Reasons Why My Critics Are Wrong: A Reply to Drange, Parsons, and Hasker," *Philosophia Christi*, 77–89.

29. See two similar tables that compare the explanatory power and scope of naturalism with that of Christian theism: Samples, *Without a Doubt*, 25; and Copan, "A Moral Argument," 114.

30. For more on Pascal's Wager, see Samples, "Why Should I Gamble on Faith?" 77–87.

31. See William Lane Craig, "The Indispensability of Theological Meta-Ethical Foundations for Morality," *Foundations* 5 (1997): 9–12, available online at Leadership U, http://www.leaderu.com/offices/billcraig/docs/meta-eth.html (accessed October 28, 2005).

32. Ibid.

Chapter 13 Postmodernism: A Skeptical Worldview Perspective

1. Miller, *Questions That Matter*, 8–9.

2. Audi, *Cambridge Dictionary of Philosophy*, s.v. "Sophists."

3. In some important ways, postmodernism does not correspond to the traditional definition of a worldview. For example, unlike Christian theism, naturalism, and pantheistic monism, postmodernism is not centered on metaphysics or ontology (ultimate reality). It is not even focused centrally on epistemology (though that is closer to the mark), but is rather oriented around creating meaning through language. For further discussion of this point, see Sire, *Universe Next Door*, 172–90.

4. Gene Edward Veith Jr., *Postmodern Times: A Christian Guide to Contemporary Thought and Culture* (Wheaton: Crossway, 1994), xii–xiii.

5. Erickson, *Christian Theology*, 166–67.

6. For sorting out how a Christian should relate to postmodernism and postmodern ideas, I recommend the following sources: Groothuis, *Truth Decay*; Veith, *Postmodern Times*; Millard Erickson, *Truth or Consequences: The Promise and Perils of Postmodernism* (Downers Grove, IL: InterVarsity, 2001); and Thomas Oden, *After Modernity . . . What? Agenda for Theology* (Grand Rapids: Zondervan, 1990).

7. Premodern, modern, and postmodern era presentations included here were influenced by Erickson, *Christian Theology*, 158–68; Groothuis, *Truth Decay*, chap. 2; Paul Copan, "What Is Postmodernism?" Apologetics (North American Mission Board), http://www.4truth.net/site/apps/nl/content3.asp?c=hiKXLbPNLrF&b=980863&ct=1318827; and "What Is Wrong (and Right) with Postmodernism?" Apologetics (North American Mission Board), http://www.4truth.net/site/apps/nl/content3.asp?c=hiKXLbPNLrF&b=980863&ct=1321233 (accessed October 27, 2005). The articles by Copan are clearly written and helpful aids in understanding postmodernism.

8. Groothuis, *Truth Decay*, 33.

9. Erickson, *Christian Theology*, 161.

10. Ibid.

11. Copan, "What Is Postmodernism?"

12. Groothuis, *Truth Decay*, 35.

13. Copan, "What Is Postmodernism?"

14. Erickson, *Christian Theology*, 163–64.

15. Groothuis, *Truth Decay*, 40–44.

16. See Thomas C. Oden, "The Death of Modernity and Postmodern Evangelical Spirituality," in *The Challenge of Postmodernism: An Evangelical Assessment*, ed. David S. Dockery (Wheaton: Victor, 1995), 23.

17. See Douglas Groothuis, "Facing the Challenge of Postmodernism," in Beckwith,

Craig, and Moreland, *To Everyone an Answer*, 238–53.

18. Copan, "What Is Postmodernism?"

19. My discussion of these postmodern characteristics was influenced by Groothuis, "Facing the Challenge of Postmodernism"; Erickson, *Christian Theology*; Groothuis, *Truth Decay*; and Copan, "What Is Postmodernism?"

20. See Jean-François Lyotard, *The Postmodern Condition: A Report on Knowledge*, trans. Geoff Bennington and Brian Massumi (Minneapolis: University of Minnesota Press, 1984).

21. Stanley J. Grenz, *A Primer on Postmodernism* (Grand Rapids: Eerdmans, 1996), 45.

22. Ibid., 43.

23. Carson and Moo, *Introduction to the New Testament*, 61.

24. Chris Rohmann, *A World of Ideas: A Dictionary of Important Theories, Concepts, Beliefs, and Thinkers* (New York: Ballantine, 1999), s.v. "deconstruction."

25. A few works of prominent postmodernist thinkers include: Jacques Derrida, *Of Grammatology*, corrected ed., trans. Gayatri Chakravorty Spivak (Baltimore: Johns Hopkins University Press, 1997); Lyotard, *The Postmodern Condition*; Richard Rorty, *The Consequences of Pragmatism: Essays, 1972–1980* (Minneapolis: University of Minnesota Press, 1982).

26. Copan, "What Is Wrong (and Right) with Postmodernism?"

27. Ibid.; see also Carson and Moo, *Introduction to the New Testament*, 62–64.

28. Copan, "What Is Wrong (and Right) with Postmodernism?"

29. Ibid.; Carson and Moo, *Introduction to the New Testament*, 64.

30. Copan, "What Is Wrong (and Right) with Postmodernism?"

Chapter 14 Pantheistic Monism: An Eastern Mystical Viewpoint

1. For information about the world's religions, see Huston Smith, *The World's Religions*, rev. ed. (San Francisco: HarperSanFrancisco, 1991); John A. Hutchison, *Paths of Faith*, 4th ed. (New York: McGraw-Hill, 1991); David S. Noss, *A History of the World's Religions*, 11th ed. (New York: Macmillan, 2002).

2. The following works provide a helpful understanding of the various aspects of pantheistic monism from the standpoint of the Christian theistic worldview and have influenced my thinking on the subject: Corduan, *Neighboring Faiths*, chaps. 7–9; Halverson, *Illustrated Guide to World Religions*, especially the section entitled "World Religions Overview," 10–30; David K. Clark and Norman L. Geisler, *Apologetics in the New Age: A Christian Critique of Pantheism* (Grand Rapids: Baker, 1990); Geisler and Watkins, *Worlds Apart*, chap. 3; Douglas R. Groothuis, *Unmasking the New Age* (Downers Grove, IL: InterVarsity, 1986), esp. chap. 1; Sire, *Universe Next Door*, chaps. 7 and 8.

3. For a detailed discussion of the various varieties of pantheism, along with a historic Christian critique, see Clark and Geisler, *Apologetics in the New Age*.

4. Corduan, *Neighboring Faiths*, 199.

5. David S. Noss and John B. Noss, *A History of the World's Religions*, 8th ed. (New York: Macmillan, 1990), 90. The 8th (and 9th) edition was written by both Nosses, father and son. David S. Noss wrote subsequent editions, including the present 11th edition, after his father died. A 12th edition is scheduled to release in 2008.

6. Corduan, *Neighboring Faiths*, 196–97.

7. Clark and Geisler, *Apologetics in the New Age*, 240.

8. For a brief but clear discussion of Advaita Vedanta Hinduism, see Corduan, *Neighboring Faiths*, 197–200.

9. For positive features of pantheistic monism, see Paul Copan, *"That's Just Your Interpretation": Responding to Skeptics Who Challenge Your Faith* (Grand Rapids: Baker, 2001), 57; Geisler and Watkins, *Worlds Apart*, 101.

10. My criticisms of the worldview of pantheistic monism were influenced by the following sources: Copan, *"That's Just Your Interpretation"*, chaps. 5 and 6; and Richard L. Purtill, *Thinking about Religion: A Philosophical Introduction to Religion* (Englewood Cliffs, NJ: Prentice-Hall, 1978), chap. 7.

11. Copan, *"That's Just Your Interpretation"*, 63.

12. Paul Copan identifies a number of other basic incoherencies with the worldview pantheistic monism: see Copan, *"That's Just Your Interpretation"*, 51–59.

13. Purtill, *Thinking about Religion*, 105–7.

14. Ibid., 107.

15. Copan, *"That's Just Your Interpretation"*, 52–53.

16. Ibid., 65–66.

17. Purtill, *Thinking about Religion*, 103; Copan, *"That's Just Your Interpretation"*, 65.

18. Purtill, *Thinking about Religion*, 104–5.

Chapter 15 Islam: A Radical Monotheistic Challenge

1. Halverson, *Illustrated Guide to World Religions*, 103.

2. Seyyed Hossein Nasr, *Islam: Religion, History, and Civilization* (San Francisco: HarperSanFrancisco, 2003), 21.

3. As of 2003 it was estimated that there were more than six million Muslims living in North America (see ibid., 23).

4. Ibid., xi.

5. The following works provide a helpful understanding of the religion of Islam and have influenced my thinking on the subject: Smith, *World's Religions*, chap. 6; John L. Esposito, *Islam: The Straight Path*, 3rd ed. (New York: Oxford University Press, 1998); John L. Esposito, ed., *Oxford Encyclopedia of the Modern Islamic World*, 4 vols. (New York: Oxford University Press, 1995); Seyyed Hossein Nasr, *The Heart of Islam: Enduring Values of Humanity* (San Francisco: HarperSanFrancisco, 2002); Nasr, *Islam*.

6. The following works provide a helpful understanding of the various aspects of the religion of Islam from the standpoint of the Christian theistic worldview and have influenced my thinking on the subject: Corduan, *Neighboring Faiths*, chap. 3; Halverson, *Illustrated Guide to World Religions*, 103–24; Norman L. Geisler and Abdul Saleeb, *Answering Islam: The Crescent in Light of the Cross*, 2nd ed. (Grand Rapids: Baker, 2002).

7. Esposito, *Islam*, 22.

8. Ibid.

9. Nasr, *Islam*, 61; Geisler and Saleeb, *Answering Islam*, 23–28.

10. Esposito, *Islam*, 21.

11. See Corduan, *Neighboring Faiths*, 89.

12. For a Muslim scholar who argues that Allah is clearly both transcendent and immanent, see Nasr, *Islam*, 60.

13. Nasr, *Islam*, 64–5; Geisler and Saleeb, *Answering Islam*, 36–40.

14. Some Islamic scholars identify the jinn as being "psychic" rather than "spiritual" beings; see Nasr, *Islam*, 65.

15. Ibid., 39.

16. Ibid., 62.

17. Corduan, *Neighboring Faiths*, 90.

18. Esposito, *Islam*, 5–8.

19. Ibid., 5.

20. Nasr, *Islam*, 46.

21. Esposito, *Islam*, 11.

22. Corduan, *Neighboring Faiths*, 91.

23. Esposito, *Islam*, 18.

24. Geisler and Saleeb, *Answering Islam*, 101.

25. Ibid., 91.

26. Nasr, *Islam*, 43.

27. Geisler and Saleeb, *Answering Islam*, 92.

28. For additional details about the Qur'an, see Esposito, *Islam*, 17–22; Geisler and Saleeb, *Answering Islam*, 91–108; and Nasr, *Islam*, 37–43.

29. See *The Koran*, trans. N. J. Dawood (New York; Penguin, 1993).

30. Concerning judgment in Islam, see Esposito, *Islam*, 25–28; Geisler and Saleeb, *Answering Islam*, 109–31; and Nasr, *Islam*, 72–74.

31. With regard to The Five Pillars of Islam, see Huston Smith, *The Illustrated World's Religions: A Guide to Our Wisdom Traditions* (New York: HarperSanFrancisco. 1994), 160–63; Esposito, *Islam*, 88–93; and Nasr, *Islam*, 91–96.

32. Nasr, *Islam*, 91.

33. Smith, *Illustrated World's Religions*, 162.

34. Nasr, *Islam*, 3.

35. Smith, *Illustrated World's Religions*, 160.

36. Nasr, *Islam*, 92.

37. Ibid.

38. Ibid., 94–95.

39. For an evaluation of the Muslim concept of jihad, see Islamic scholar Nasr, *Islam*, 34, 91, 96–7; and Christian scholar Corduan, *Neighboring Faiths*, 102–3.

40. See the Muslim discussion of "Islam in the Contemporary World," in Nasr, *Islam*, 173–86.

41. Ibid., 178–82.

42. For a summary of Islam's intellectual achievements in the Middle Ages, see Lawrence

Cunningham and John Reich, *Culture and Values: A Survey of the Western Humanities*, vol. 1, 2nd ed. (Fort Worth, TX; Holt, Rinehart and Winston, n.d.), 305.

43. For a brief discussion of Islam's scientific emphasis, see Nasr, *Islam*, xxi–xxii.

44. For a defense of the Qur'an on the basis of science, see Muslim apologist Maurice Bucaille, *The Bible, the Qur'an and Science*, trans. Alastair D. Pannell (Indianapolis: American Trust Publications, 1979). For a specific Christian response to Bucaille's work, see William Campbell, *The Qur'an and the Bible in the Light of History and Science* (Upper Darby, PA: Middle East Resources, 1992).

45. Esposito, *Islam*, 18.

46. For textual studies that refute the Islamic claim of substantial corruption of the Bible, see Geisler and Nix, *General Introduction to the Bible* and Bruce M. Metzger, *The Text of the New Testament: Its Transmission, Corruption, and Restoration*, 3rd ed. (New York: Oxford University Press, 1992).

47. See Gerald Bray, *Creeds, Councils and Christ* (Ross-shire, UK: Mentor, 1997); Louis Berkhof, *The History of Christian Doctrines* (Grand Rapids: Baker, 1975); Kelly, *Early Christian Doctrines*.

48. Nasr, *Islam*, 37–38.

49. Esposito, *Islam*, 22.

50. See Nasr, *Islam*, 62.

51. For more on the life and thought of Augustine of Hippo, see Augustine Fellowship Study Center, http://www.augustinefellowship.org/.

52. Pascal, *Pensées*, 131/434. The *Pensées* have been translated into two basic versions. The numbering of the sections from both translations is provided. For more discussion of Blaise Pascal and his views on human nature, see Samples, "Why Should I Gamble on Faith?" 77–87.

Chapter 16 Testing the Christian Theistic Worldview

1. Heidelberg Catechism, Question and Answer #1 in *Ecumenical Creeds and Reformed Confessions*, 13.

2. Many people prayed for me and graciously reached out to my family during my health crisis. I discovered later that some people who I had never actually met learned of my illness and prayed for me while I was sick. This discovery deeply touched me and left me with a genuine sense of gratitude.

3. John Jefferson Davis, *Foundations of Evangelical Theology* (Grand Rapids: Baker, 1984), 117.

4. For a defense of the doctrine of the Trinity against the charges of incoherence, see Samples, "How Can God Be Three and One?" 63–76; Thomas D. Senor, "The Incarnation and the Trinity," in *Reason for the Hope Within*, ed. Michael J. Murray (Grand Rapids: Eerdmans, 1999), chap. 10, 238–60; Moreland and Craig, *Philosophical Foundations for a Christian Worldview*, chap. 29, 575–96.

5. See Calvin, *Institutes of the Christian Religion*, 2.13.4, 1:481.

6. Milne, *Know the Truth*, 146–47.

7. For a defense of the doctrine of the Incarnation against the charges of incoherence, see Samples, "How Can Jesus Christ Be Both God and Man?" 120–33; Thomas V. Morris, *The Logic of God Incarnate* (Ithaca, NY: Cornell, 1986); Moreland and Craig, *Philosophical Foundations for a Christian Worldview*, chap. 30, 597–614.

8. For a historic Christian response to the problem of evil, see Samples, "How Can a Good and All-Powerful God Allow Evil?" 239–54; Alvin Plantinga, *God, Freedom, and Evil* (Grand Rapids: Eerdmans, 1974); Nash, *Faith and Reason*, chaps. 13–15.

9. For a discussion of the possibility of having goodness and evil without God, see Samples, *Without a Doubt*, 244–46.

10. Wainwright, *Philosophy of Religion*, 171–72.

11. Ibid., 172.

12. Oxford philosopher Richard Swinburne argues for God's existence as an adequate explanation of reality. For a more popular treatment, see Richard Swinburne, *Is There a God?* (Oxford: Oxford University Press, 1996); for a more technical, philosophical treatment, see Richard Swinburne, *The Existence of God* (Oxford: Clarendon, 1979).

13. For a discussion of the Christian worldview's impact on the emergence of science, see Samples, "Aren't Christianity and Science Enemies?" 187–200; Nancy R. Pearcey and Charles B. Thaxton, *The Soul of Science: Christian Faith and Natural Philosophy* (Wheaton:

Crossway, 1994); Rodney Stark, *For the Glory of God: How Monotheism Led to Reformations, Science, Witch-Hunts, and the End of Slavery* (Princeton, NJ: Princeton University Press, 2003); Stanley L. Jaki, *The Savior of Science* (Grand Rapids: Eerdmans, 2000).

14. For a defense of the historicity of the person of Jesus of Nazareth, see Gary R. Habermas, *The Historical Jesus: Ancient Evidence for the Life of Christ* (Joplin, MO: College Press, 1996); John Warwick Montgomery, *History and Christianity* (Minneapolis: Bethany, 1965); R. T. France, *The Evidence for Jesus* (Downers Grove, IL: Inter-Varsity, 1986); Edwin Yamauchi, "Jesus Outside the New Testament: What Is the Evidence?" in J. P. Moreland and Michael J. Wilkins, eds., *Jesus under Fire: Modern Scholarship Reinvents the Historical Jesus* (Grand Rapids: Zondervan, 1996), chap. 8.

15. For apologetic evidence of the resurrection of Jesus as well as critiques of alternative naturalistic theories, see William Lane Craig, *Knowing the Truth about the Resurrection* (Ann Arbor, MI: Servant, 1988); William Lane Craig, *Reasonable Faith: Christian Truth and Apologetics* (Wheaton, IL: Crossway Books, 1994), 255–98; William Lane Craig, *Assessing the New Testament Evidence for the Historicity of the Resurrection of Jesus* (Lewiston, NY: Edwin Mellen, 1989); Stephen T. Davis, *Risen Indeed: Making Sense of the Resurrection* (Grand Rapids: Eerdmans, 1993); Norman L. Geisler, *The Battle for the Resurrection* (Nashville: Thomas Nelson, 1992); Moreland, *Scaling the Secular City*, 159–183; Kreeft and Tacelli, *Handbook of Christian Apologetics*, 175–198.

16. For a Christian discussion of the dark periods in Christian history, see Samples, "Doesn't Hypocrisy Invalidate Christianity?" in *Without a Doubt*, 201–10.

17. Richard Purtill, *Thinking about Ethics* (Englewood Cliffs, NJ: Prentice Hall, 1976), 136.

18. Ibid., see also Matthew 7:12; Romans 15:1; James 2:14–26.

SELECTED BIBLIOGRAPHY

Bandow, Doug. *Beyond Good Intentions: A Biblical View of Politics.* Wheaton: Crossway, 1988.

Beckwith, Francis J., William Lane Craig, and J. P. Moreland, eds. *To Everyone an Answer: A Case for the Christian Worldview: Essays in Honor of Norman L. Geisler.* Downers Grove, IL: InterVarsity, 2004.

Blamires, Harry. *The Christian Mind: How Should a Christian Think?* Ann Arbor, MI: Servant, 1978.

Bush, L. Russ. *A Handbook for Christian Philosophy.* Grand Rapids: Zondervan, 1991.

Carson, D. A., gen. ed. *Telling the Truth: Evangelizing Postmoderns.* Grand Rapids: Zondervan, 2000.

Clark, Gordon H. *A Christian View of Men and Things: An Introduction to Philosophy.* Grand Rapids: Eerdmans, 1951.

Clouser, Roy A. *The Myth of Religious Neutrality: An Essay on the Hidden Role of Religious Belief in Theories.* Rev. ed. Notre Dame, IN: University of Notre Dame Press, 2005.

Colson, Charles, and Nancy Pearcey. *How Now Shall We Live?* Wheaton: Tyndale, 1999.

Copan, Paul. *"That's Just Your Interpretation": Responding to Skeptics Who Challenge Your Faith.* Grand Rapids: Baker, 2001.

Dockery, David S., and Gregory Alan Thornbury, eds. *Shaping a Christian Worldview: The Foundations of Christian Higher Education.* Nashville: Broadman & Holman, 2002.

Dooyeweerd, Herman. *Roots of Western Culture: Pagan, Secular, and Christian Options.* Trans. John Kraay. Lewiston, NY: Edwin Mellen Press, 2003.

Doran, Robert. *Birth of a Worldview: Early Christianity in Its Jewish and Pagan Context.* Lanham, MD: Rowman & Littlefield, 1999.

Eckman, James P. *The Truth about Worldviews: A Biblical Understanding of Worldview Alternatives.* Wheaton: Crossway, 2004.

Erickson, Millard J., Paul Kjoss Helseth, and Justin Taylor, eds. *Reclaiming the Center: Confronting Evangelical Accommodation in Postmodern Times.* Wheaton: Crossway, 2004.

Geisler, Norman L., and William D. Watkins. *Worlds Apart: A Handbook on World Views,* 2nd ed. Eugene, OR: Wipf and Stock, 2003.

Godawa, Brian. *Hollywood Worldviews: Watching Films with Wisdom and Discernment.* Downers Grove, IL: InterVarsity, 2002.

Groothuis, Douglas R. *Truth Decay: Defending Christianity against the Challenges of Postmodernism.* Downers Grove, IL: InterVarsity, 2000.

———. *Unmasking the New Age.* Downers Grove, IL: InterVarsity, 1986.

Halverson, Dean, gen. ed. *The Illustrated Guide to World Religions.* Bloomington, MN: Bethany House, 2003.

Halverson, William H. *A Concise Introduction to Philosophy.* 4th ed. New York; Random House, 1981.

Harris, Robert A. *The Integration of Faith and Learning: A Worldview Approach.* Eugene, OR: Cascade, 2004.

Holmes, Arthur F. *All Truth Is God's Truth.* Grand Rapids: Eerdmans, 1977.

———. *Contours of a World View.* Grand Rapids: Eerdmans. 1983.

Honeysett, Marcus. *Meltdown: Making Sense of a Culture in Crisis.* Grand Rapids: Kregel, 2005.

Kline, Meredith G. *Kingdom Prologue: Genesis Foundations for a Covenantal Worldview.* Eugene, OR: Wipf and Stock, 2006.

Kreeft, Peter. *Three Philosophies of Life.* San Francisco: Ignatius, 1989.

Kuyper, Abraham. *Lectures on Calvinism.* Grand Rapids: Eerdmans, 1931.

McCallum, Dennis, gen. ed. *The Death of Truth: Responding to Multiculturalism, the Rejection of Reason and the New Postmodern Diversity.* Minneapolis: Bethany, 1996.

Middleton, J. Richard, and Brian J. Walsh. *Truth Is Stranger than It Used to Be: Biblical Faith in a Postmodern Age.* Downers Grove, IL: InterVarsity, 1995.

Moreland, J. P., and William Lane Craig. *Philosophical Foundations for a Christian Worldview.* Downers Grove, IL: InterVarsity, 2003.

Moseley, N. Allan. *Thinking against the Grain: Developing a Biblical Worldview in a Culture of Myths.* Grand Rapids: Kregel, 2003.

Mouw, Richard J. *He Shines in All That's Fair: Culture and Common Grace.* Grand Rapids: Eerdmans, 2001.

———. *When the Kings Come Marching In: Isaiah and the New Jerusalem.* Grand Rapids: Eerdmans, 1984.

Myers, Kenneth A. *All God's Children and Blue Suede Shoes: Christians and Popular Culture.* Wheaton: Crossway, 1989.

Nash, Ronald H. *Faith and Reason: Searching for a Rational Faith.* Grand Rapids: Zondervan, 1988. Chapters 2–4.

———. *Life's Ultimate Questions: An Introduction to Philosophy*. Grand Rapids: Zondervan, 1999. Chapter 1.

———. *The Meaning of History*. Nashville: Broadman & Holman, 1998.

———. *Worldviews in Conflict: Choosing Christianity in a World of Ideas*. Grand Rapids: Zondervan, 1992.

Naugle, David K. *Worldview: The History of a Concept*. Grand Rapids: Eerdmans, 2002.

Netland, Harold. *Dissonant Voices: Religious Pluralism and the Question of Truth*. Vancouver, BC: Regent College Publishing, 1999.

Newport, John P. *The New Age Movement and the Biblical Worldview: Conflict and Dialogue*. Grand Rapids: Eerdmans, 1998.

Noebel, David A. *The Battle for Truth: Defending the Christian Worldview in the Marketplace of Ideas*. Eugene, OR: Harvest House, 2001.

———. *Understanding the Times*. Eugene, OR: Harvest House, 1994.

Orr, James. *The Christian View of God and the World*. Grand Rapids: Kregel, 1989.

Palmer, Michael D., comp. and ed. *Elements of a Christian Worldview*. Springfield, MO: Logion, 1998.

Pearcey, Nancy R. *Total Truth: Liberating Christianity from Its Cultural Captivity*. Wheaton: Crossway, 2004.

Pearcey, Nancy R., and Charles B. Thaxton. *The Soul of Science: Christian Faith and Natural Philosophy*. Wheaton: Crossway, 1994.

Phillips, W. Gary, and William E. Brown. *Making Sense of Your World: A Biblical Worldview*. Salem, WI: Sheffield, 1991.

Plantinga, Cornelius, Jr. *Engaging God's World: A Christian Vision of Faith, Learning, and Living*. Grand Rapids: Eerdmans, 2002.

Purtill, Richard L. *Thinking about Religion: A Philosophical Introduction to Religion*. Englewood Cliffs, NJ: Prentice-Hall, 1978.

Samples, Kenneth Richard. *Without a Doubt: Answering the 20 Toughest Faith Questions*. Grand Rapids: Baker, 2004.

Schaeffer, Francis A. *The Complete Works of Francis A. Schaeffer: A Christian Worldview*. 5 vols. Wheaton: Crossway, 1985.

Schlossberg, Herbert, and Marvin Olasky. *Turning Point: A Christian Worldview Declaration*. Wheaton: Crossway, 1987.

Sire, James W. *Naming the Elephant: Worldview as a Concept*. Downers Grove, IL: InterVarsity, 2004.

———. *The Universe Next Door: A Basic Worldview Catalog*, 3rd. ed. Downers Grove, IL: InterVarsity, 1997.

Smith, Ralph A. *Trinity and Reality: An Introduction to the Christian Faith*. Moscow, ID: Canon, 2004.

Sproul, R. C. *Lifeviews*. Grand Rapids: Revell, 1990.

Van Til, Henry R. *The Calvinist Concept of Culture*. Grand Rapids: Baker, 1972.

Veith, Gene Edward Jr. *God at Work: Your Christian Vocation in All of Life*. Wheaton: Crossway, 2002.

———. *Postmodern Times: A Christian Guide to Contemporary Thought and Culture.* Wheaton: Crossway, 1994.

———. *State of the Arts: From Bezalel to Mapplethorpe.* Wheaton: Crossway, 1991.

Wainwright, William J. *Philosophy of Religion.* Belmont, CA: Wadsworth, 1988.

Walsh, Brian J., and J. Richard Middleton. *The Transforming Vision: Shaping a Christian Worldview.* Downers Grove, IL: InterVarsity, 1984.

Wells, David F. *No Place for Truth, Or, Whatever Happened to Evangelical Theology?* Grand Rapids: Eerdmans, 1993.

Wolters, Albert M. *Creation Regained: Biblical Basics for a Reformational Worldview.* Grand Rapids: Eerdmans, 1985.

Scripture Index

General Index

Adam, 186–87
  and Eve, 95, 164–65
Adler, Mortimer J. 107–8
Age of Reason, 222
agnosticism, 207
Allah, 248–50, 260–61
angels, 164, 175, 250
antisupernaturalism, 207
apocalypse, 85
Apostles' Creed, 88–104
apostolic writings, 118, 123–24
Aquinas, Thomas, 125
Articles of the Church of England, 116–17
atheism, 207, 281n1
Atonement, 96–103
Augustine, 84–85, 125, 179, 266
axiology, 25–26

Barna survey, 15
beatific vision, 85
Belgic Confession, 110, 116
Bible, the, 108–9, 127–28. See also Scripture
big bang, 163, 215
Bruce, F. F., 115
Buddhism, 239

canon of Scripture, 114–16, 126–27, 285n3
catholic, 102
Catholic teachings, 125–27, 285n3
Chicago Statement on Biblical Inerrancy,
  113, 117

Christian theism, 74. See also Christian
  worldview
Christian worldview, 277
  creation, 154–65
  God, 139–51
  history, 27–28, 83–85
  humanity, 172–88
  knowledge, 78–83
  moral values, 190–96
  providence, 165–69
  Scripture, 127–28
  tests, 266–76
  truth, 74–78
City of God, 84–85
City of God, The, 84
City of Man, 84–85
common grace, 283n18
confessional statements
  Articles of the Church of England, 116–17
  Belgic Confession, 110, 116
  Chicago Statement on Biblical Inerrancy,
    113, 117
  Formula of Concord, 117
  Westminster Confession of Faith, 117
creation ex nihilo, 92, 154–65
creeds
  Apostles' Creed, 88–104
  early Christian, 89–90

Darwinian evolution, 206–7
deconstructionism, 225–27, 229
doctrine, Christian

Kenneth Richard Samples serves as senior research scholar with a focus on theological and philosophical apologetics at Reasons To Believe (RTB). A nonprofit and interdenominational organization, RTB provides research and teaching on the harmony of God's revelation in the words of the Bible and the facts of nature.

An avid speaker and debater, Kenneth has appeared on numerous radio programs across the country including *Religion on the Line, VoiceAmerica, Newsmakers, Talk New York, Stand to Reason, The Frank Pastore Show, The White Horse Inn, The Bob Grant Show, Issues Etc.*, and RTB's *Creation Update*.

Prior to joining RTB in 1997, Kenneth worked as senior research consultant and correspondence editor at the Christian Research Institute (CRI) for seven years. During that time he regularly cohosted the popular call-in radio program *The Bible Answer Man*.

Kenneth is the author of *Without a Doubt: Answering the 20 Toughest Faith Questions*. He also contributed to *Lights in the Sky and Little Green Men: A Rational Christian Look at UFOs and Extraterrestrials*, as well as several other books. In addition, his articles have been published in *Christianity Today, Christian Research Journal*, and *Facts for Faith*.

An experienced educator and author, Kenneth has taught courses in philosophy and religion at several colleges and is an adjunct instructor of apologetics at Biola University and at Providence Christian College, both in Southern California. He's also an instructor of adult education at Christ Reformed Church in Anaheim, California. Undergraduate degrees in philosophy and social science, and a master's degree in theological studies led to memberships in the American Philosophical Association, the Evangelical Philosophical Society, and the Evangelical Theological Society.

Kenneth lives in Southern California with his wife, Joan, and their three children. He is a serious student of the American Civil War and World War II and is an avid Los Angeles Lakers fan.

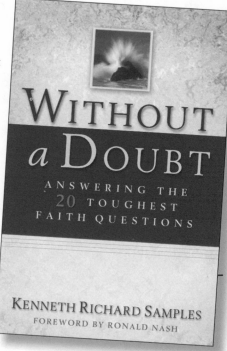